HEALTHY STEPS
4
HEALTHY KIDS

IS MY CHILD BEHAVING OK?

DR. MAURICE LEVY
M.D, M.Sc., F.A.A.P., F.R.C.P (C)

First Printing: 2012   Printed in USA .

Library and Archives Canada Cataloguing in Publication

Ordering Information for Canada and USA can be obtained through bookstores or by visiting the website below.

Publisher: Dr. Maurice Levy

ISBN : 978 – 0 – 9877909 – 0 – 3

Healthy Steps 4 Healthy Kids
Is My Child Developing OK?
- Dr. Maurice Levy -

1. Baby and child
2. Health
3. Parenting
4. Development and Behaviour
5. Pediatrics
6. Child rearing

For more information visit
www.drlevy4kids.com

INTRODUCTION
GENERAL ASPECTS

The first few years are the most important for the child's health and behavior. The early years set the stage for self-confidence, well being and readiness to learn at school. It is a time of rapid brain growth during which nerve connections are made, the brain differentiates and develops higher functions along with the body's natural growing and maturing stages.

It is estimated that 15-18% of all children experience behavioral or developmental disabilities. Studies show that the better-educated parents are, the earlier problems are identified and the sooner intervention can begin. About 70% of mothers in one study expressed behavioral or developmental concerns regarding their child. About 40% report having concerns, but not sharing them with the child's health professional (mainly due to lack of knowledge). As a result, the progress and outcome will be better with earlier intervention and include improving the child's development and preventing additional concerns (e.g. behavioral issues).

Behavior refers to an individual's actions, typically in response to various physical and environmental influences. Their overall development, environment and the adults who care for them influence children's behavior. Each child is unique and differs in terms of their activity levels, distractibility and sensitivity. Parents and caregivers who accept and understand these differences will be in a better position to offer effective and appropriate guidance.

The behavior of young children is a common parental concern since guiding behavior early in life sets the foundation for successful interactions in the future. Understanding the basic principles and practices related to child behavior is important for appropriate child development. Children's behavior reflects their level of development; achieving an understanding of appropriate developmental issues allows parents to be more effective in dealing with them. In this way, children will be able to gain confidence, competence and social problem-solving skills.

This book promotes behavioral strategies and techniques for dealing with various child behaviors'. It not only includes strategies of intervention, but prevention along with an overview of the attitudes, knowledge and skills that are beneficial to parents, caregivers and professionals in their day-to-day relationships with children. Concrete suggestions and examples are offered within a practical framework that allows parents to guide their child's behavior. Developing respect, self-control, self-confidence and sensitivity in a child is a constant goal for parents. As such, the purpose of this book is to offer recommended practices for guidance in instilling these behavioral characteristics including effective parenting strategies, quality family time, improving appropriate behaviors' and listening skills, and much more!

ABOUT THE BOOK

THE BOOK
How it is Written & What it Provides

- The book is written in an **easy, point-by-point format**. Parents do not have the time to read between the lines or look for the answer in a long story. This easy guide is designed to offer direct and clear answers, saving parents lots of time.
- It is a **comprehensive guide** that provides parents with answers to daily concerns, often asked in the pediatric setting.
- The step-by-step guide allows parents to calm, connect and communicate with their little ones from birth to middle school-aged children and beyond.
- The book is full of **practical and useful content** that is applicable to most infants and children; it is **simple yet individualized advice**.
- The **most recent research** (sound scientific evidence) in development and behavior along with training and professional experience are included.
- Each chapter begins with a general introductory note to better define the issue at hand.
- For each step, situation or problem in behavior, the tools for early identification or warning signs, red flags, what to do and when to seek help is provided.
- Although the information provided in this book equally applies to both sexes (i.e. he or she), each sex is alternated through the chapters to prevent the awkward use of "he/she". If a particular problem is related to one sex more than the other, it is explicitly stated. Otherwise, it is equal to both sexes without the intent of offending.
- Essentially, this book is a useful guide that benefits parents and health professionals with multiple pictures, tips and variations that make it concrete and memorable.

Different Sections of the Book
The book contains:

- Sections on misbehavior and discipline
- General behavior issues
- Social-emotional related behaviors
- Behavior with family and friends
- Physical behaviors
- Sexuality issues
- Learning and school issues
- Miscellaneous Parent concerns

By looking through the table of contents, you should easily find the chapters that you are interested in or have questions/concerns about your child.

Each chapter includes a general introduction, normal parameters for often-transient conditions, causes and signs of troublesome conditions. When to seek professional help and intervention is indicated followed by a section on 'what to do'.

The book contains general information along with advice. It should be used to supplement rather than replace the regular care and advice provided by your child's physician and other appropriate health care professionals. The author and publisher expressly disclaim responsibility for any adverse effects that may result from the use of the application of the information contained in this book.

SECTION SUMMARIES

Misbehavior & Discipline
All children misbehave; they are children after all! They are always testing various behaviors and learning what they can get away with and what they can't. If you understand why children misbehave, then it may be easier to distinguish between misbehavior that is a normal part of growing up or those that are related to the home or school environment.

One of the most common parental concerns heard is: "I don't understand why my child is doing that!" The cause for misbehavior and the child who "acts up" is doing so for a reason. For example, the "bully" does not have the same reason for bullying as the class clown does. The vast majority of misbehaviors arise from a lack of attention, lack of power, revenge or lack of self-confidence. Without knowing the reason for the misbehavior, it may be difficult to effectively deal with it.

Difficult behaviors included in this section are aggressive behaviors, hitting, biting, temper tantrums, food throwing, swearing, lying and so forth. Subsections in these chapters include how to deal or respond (e.g. time-outs, responding to outbursts, discipline, teaching appropriate manners) to difficult and misbehaviors. Both children and parents benefit from teaching and learning right from wrong and what is acceptable and unacceptable behavior. A child who is disciplined well and learns appropriate behaviors will grow to be self-confident, self-disciplined and self-controlled.

General Behavioral Issues
Knowing what to expect from your child at every age and how to respond to various behaviors allows parents to effectively prepare and deal with everyday behaviors. Some of these general behavioral issues include nightmares, toilet training (when and how to start), boredom, sleep problems (waking up in the middle of the night, sleeping through the night), difficulties falling asleep, handling expensive requests, nail biting (what to do), thumb sucking (how to wean), and so forth. These are everyday concerns that many parents face. This section offers parents the information required to offer reassurance to their typically developing child.

Social-Emotional Behaviors

Social-emotional behaviors refer to the positive interaction and healthy emotional state of a child. Fostering and promoting healthy development of social-emotional behaviors leads children to grow into adults who understand and know how to control emotions while socially interacting in an acceptable manner with others.

This section discusses how to offer reassurance to the shy child and when shyness is abnormal, how to deal with common fears such as fear of animals, doctors, bathing, and so forth. The importance of the imaginary friend in the well-developed child and when it becomes abnormal is discussed along with how to deal with separation anxiety, developing self-esteem, emotional health, establishing friendships, sharing, et cetera. The causes of a whiny child, sensitive child and how to respond are shared in this section in an informative and detailed manner for parents and caregivers.

Behavior with Family & Friends

This section discusses the relationships children have with family and friends such as parent-child communication, raising a grateful child, ignorance, preferring one parent over the other, how to deal with disruptions and so forth. In addition, this section includes how to ease certain challenges with children such as dressing toddlers, brushing teeth, sibling rivalry, spoiling and more!

Physical Behaviors

Many physical symptoms are a manifestation of behavioral or emotional issues including tics (eye blinking), stuttering, tiptoe walking, teeth grinding, head banging, abnormal head shape, handedness and so forth. This section informs parents of the expected physical behaviors at every age as well as behaviors that require further consultation and examination by health care professionals.

Sexuality Issues

It is often difficult for parents to discuss issues relating to a child's sexuality. Many times, parents are not even aware or prepared for certain sexual behaviors that arise in childhood.

This section provides parents to effectively prepare and deal with issues relating to sexuality including masturbation, naked toddlers, sexually curious children, bath time, erections, touching genitals and how to talk about sexual issues with children. It is an informative section that helps put parents at ease when discussing or dealing with children's sexuality.

Learning & School Issues

Parents are the first individuals to teach children early learning and education. Spending time with your child reading, writing, drawing, and participating in activities together allows your child to grow and develop the necessary skills required to enter and excel in the school system.

Various topics that are related to learning and the school environment are covered in this section including readiness for preschool or grade one, language stimulation, language delays, encouraging reading in uninterested children, how to improve comprehension in the older child, bilingualism, the gifted child (how to identify and what to do) and so forth.

DISCLAIMER

Despite the fact that the best efforts have been made to ensure that this book is detailed and very practical, and in most cases, will fit your child's case, you must always work in concert with your child health professional. This is because your doctor knows your child's unique needs and over time, recommendations may change or differ according to individual consideration.

The contents of this book are not intended and should not be taken as a substitute for your doctor's advice. It is meant purely for informational purposes. Anything contained in this book should not be considered as specific medical advice with respect to any specific condition and/or person. It is meant to ease your concerns and give you knowledge that complements the information your health professional provides.

Thus the author respectfully and specifically disclaims any liability, risk (personal or otherwise) that may be incurred as a consequence (directly or indirectly) from the use or application of any of the information provided in this book.

For more information and parenting books published by Dr. Levy, please visit:

www.drlevy4kids.com

Dedication

In Loving Memory & Dedication to,
My parents, Jacob & Heftzibah Levy who gave me life and taught me how to persevere in it. To my in-laws, Joseph and Fani Hazan who have always supported my endeavors.

To my beautiful wife,
Brigitte, who is always supportive, understanding and loving in my professional life.

To the joys of my life,
My four children, Lital, Liran, Roy and Jonathan for their support and patience during the writing of this book.

Special thanks:

My eldest daughter *Lital*, for her tireless efforts to transform my ramblings and lengthy details into the simple and easy to read, wonderful book you have before you.

My youngest daughter *Liran*, for her patience and dedication to transform the edited pieces into the colorful designs and lovely photographs you have before you.

Thank you to all the health professionals for their insight and interest in providing me with all their helpful comments and suggestions in support of the development of this book.

ACKNOWLEDGEMENTS

I wish to acknowledge and offer my sincere appreciation and thanks to all those who have provided invaluable feedback and comments on this book including the following psychologists, physicians and other health professionals.

Danielle L. Piver, PhD (Buffalo, New York)

Dr. K. Haka-Ikse, Associate Professor of Pediatrics, University of Toronto and the Hospital for Sick Children (Emer), Toronto, Ontario.

Dr. John Hsuen, Associate Professor of Pedatrics, North York General Hospital, Toronto, Ontario.

Marlene Bedzow-Weisleder, Speech-Language Pathologist M.S. CCC SLP Reg.CASLPO

Dr Anna Stuckler, PhD, Registered Clinical Psychologist, Toronto, Ontario

Dr. Kurt Andre, Pediatrician, York Central Hospital. Richmond Hill, Ontario

I am truly grateful for all of your time and support.

I would also like to thank all the parents from my clinic who read and provided helpful comments on my book. I appreciate your time and genuine comments. Thank you.

About Dr. Maurice Levy
The Author at a Glance

Dr. Maurice Levy has 35 years of medical experience in hospitals and in his active pediatric primary care and consultation clinic. As the former Chief of Pediatrics and currently, the Head of Research at North York General Hospital in Toronto, Ontario, Dr. Levy has completed numerous degrees and diplomas besides his medical degree in the areas of pediatrics, nephrology, pharmacology, and more. As the leading expert in his field of pediatrics, Dr. Levy has received many awards and published various articles for both health professionals and parents. The following is a brief overview of Dr. Levy's extensive work with children:

- 35 years of medical experience in hospitals & private practice across the globe

- Trained & worked in various prestigious hospitals in Canada, France and Israel (e.g. Hospital for Sick Children, Toronto, Canada)

- Formerly Chief of Pediatrics in the Pediatric Department at North York General Hospital (formerly known as North York Branson Hospital), Toronto, Canada

- Currently Head of Research at North York General Hospital, Toronto, Canada

- Diploma in Pediatric Clinical Pharmacology obtained from The Hospital For Sick Children, Toronto, Canada

- Pediatric Nephrology training at The Hospital For Sick Children, Toronto, Canada

- Research Degree in Clinical Science –University of Montreal, Canada

- Published articles in medical & parenting journals (e.g. "La-Isha", a journal for parents in Israel; "Toronto4Kids"website for parents; "Life for a Baby" Toronto website for parents)

- Formerly member of various committees & associations such as The College of Physicians & Surgeons of Ontario and the Canadian Pediatric Society and many more

- Received various awards & recently awarded the PTPA (Parent-Tested and Parent-Approved) award winner for a book about feeding & nutrition for babies & children, written for parents in 2010

TABLE OF CONTENTS

-BEHAVIOUR ISSUES AND PARENT CONCERNS-

MISBEHAVIORS AND DISCIPLINE

GENERAL BEHAVIOR ISSUES

SOCIAL-EMOTIONAL RELATED BEHAVIORS

BEHAVIOR WITH FAMILY AND FRIENDS

PHYSICAL BEHAVIOR

SEXUALITY ISSUES

LEARNING AND SCHOOL ISSUES

Miscellaneous Parent Concerns

Misbehavior and Discipline

TODDLER TEMPER TANTRUMS

GENERAL

- A **temper tantrum** is an unplanned and unintentional expression of anger that is often associated with verbal and physical outbursts. It can sometimes involve spectacular explosions of anger, frustration and inappropriate behaviour.
- Anger is a response to feelings of helplessness. An angry child is crying out to be heard, understood and reassured. Most angry children are not out of control, however a temper tantrum can erupt when a child becomes out of control.

- They can be incredibly frustrating but as parents, you must treat tantrums as opportunities to learn about your child.
- Temper tantrums are a common occurrence in 60-90% of children between the ages of one and four (most common at the age of 2 years); they are equally common in both boys and girls.
- It is not a cause for concern as it generally disappears on its own, as the child matures developmentally and the frustration levels decrease.
- Between 12-18 months, parents will start to notice the difference between a distressed cry and a tantrum. Between 18 months – 3 years, tantrums are more purposeful or used as a way of manipulation.
- Tantrums can become upsetting to parents because they are embarrassing, challenging, and difficult to manage.
- Temper tantrums typically last anywhere from 30 seconds to 5 minutes and are most intense at the onset, occurring about 5-9 times per week. Occasionally, tantrums last longer and consist of more aggressive behaviour such as biting, hitting, or punching.

CAUSES

- Temper tantrums are usually a **normal part of development**. Unlike adults, young children do not have inhibitions or control.
- Toddlers are **unable to cope with their feelings** including feelings of hunger, sickness, confusion, helplessness, frustration, anger, or even fear. Temper tantrums are the toddler's main way of communicating these feelings.
- **Toddlers generally understand more than they can express, not allowing them to communicate their needs.** This creates a frustrating experience that may precipitate the onset of a tantrum (tantrums tend to decrease as language skills improve).

- Toddlers are faced with the **increasing need for autonomy**; they want to feel a sense independence and control over their surroundings. When the child realizes that he cannot do something himself or cannot have everything he wants, then the stage is set for a tantrum.
- Temper tantrums **learn from past experiences** when a tantrum is rewarded. By getting what he wanted as a result of the tantrum, your toddler may have more tantrums to force his will on a situation.
- General causes of temper tantrums may include a **child's temperament, stress in the environment and/or underlying behavioural/developmental problems** (e.g. language delays, learning disabilities, Autism/Asperger's Syndrome, chronic illness, hearing problems). Medical causes for temper tantrums are less common.

TIP: Parenting and Temper Tantrums: Temper tantrums do not result from inadequate parenting, spoiling or under-disciplining the toddler.

THE TANTRUM EPISODE

Factors that may trigger a temper tantrum include bedtime, supper time, morning wake, getting dressed, bath time, watching television, talking on the phone, home visitors, car rides, public places, peer interaction, directions given by the teacher, group activities, and so forth.

Temper tantrums typically occur when the child is:
- Frustrated due to the inability to do something
- Angry and needs to get rid of his anger
- Seeking attention or demanding (wants your undivided attention)
- Hungry or excited
- Over-tired or fatigued
- Uncomfortable
- Asked to do something he does not want to do

Tantrums are limited bursts of anger and run their course fairly quickly. During a tantrum, your child may kick, bite, throw, hit and scream, punch, run around, bang his head, hold his breath (breath holding), whine, cry, flail his arms and legs, pound the floor or wall, slam the door, behave aggressively or disruptively, fall down, stiffen limbs, arched back, and in some cases, he may even break objects or vomit.

Occasionally, he will have a hard time stopping the tantrum. In these cases, it may help to say, "*I will help you settle down now*". **Do not reward** your child after a tantrum by giving in since this will only reinforce the notion that tantrums are effective. Instead, verbally praise your child for regaining control. The child may be especially vulnerable after a tantrum when he knows he has been less than adorable. Now is the time for a **hug and reassurance that he is loved**, no matter what.

If your child is capable of verbal exchanges, **find out what caused or triggered the tantrum**. Allow him to vent his remaining anger so that he can let out his frustrations.

DEALING WITH TEMPER TANTRUMS
GENERAL
The first step in handling temper tantrums is to realize that the child is out of control and that you cannot take the tantrum personally. It is not a conscious attempt on the child's part to embarrass you. You can try the following suggestions to help avoid tantrum situations and handle them when they arise.

AVOIDING TANTRUMS & SUGGESTIONS
- Do not ask the child if he wants to have dinner at a specified time. Instead, firmly state that "it is supper time now".
- Give some control by asking questions such as "which do you want first – to put your pyjamas on or brush your teeth?"
- Remove any potential triggers for a tantrum by offering distracting activities to keep him away.
- Teach how to request something he wants and honour that request. You can say: "Try asking for that toy nicely and I will get it for you".
- Avoid fighting over minor things.
- Prepare for the transition of finishing one activity and beginning another. You can let him know that the activity will finish in about 5 minutes and that the next activity will begin.
- Keep objects out of reach and out of sight. For example, keep scissors away from your child's grasp.
- When there is a safety threat, use a time out or hold the child firmly for several minutes. Let him know that you are inflexible on safety issues; be firm and consistent, so that he understands the importance of safety.

ATTENTION-SEEKING (DEMANDING) TEMPER TANTRUMS

- When children are seeking attention or being demanding, it is often when the child is left with a babysitter, acts against parent wishes, wants candy, and so forth. With these types of temper tantrums, **ignore** your child's behaviour. When ignoring behaviour, continue your activities and pay no attention to your child (but have him remain in sight). Do not leave him alone, otherwise he may feel abandoned on top of all the other uncontrollable emotions!

- **Leave him alone** and ignore the behaviour as long as he stays in one place and is not too disruptive (and is harmless), you can:
  - Try to **shift his attention** onto something else if you recognize that a certain event is going to "push him over the edge". **Do not give in** to your child's tantrum.
  - **Do not reward** your child.
  - Let him know that **you are not afraid** of his tantrum. This not only gives him the sense that his anger is containable and manageable, but it helps you set reasonable limits.
  - **Move** to a different room, so that your child no longer has an audience.
  - **Do not try to reason** with him since this will only make the tantrum worse.

DISRUPTIVE TANTRUMS

- Disruptive tantrums include clinging, following you around during a tantrum, hitting, screaming or yelling at you for long periods of time, having a tantrum in a public place (e.g. restaurant), and so forth. With these temper tantrums, use **time outs**.
- Take or **send him to his room** for 2-5 minutes.
- In a public setting, you need to **move your child to another place** for a time out; the rights of others need to be protected.
- For this type of tantrum, it is too disruptive to ignore the behaviour. Refer to the section on *Time Outs* for further details of a proper time out.

REFUSAL-TYPE TANTRUMS

- A refusal-type tantrum is when the child refuses to do something. **Physically remove** him from the area and take him to his room.
- Your child needs to learn that he cannot avoid doing something by having a tantrum. **Be firm and consistent** with your rules and ensure that he follows them for important matters (e.g. brushing teeth, going to day care or bed). If your child refuses something that is unimportant (e.g. snack), then let it go before a tantrum begins.
- **Prepare** your child for what he needs to do. For example, when your child has to go to bed, give him a 5 minute warning instead of asking him to suddenly stop what he is doing.

HARMFUL TANTRUMS

- When a child is having a harmful or rage-filled tantrum, then you need to **hold him tightly**.
- You need to hold him when he is totally out of control or there is a danger of self-injury (e.g. throwing himself backwards) until you feel he is beginning to relax.
- Some children do not want your comfort, so only hold them if it helps.

FRUSTRATION OR FATIGUE-RELATED TANTRUMS

- **Support and help** the child who is frustrated or fatigued.
- **Encourage** your child when he is frustrated with something he cannot do.
- **Offer help and praise** for not giving up on a task when he is frustrated.
- **Steer him away** from something he is really tackling. Redirect him to a different activity.
- **Put your child to bed** when he is tired, especially since children tend to have more tantrums when they are fatigued.
- **Offer him a snack**, if he seems to be hungry.
- Try to **comfort** the child when he is ill since tantrums increase during times of illness.

WHEN TO SEEK HELP

Consult your child's health professional when:

- You have questions about what you or your child is doing
- You are uncomfortable handling tantrums
- You keep giving in to your child's demands
- The tantrum arouses many negative feelings
- The child continues to have tantrums above the age of 4 years (studies show that these children tend to display more difficulties managing anger later in life)
- Tantrums increase in frequency, intensity or duration
- The tantrum escalates into violent behaviour that results in self-inflicted injuries or harm to others

Parent Concerns

How do I control a tantrum in public settings?

- Public places are the most embarrassing tantrums. Stares by strangers and unhelpful comments make the situation worst. Try not to let it bother you, because you know you are a good parent and that is all that matters.

- If you know your child does not enjoy specific outings (e.g. shopping, playground), then try to arrange these outings without him. If it is unavoidable, make it easier for your child by trying the following:
  - ✓ Keep the trip as short as possible. Know exactly what you need to buy and stick to it, so that you can leave sooner.
  - ✓ Use distractive methods such as taking a toy for him to play with (it also helps to keep a snack handy).
  - ✓ Involve your child in the outing. For example, when you are at the grocery store, you can ask your child to get the cereal or choose a breakfast item.

- If a tantrum does occur, then try the following suggestions:
  - ✓ Remain calm and quietly talk to him. By staying calm, you are in a better position to settle the tantrum.
  - ✓ Explain that the behaviour is unacceptable.
  - ✓ Carry your screaming child to the washroom or even the car.
  - ✓ Offer drinks or food in case he is hungry or thirsty.
  - ✓ Present relaxation techniques such as breathing slowly.
  - ✓ Focus only on the child and ignore any stares or comments.
  - ✓ Try whispering rather than yelling at your child. Sometimes, he will quiet down just to hear what you are saying.
  - ✓ You may have to return home, if the tantrum is uncontrollable.

TIP: When Strangers Butt In ...

When strangers offer comments or try to intervene, you can politely say:
- "Thank you. My doctor recommended this approach, so I think I will stick with it".
- "We will have to agree to disagree on that".
- "Do not judge my parenting in the few minutes you see my child and I".
- "I appreciate your concern".
- Smile at the stranger who is staring at you; this always unsettle them.

Is time out the only way to curb attention-seeking behaviors?

- Children need to feel a sense of belonging, control and connection over themselves. If they are unable to find this type of attention through positive behaviour, they may resort to negative attention-seeking behaviours.

- Some strategies to stay calm and deal with the behaviour include:
  - ✓ Ignore the behaviour and redirect.
  - ✓ Say it once and mean it. Follow through on your words and be consistent. There is nothing more ineffective than idle threats and repeating them.
  - ✓ Offer choices.
  - ✓ Breed independence by allowing the child to experience consequences.
  - ✓ Avoid a battle of the wills. Do not say "no" too many times and if you need to, then offer options for what is acceptable or allowed.
  - ✓ Do not call your child "bad"; it is the behaviour that is bad, not the child.
  - ✓ Do not over-use time out techniques. You can also ask if he is going to calm himself down.
  - ✓ Consequences need to be logical, respectful, related and revealed in advance.

Remember that toddlers are usually accepting of rules and limits. They just need to learn these rules early to pave the way for better behaviour, as they grow older.

HITTING

GENERAL

- Toddlers hit or kick other children when things do not go their way (e.g. just because he wants the toy the other child is playing with). Sometimes hitting happens out of nowhere.
- It is fairly normal for children between the ages of 15 months and 4 years. This aggression is probably more of an indicator of age than of future personality. It is a stage that the child will outgrow.

- The act of hitting others is seen in boys and girls; however boys tend to be more aggressive.
- Hitting is not necessarily a reflection of bad parenting.

PREDISPOSING FACTORS

- Predisposing factors for hitting include frustration, reaction to stress, overcrowding or too much discipline.
- Toddlers are beginning to assert their independence and view themselves and their needs as comprising the center of the universe; most do not have emotional maturity to understand or feel 'bad' when a playmate is hurt.
- The only way for a toddler to deal with frustration is to release that frustration through anger. He may hit when he is angry about not getting what he wants, whether it is a toy or treat.
- Poor impulse control is characteristic of toddlers. Even if he has the ability to understand that hitting hurts, he is unable to anticipate consequences.
- Hitting is an attention-getting device. Toddlers may hit their playmates or siblings as a way of gaining attention.
- Children are curious and want to experiment cause and effect relationships. They want to see the reaction elicited from another who has been hit (the reaction of his "victim") and to see your reaction to his behaviour.
- Role-models (e.g. parent, caregiver, media, etc) in the child's life who exhibit aggressive behaviour such as hitting, may think/learn that this is appropriate behaviour.
- Developmentally, toddlers are in the pre-verbal stage of language. Hitting is a form of communication that something made the child mad or that his needs are not being met.
- Shortage of social skills requires toddlers to have more direction and guidance on how to control aggressive feelings or emotions. Social skills need to be learned and practiced over time.

WHAT TO DO

- Toddlers do not usually mean to act 'badly' or inappropriately. Keeping this in mind will help parents calmly discipline the youngster (unless the child is older, then it is an entirely different matter).
- If you or the teacher is near the scene of the hitting incident and catch him in the act, then correcting behavior is appropriate. However, if you are nowhere near the scene of the hitting and you did not witness him hitting first, then discussing with your child hours after the fact will not do any good. Children at this age cannot remember what happened hours ago.
- Ensure that the victim is okay.
- Respond immediately, firmly and calmly.
    - ✓ Ensure that your child clearly understands that hitting is not okay by walking over to him, getting down on both knees, holding his hands down by his sides (not forcibly, but to offer comfort and further engagement), looking him in the eyes with a look of disappointment and saying "no" in a quiet, firm tone.
    - ✓ Maintain eye contact and ensure that he is looking at you (you may have to wait on this).
    - ✓ If he falls to the floor, wait beside him and start over again when he is ready.
    - ✓ The key here is to model calmness – he is not in trouble; he is in focus.

- **Express empathy** and avoid acting in ways that draw the child's attention away from his poor choices.
- **Do not yell** at your child or show anger.
- **Do not give a mini-lecture** about the evils of hitting.
- **Do not hit** the child back.
- Before the child returns to his activity, he needs to learn that his actions had an impact on his 'victim' (**empathy training** is also known as emotional intelligence). Bring your toddler face to face with the other child and allow him to say sorry.

- At this point, your child knows that hitting is not okay. If he continues to hit (more than 3-4 times), **state the consequences** and be sure to follow through with your warnings. You can try the following consequences:
    - ✓ "You hit, you sit"; brief time-out.
    - ✓ Get him to sit nearby to motivate him to change his behaviour in order to re-join the group; you can also have him go to his room.

✓ Let him decide when he is ready to return or until you come back to him. Tell him that he is welcome to return as soon as he decides to play without hitting.
✓ Stay calm and avoid showing anger or disappointment, so that he can solely focus on his behaviour.
✓ Use this time to comfort the child who was hit.

FURTHER COMMENTS

a. Give your attention to the victim rather than focusing on the aggressor. If you catch your son in the act of hitting, remove him immediately from the situation.
b. Time out is particularly effective in children over the age of 2 ½ years (see *Time Out*).
c. Avoid warnings to your child such as "if you hit again, then you will be in time out".
d. Avoid giving a mini-lecture for why he is in time-out.
e. Avoid scolding the child such as "you should never hit; hitting is not ok".
f. Talk to your child about appropriate ways to act before he joins others in a play group.
g. Prepare to react quickly.
h. Redirect any behaviour that could lead to physical hitting.
i. Supervise your child by not allowing him to play unattended with another child who consistently demonstrates hitting behaviour.

WHEN TO CONSULT YOUR CHILD'S DOCTOR

Consult your child's doctor when (a) a child continues to hit other children or adults at home, day care or preschool; (b) your child is exhibiting other problem behaviours, since there may be a more serious underlying issue; and (c) you have any concerns.

TIP: Aggressive Behavior in Older Kids
- Children of any age may respond to models of aggressive behavior in their environment. e.g. child who watches TV shows with violence may exhibit aggression.
- **What to Do:**
- Eliminate or reduce exposure to acts of aggression
- Include outdoor physical activity to provide outlets of energy
- Supervise
- Teach alternative ways to solve problems
- Teach him to be verbally assertive
- Recognize and comment on good behavior

BITING

GENERAL

Forms of aggressive behavior include hitting, punching, pulling hair, pushing, slapping, and biting. The most common form of aggressive behavior is biting, which occurs particularly among boys. Almost all children bite at some point during the first three years of life; in fact, some studies estimate that about 50% of toddlers are biters.

Biting is an unacceptable behavior. The act of biting should be removed from the child's repertoire the moment it starts. To be successful in doing so, parents must recognize the reasons for biting, react appropriately, and take the proper measures to prevent further incidents.

CAUSES

Developmental

- The first peak of biting is typically present during **teething and teeth eruption**.
- The next peak of biting is between **8-12 months of age** when biting is an expression of excitement.
- During the **second year of life**, children do not yet have the verbal skills necessary to fully express themselves. Delayed abilities in expressive language and fine motor skills may set the child up for frequent outbursts, particularly in various social situations.
- At the **toddler age**, biting becomes a form of communication where the child wants to be independent, yet lacks the necessary verbal skills to do so. Temper tantrums can develop as a way of expressing feelings and needs and biting may be a severe form of a temper tantrum.
- **Comment:** For information on biting on the breast, see the *Complete and Practical Guide to Feeding & Nutrition for Babies and Toddlers*.

Social/Environmental

- It is usually difficult for young children to express and control both positive and negative emotions. These emotions can be caused by over-excitement, frustration, fatigue, fear of being separated from loved ones and so forth. As such, children may **react and express their emotions** through various forms of aggressive behavior such as biting.
- **Role models** in the child's life (parents/caregivers) who exhibit aggressive behavior are teaching the child that this type of behavior is allowed. Aggressive behavior is learned from the environment, whether it is family members, other children or the television.

- Children are more likely to bite others when they are in social situations beyond their coping abilities. In these situations, biting is usually included for the purpose of **obtaining objects, gaining attention from adults or expressing anger/frustration**.
- Children undergoing **stressful situations** (e.g. separation at the daycare) may derive satisfaction from causing distress to others by biting.

HOW TO DEAL WITH BITING

Parents need to understand that biting is a normal developmental phase and does not usually predict later aggression. Children who engage in acts of aggression need to learn more appropriate ways of dealing with conflict and frustration. The best way to stop biting is to know when it starts and do something about it immediately. As such, parents/caregivers should learn how to manage and deal with the problem of biting effectively to help eliminate its incidence.

The following are some suggestions of how to react once your child bites:
- Look your child straight in the eye and in a loud, sharp voice; **say, "no biting!"** Explain that biting is not allowed and that it is not okay to bite another person.
- To interrupt a biting episode, you may **shout** to declare the seriousness of the incident.
- Place your child in a **time-out** with a short explanation of what he can do the next time he experiences emotions that cause him to bite. Make sure that there is no eye contact or interaction when your child is in the time-out.
- **Sympathizing with the victim** that's been bitten may be helpful and avoid secondary gains for the biter.
- Finish the interaction on a positive note. Reassure your child that you **still care** and love him.
- Do not bite back since parents are supposed to be the **example** for the child.
- Do not wash your child's mouth with soap, pinch their cheeks or slap their face.
- Make sure siblings **do not laugh** when a younger child is biting.
- Later, the incident can be reviewed and **alternatives** can be discussed for negotiating conflicts and expressing feelings.

To decrease/prevent biting, you can:
- Provide close **supervision** of your child.
- **Avoid physical punishment** or exposure to violence.
- **Set consistent limits**, especially on aggressive acts.
- **Stay in control** and express negative emotions verbally.
- Try diffusing potential biting situations before any trouble occurs by **learning** the situations that cause biting in the first place. When your child looks as though he is about to bite, send him to a "time out".

- **Re-direct** your child when anger or frustration appears. You can re-direct your child to another area. This may mean feeding him, putting him down for a nap or involving him in another activity.
- Do not give your child something else to bite (e.g. towel, stuffed animal). The **message should be clear**: biting is bad!
- **Praise appropriate** social interactions and behavior.
- **Encourage the use of words** to express feelings, emotions and recognize good behavior when it happens. You may need to teach your child words that are appropriate, because the child who can verbally express himself will be less likely to lash out physically.
- Most children look for attention. If children get **attention during positive behaviors**, they are more likely to continue these behaviors.
- **Teach** your child empathy so he understands how the victim feels.

BITING IN THE DAY CARE

Biting in the day care is a challenge, but a common one. Initially, the day care staff will let parents/caregivers know of biting incidents that occur, stressing the mildness or severity of the problem and assure parents that reprimands were given. As such, further reprimands are not necessary.

You can work with your child's day care on a plan of action that will also be reinforced at home with specific measures to prevent further incidents such as those listed above. In addition, you should check the following:
- If your child is a good match with his day care program, it should have **sufficient equipment** to meet your child's needs. For example, the day care should have enough space so that he can move around freely without bumping into other children and enough toys for no conflicts to erupt between children.
- The day care staff should know the **temperaments** of your child and should help in teaching your child ways of expression that is not aggressive.
- Look for a **pattern** of frequent biting. If there is a particular time of the day the biter has difficulty with, then make sure that you or the day care staff is ahead of those times to help him.
- The nature of **supervision and activities** should be evaluated. Discuss how your child is being cared for and how they are reprimanded with the day care staff to ensure a consistent plan is carried out both in the day care and at home. You may need to move your child to a smaller, more closely supervised setting with fewer aggressive children. Finding a day care whose staff is better able to deal with biting may also be helpful.
- **Remember:** Preschool children need an active curriculum focused on small group play with responsive adults who are positive in their interactions and able to redirect aggressive behaviors.

If your child continues to bite in the day care and all measures have been tried and unsuccessful, then the program your child is in may not be a good match for him. In this case, the best thing to do is to move the child to another day care setting. At this point, it is important to be helpful and compassionate since the move may be upsetting for your child. Seek professional help for further advice and if required, consider shorter day care stays.

BITING & THE HEALTH PROFESSIONAL

- Discuss with a health professional, especially if your child is older than three years of age and continues biting. In children over three years of age, biting should only occur in extreme circumstances (e.g. losing a fight or perceived survival is threatened).
- Consult your health professional if there are any signs of infection or risk of transmission of infection. Although the risk of infection is minimal, the level of parental anxiety may be high. Most bites do not break the skin and result in superficial minor abrasions. A bite that results in a breaking of the skin has the potential to transmit a virus.
  - ⇨ Blood-borne viruses (e.g. Hepatitis B virus, Hepatitis C virus and HIV) are unlikely to be transmitted in childcare settings.
  - ⇨ Bites in young children rarely lead to bacterial infections.
  - ⇨ However, the biter and the victim can be seen for medical evaluation to assess the need for a tetanus immunization, antibiotic use for bites with severe tissue damage, Hepatitis B status of both victim and biter, and any need for immunoglobulin injections for the prevention of Hepatitis B.

The Health Professional: Clinical Questions
The following are some key clinical questions your health professional may ask about your child's biting and aggressive behavior. ■ When did the biting start? At what age? ■ Are there any acute stressful events in the child's life? ■ Was the biting coincidental with any new developmental milestones? ■ What situations have caused your child to bite? (Frustrating situations are commonly noticed during biting incidents) ■ Does your child bite only in the day care or at home or both? ■ How are the parents/caregivers handling the problem so far? ■ How does your child's day care handle the problem so far? ■ Are there any secondary gains for the child to continue biting? ■ Are there any other concerns you have about your child's behavior or development? Any developmental delays? (Sometimes points to a more pathological process) ■ How is anger expressed in your home? (Children may model other family members behavior) ■ Do you have any concerns about how your child is cared for (e.g. abuse, neglect, violence, poor quality care)?

BREATH HOLDING SPELLS

GENERAL

- **Breath holding spells** are episodes in which children hold their breath (involuntary pause), sometimes losing consciousness, after a particular triggering event (e.g. frightened, surprised, and upset). It is especially frightening for parents who may think that the child has a seizure or cardiac arrest.

- These spells are caused by an abnormal reflex that allows the child to hold his breath long enough to actually pass out or faint. It is thought to be a **reflexive behaviour**, rather than intentional; it is not caused by a health problem and only occurs when the child is awake.
- About 1-5% of toddlers hold their breath.
- The onset of breath holding spells occurs between 6 months and 2 years, peaking between 18 months and 3 years of age. It is most commonly seen during the ages of 1-6 years.
- Breath holding spells can occur from 1-3 times per day or 1-3 times per month.
- Usually, attacks disappear by 6-7 years of age. They are not typically dangerous and do not lead to epilepsy or brain damage.

> **Parent Concern**: My 2 ½ year old son clipped his finger in the door, cried, held his breath & fainted. The same thing happened a few months ago when he was very excited; he seems to hold his breath when he is excited or having a temper tantrum. What are these breath-holding spells &what should I do?

TYPES OF ATTACKS
Blue Attacks (75% of Cases)

- A blue attack occurs when the child is angry or frustrated, experiencing behavioral difficulties (e.g. temper tantrum), sudden fear, pain or surprise.
- In a healthy toddler, blue attacks can be part of a tantrum and is rather dramatic attention seeking behaviour.
- Usually, children give out a short cry, breathe out, or stop breathing. They can turn blue quickly, and sometimes appear unconscious and floppy.
- If your child holds his breath long enough, his skin will turn blue and he will pass out.
- A few muscle twitches may occur similar to a fit (e.g. a short seizure-like movement that is not harmful), and then recover fully.
- Breath holding spells typically **last anywhere from 2-20 seconds**, but it can last longer (a minute or more).

White Attacks (25% of Cases)

- White attacks typically occur when the child is hurt or startled in response to fear or injury.
- The child will become limp, pale and fall to the ground as though he is fainting. Unlike the blue attack, the child in the white attack will not screech or hold his breath.
- Children who experience white attacks are often from families that have a history of fainting/syncope. They have an increased risk of fainting/syncope attacks as adults.

HOW TO MANAGE

What to Do During the Attack

- Essentially, attacks are **harmless** and **end on their own.**
- Have your child lie flat to increase blood flow to the brain.
- If necessary, help avoid injury by **keeping his arms, legs and head from hitting anything** hard or sharp.
- **Move your child somewhere safe**. The biggest risk with breath holding spells is head injury, due to falls during spells.
- When safety is not an issue, pretend to ignore your child's behaviour. The less attention your child receives, the fewer breath holding spells there will be.
- Leave him lying flat on the ground until he recovers (it is a fairly quick recovery).
- **Do not place anything in your child's mouth** since this can be a choking hazard.
- If the attack results in a genuine fear of being hurt, cuddle and reassure your child; be sure **not to overcompensate** for his sensitivity.
- If you are unsure about your child's attack, then consult your child's doctor.

After the attack

- **Do not give any extra attention** since this may act as a reward for your child's breath holding spell.
- **Do not punish** him since he is not old enough to understand what is happening.
- Give your child a brief hug and go about your business as usual.
- If you are anxious or frightened, do not let your child be aware of it.
- **Do not give into him** after the attack. Do not change your limits or house rules to accommodate blue attacks.
- When your child is conscious, **refrain from discussing** the attack.

WHEN TO BE CONCERNED
- ✓ You are very anxious and/or have questions/concerns
- ✓ Your child is unconscious for more than 1 minute
- ✓ Muscle jerks occur during the attack

Your child's health professional may refer your child to a neurologist, psychiatrist/psychologist and/or a cardiologist if: (a) the diagnosis is unclear; (b) parents are unable to manage the child's behaviour and set limits; and/or (c) parents are concerned and request a referral. Sometimes, an EEG is done when it is difficult to differentiate between the seizure-like movements of a breath holdings spell from an actual seizure.

ADDITIONAL PARENT CONCERNS

Is there a reason for frequent attacks? What should I do?
- Frequent or daily attacks may occur, because the child has learned to trigger the attacks himself.
- Attacks may occur more frequently when parents provide attention to the child immediately following an attack (e.g. parents run and pick up the child every time he is about to cry).
- A possible negative effect of breath holding spells is a spoiled child, since attacks are dramatic attention seeking behaviour. Running to your child every time he is about to cry or trying to prevent a breath holding spell will result in a tyrannical toddler who will not learn to handle frustrations, surprise, excitement, disappointment and limits.
- Do not allow your child to manipulate you. Ensure that you set appropriate age limits and do not change house rules or settings as a result of your child's behaviour.
- It can also help to keep the child on regular routines, set limits and avoid things that are sure to frustrate him and trigger a tantrum (e.g. allowing him to get hungry or overly tired).
- Consult your child's doctor if and when attacks become more frequent.

Since breath holding spells sometimes include jerky movements, how do I know that my child is not experiencing a seizure?
- Breath holding spells take place only when the child is awake, after an exciting event and never during sleep (unlike epileptic seizures).

- Symptoms of seizures include the following:
  a. Usually no preceding crying or tantrum
  b. Can last longer than one minute
  c. Occurs at any age (below 6 months and above 4 years)
  d. Arm-leg movements are more prominent
  e. May turn blue during or after a seizure, not before
  f. May need to go to sleep after an episode

- The health professional will assess the situation by looking at the child's history and doing a physical examination. Typically, the examination is normal and the diagnosis of breath holding spells is based on history. In addition, laboratory tests are not necessary most of the time (unless it is not a clear-cut case).

MORE TO KNOW: Iron Supplements & Breath Holding Spells Attacks
In children who are not even iron-deficient, iron supplements have been shown to reduce the number of breath holding episodes and their severity. The mechanism of its action is not clear.

SWEARING

GENERAL
- Swearing by your child, especially when he is angry or frustrated, can be an embarrassing/ shaking moment to experience.
- The fact that the child is swearing does not mean that you are a bad parent.

WHY CHILDREN SWEAR
- **Experimenting with language**: As a child grows, his vocabulary expands by listening to the people surrounding him (e.g. parents, family members, day care teachers, peers). Young children are fascinated with the power and magic of language, often saying words without truly understanding their meanings. Swearing is one way children explore language and learn how to express their feelings without understanding that these are bad words.
- **Reaction response & attention-seeking device**: A child may swear to see a parent's reaction to it and the power the word has in grabbing attention. If you respond by laughing, then your child will continue swearing thinking that it is a funny or cute word. If you respond by getting angry at your child for swearing, then he may be tempted to say the bad word when he is angry and wants to upset you.
- **Modeling behaviour**: If you swear a lot, then you are modeling this type of behaviour. You need to stop swearing yourself if you do not want your child to swear as well.

TIP: Common Swearing
Swearing is most common in children between the ages of 4 to 8 years of age. Children first hear swear words around 3-4 years of age. Understanding language at this age is not yet sophisticated. The parent's job is to model behaviour and create an environment in which the child learns how words and actions affect others.

WHAT TO DO
For Toddlers
- Both parents need to discuss what is and what is not acceptable so that the **child does not receive mixed message**
- Provide a good example and role model.
- **Think about the source of swear words** (i.e. where is he learning these bad words?). If your child is learning swear words from the television or friends, then you will have to limit access to the television and supervise him when he is with his friends. If these friends come from school or home, then alert the teacher or the parents. In addition, ensure that no one in the family or in the home is swearing.

- Set a good example for your child by **modeling appropriate behaviour** (i.e. do not swear in front of your child).
- A basic rule for dealing with unacceptable behaviour is to **ignore it** if you do not want to reinforce it; it is the best strategy. Try **not to laugh** or give away body language that lets the child know the swear word is funny or interesting. Calmly say that you do not like the word and you do not want to hear it again. If your child experiments with "off-limits" word again, then try to ignore it and avoid responding. Once he sees that the word has no effect on you, he will be less likely to use it again.
- **Provide alternative words or phrases**. Suggest other words that will effectively communicate how your child is feeling and why. This may help take you directly to the source of the problem in that he may not know how to express his feelings in an appropriate manner. **Teach alternative words** (e.g. mad, frustrated, angry) and when he absolutely feels the need to swear, tell him to do so only in the privacy of his own room (so that you don't have to hear them).
- **Explain** that swear words are offensive to many people and can hurt their feelings.
- **Give your child a little time to stop using the word**. It may be difficult for a 3 year old to give up an exciting new word that he just learned. Gently remind him that he has to find other words to use. You can even ignore it some of the time.

For Children between 3-6 Years of Age
- **Ignore** your child's swearing or quickly ask him not to say that or give him a **time out**.
- **Do not swear yourself**.
- Swearing is common on the television, so **limit or supervise television** viewing.
- **Make up another word** that you can suggest trying instead of swear words; you can say "I know a better word than that".
- **Explain** to your child what swear words really mean, rather than making a big fuss over the word. Provide alternative words or phrases to help him express what he is feeling.

COMMENT: Swearing in Older Children
Swearing in older children has different causes and consequences. Typically, older children will swear to impress friends or because it is part of their school yard language. You can:
✓ **Explain** that swear words offend others and are not positive words. You can also explain that swear words do not make you sound smart, but rather have the opposite effect.
✓ **Do not turn the issue into a big battle**. Talk when you are both relaxed and ask why he is swearing. If swearing continues, use consequences.

FOOD THROWING

GENERAL

- Feeding on demand is replaced with scheduled meals with the family around 12 months of age.
- Scheduled snacks and meals have advantages for the child in teaching good eating habits, assuring hunger satisfaction and an appropriate appetite.
- It is not uncommon for young children to play or toss their food around repeatedly, since they (1) have a hard time controlling their impulses to touch, grab and throw; (2) enjoys the new skill of being able to

throw around food, developing and mastering new skill; (3) testing the limits of her will against yours to assert her independence; and (4) letting you know that they are bored with their food.

MINIMIZING FOOD THROWING

- Rather than trying to stop your toddler's food throwing, **concentrate on limiting** what she throws and where she throws it instead.
- Try using a **special toddler plate** with plastic "suckers" that fasten to the table or high chair tray. This will make it hard for the child to throw away an entire plate, though it may not stop the determined child.
- **Do not overwhelm** your child with too much on her plate. Offer a small amount of food at first and only offer more if she asks for more.
- Limit your child's food choices.
- If she throws her food, **say firmly and quickly** that "it is not ok to throw your food" and that "food should be on the plate or in the mouth and nowhere else". You can also let her know that the food will be taken away unless she is ready to eat within a reasonable period of time (around mealtime). If your child is not ready to eat during mealtime, then you can calmly tell her when the next mealtime is and ignore any further requests or distract her; a consequence of throwing food.
- **Pick your battles**. If your child throws a small piece of bread on the floor, this is certainly not worth getting upset about.
- Take your child out of the high chair and place her in a **time out** for throwing food, while the rest of the family continues eating.
- **Praise** her for not throwing any foods and eating properly. Similarly, fuss about thrown foods at minimum.
- **Do not reward** any behaviour with attention. You can simply comment on good behaviour by praise.
- Be **firm and consistent**, yet with love and understanding.

TIPS: Choices with Food
<ul><li>Provide comfortable seating at a good height when eating at the table or in a high chair. Make sure your child's feet are supported.</li><li>Offer choices between two healthy types of food.</li><li>Offer one food choice that you know your child enjoys along with a lesser favoured food or new food.</li></ul>

BREAKFAST BATTLES

GENERAL

- About 40% of children do not eat breakfast.
- It is well established that breakfast is the most important meal of the day.

- Children who eat breakfast show an increased level of concentration, positive attitude and behaviour, better performance in school (attending school more frequently) along with a clearer and quicker thought process. These children are also less likely to be overweight, complain of stomach pain, or have high cholesterol levels. Essentially, children who eat breakfast show improved mental health.
- Eating breakfast will allow children to meet their daily nutritional needs. They are more likely to consume adequate levels of minerals such as calcium, phosphorous, magnesium and vitamins A, B12, C and folic acid.
- Kids who skip breakfast present with worse aspects of the above, miss makeup calories at other meals, are irritable, easily distracted, restless and show impaired memory.
- The entire point of breakfast is to provide your child's body with the necessary carbohydrates, protein and energy required to start the day.

Tip: Why Children Miss breakfast
Most children miss breakfast because of the following reasons:
✓ Rushing in the morning (no time for a nutritious breakfast)
✓ Late sleepers leave no time for breakfast before school
✓ Pressure to be on-time for school
✓ Child says he is not hungry or is bored with food

WHAT IS A GOOD BREAKFAST?

- A good breakfast is a balanced breakfast that includes fruits, whole grain products and protein sources.
- Whole grain products include hot and cold cereals, toast, muffins, waffles and pancakes.
- Healthy fruits are those that are fresh, dried or canned.
- You can offer pure fruit juice rather than carbonated juice drinks.
- Offer milk and dairy as part of a healthy breakfast to provide your child with vitamin B, calcium and protein.

WHAT TO DO

- **Prepare breakfast the night before** so that your child does not miss breakfast because you're rushing.
- **Never force** your child to eat any meal.
- Encourage her to eat something in the morning, **even if it is only a small piece** of fruit.
- **Offer a variety** of healthy food choices such as ready-to-eat cereal with fruits and milk, toasted bagel with cheese, waffles with yogurt, or peanut butter on whole-wheat bread.
- **Start by offering her a small piece** of fruit, cheese cubes or a cup of yogurt to get him eating in the early morning.

- Let breakfast be a drink by offering a smoothie made of yogurt and fruits or a pre-packaged instant drink.
- **Allow your child to be part of the preparing** breakfast process by allowing her to pour the milk in her cereal, add the fruits to her yogurt, and so forth.
- **Pack breakfast in a "grab 'n' go"** manner so that he can eat on the way to school. You can pack a cereal box, sandwich or bread roll.
- If your child does not eat breakfast because she is bored with food, then you can break up the traditional breakfast routine by offering non-traditional breakfast foods (e.g. veggie sticks, baked pasta).
- **Be a role model** and eat breakfast yourself with your child.
- Additional healthy breakfast ideas:
  - ✓ Fruits with yogurt
  - ✓ Baby carrots
  - ✓ Low-fat milk or calcium-enriched soy milk for a smoothie
  - ✓ Celery sticks with peanut butter (for older children)
  - ✓ Grilled cheese sandwich with juice
  - ✓ Breakfast burrito (includes scrambled eggs, cheese and veggies wrapped in a flour tortilla)

More to Know: Skipping Breakfast & Obesity
It is possible that children and adults who skip breakfast may possess less healthy habits. They are less likely to be active or exercise, will snack more and pick less nutritious foods throughout the day. In the long run, this may increase the risk of becoming overweight or obesity.

LYING

GENERAL

- All children lie at one time or another. It can be upsetting to parents and many wonder how to handle children's lies.
- Handling lies depends not only on the child's age, but on the specific situation and the established family rules that exist about lying.

WHY CHILDREN LIE

- Many children do not know the difference between wishful thinking, imagination and reality.

(a) Before the age of 4 years, toddlers do not understand truths and lies. Toddlers lie due to difficulties distinguishing between reality and fantasy or faulty memories.

(b) Generally, preschoolers tell 2 types of lies:

- (1) **Tall tales**: Children make up a story that is not true or greatly exaggerate something that is true. Tall tales are told because the child has a vivid imagination and is learning the difference between fantasy and reality.
- (2) **Wishes**: Often, preschoolers will lie to get something they want or avoid something they don't want. For example, lying to avoid an unwanted consequence (such as punishment) is an adaptive response.

(c) School-age children are able to predict what is going to happen, so lying seems better than telling the truth in some cases. For example, a school-aged child may lie to avoid being reprimanded for losing a book. At this age, children understand the concept of consequences better and may lie to avoid these consequences.

- Generally, children lie to avoid getting in trouble and may lie for the following reasons:
  - ✓ To impress others
  - ✓ To gain love and acceptance
  - ✓ To boost self-esteem and self-image
  - ✓ To gain something
  - ✓ To protect others
  - ✓ They hear parents lying
  - ✓ Not good at differentiating between fantasy and reality

- Expecting a child under the age of 7 years to tell the truth at all times is not exactly feasible. After the age of 7, we can increasingly expect children to know the difference between truth-telling and lying.

- Children that are older than 7 years of age lie for the same reasons as adults (e.g. to cover up actions, avoid disapproval or disappointment, boost self-image).

WHAT TO DO

TODDLERS	<ul><li>React in a calm manner.</li><li>Make it easy for your toddler to tell the truth by asking questions such as "did you..." or "I saw you..."</li><li>Show appreciation for honesty by saying things like "I like it when you tell me the truth."</li><li>Do not force lying by placing too much pressure, having high standards or severe punishment.</li><li>Do not insist on an admission of guilt when the child maintains his stance that he did not do something. Instead, say that what was done is unacceptable.</li><li>Let your child know you trust him.</li><li>Make honesty your policy (e.g. do not lie and say the vaccine won't hurt when it will).</li><li>Focus on fixing the problem together (e.g. help mommy clean it up).</li></ul>
PRESCHOOLERS	<ul><li>You can listen to your preschoolers tall tales and either leave it at that or try to interject reality into his story.</li><li>When the child lies to avoid consequences or get something he wants, simply get to the point and state that it is wrong to lie; it is important to tell the truth.</li></ul>
SCHOOL-AGE & OLDER	<ul><li>Actively and continuously teach moral values.</li><li>Help understand what is wrong with lying. Explain that lying breaks down trust and that it is important to trust one another.</li><li>Try not to punish, especially when the child is afraid of punishment. Avoiding punishment opens the line of communication so that he can come to you for help in any situation.</li><li>Deal with the original misdemeanour that caused the child to lie to help him come up with a solution.</li><li>Share values in words and actions. Parents should not lie in front of the child and try to model truthfulness.</li><li>Appreciate honesty when your child tells you the truth and let him know it. Praise him for being honest.</li><li>Discipline him for lying. Set rules for lying and the consequences of doing so.</li><li>Be consistent when dealing with lying.</li><li>Do not shame him for lying and avoid sending the message that he is bad; do not make him feel guilty.</li><li>If he lies frequently, then find out what's causing him to lie so</li></ul>

much (chronic liars do not usually feel good about themselves). The child may require more emotional support, increase in confidence and praise.

CAN PARENTS LIE?

- Parents should not lie to children.
- When you do not want to say the whole truth to a young child (e.g. family member is dying), then simply focus on the facts (e.g. "he is still with us").
- When your child asks questions that you do not want to answer (e.g. "Am I fat?"), go around the question and ask how he arrived at the question.
- Respond to your child's concerns and focus on the answer.

WHEN TO SEEK HELP

Professional help should be sought when:

- Lies are compulsive and widespread
- Accompanies aggressive and antisocial acts (violation of rules, stealing, substance abuse, other delinquent acts)
- Repeated lies about social status are a sign of trouble. These indicate negative attitudes that the child has about himself (Ask yourself why he might be feeling worthless, humiliated, etc)

BULLYING

GENERAL

- Bullying is the intentional and repeated words and actions designed to intimidate and hurt others.
- It is not and should not be considered a normal part of growth. It does not disappear on its own, but instead, becomes worse with time.
- A US study found that 10% of children report being bullied, 13% report being a bully and 6% report being both the victim and the bully.
- Although bullying is common, some studies report that only half of children report the bullying to a part and even fewer, report to a teacher.
- Bullying is most commonly found in the younger age group (17% in grade 2), however it does present in the junior teenage years (5% in grade 9) as well. Bullying tends to peak around grade 6.
- Although many children occasionally bully, only a small percentage of children engage in frequent bullying over an extended period of time.
- Bullying typically occurs in the neighbourhood, school or camp. Sometimes, it occurs at home.
- Bullying makes children feel upset, lonely, unsafe, unhappy and frightened.
- Bullied children can lose confidence and may lose the desire to attend school or play-dates.
- There can be long-term physical and psychological consequences that include shyness, withdrawal from family and school activities, wanting to be left alone, headaches, stomach aches, panic attacks, sleep disturbances, nightmares, stress and anxiety (can affect learning), difficulties concentrating, shame, violent behaviour and even, suicide.
- Victims of bullying are often rejected by peers and are at risk of depression and dropping out of school.

IDENTIFYING BULLIES & THE BULLIED
The Bully

- The bully tends to be an aggressive child who frequently lack empathy for others. He is generally not amenable to talking about feelings or trying to understand his behaviour. He is usually anxious, depressed, angry and hurt children.
- An imbalance of power, either physical or psychological, tends to exist between the bully and his victim.
- The child who bullies uses aggression and control to maintain a position of power over the victimized child.

The Bullied

- Children that are the victims of bullying are often nervous, worried, and insecure.
- In many ways, the bullied children express the same feelings bullies try to repress.
- Becoming a victim of frequent bullying causes children to become traumatized, often retreating from parents and developing somatic symptoms or school phobias to avoid the harassment and embarrassment.

TYPES OF BULLYING

The basic elements of bullying include both direct (i.e. face to face) and indirect (i.e. behind one's back) actions, repetitive behaviour and hurtful words or actions. It may involve money and possessions or in more serious cases, assault and sexual submission. There are two types of bullying that generally occur within schools, playgrounds and areas where adults are not present or where there is little supervision and these include:

- **Physical or harmful bullying** includes hitting, kicking, punching, pushing or shoving and stealing.
- **Psychological or hurtful bullying** includes verbal bullying (e.g. name calling, threats, insults) and social bullying (e.g. gossiping, rumours, ignoring, excluding).

WHAT TO DO

- Do not expect your child to solve the problem on his own and do not believe that it will go away on its own.
- Regardless of the child's age, encourage him to talk about any problems either with his parents, friends, or teachers.
- Make sure your child does not feel alone in offering help and support in all situations.

- Do not teach your child to talk or hit back to the bully. Explain that he should walk away and get help or join other children in an activity. You can also tell him to tell the bully, straight in the eyes, that you don't like what he is doing.
- Explain to your child that staying and watching an act of bullying makes him part of the problem rather than part of the solution.  When other children intervene in a bullying situation (usually only 10-19% of peers intervene), more than 50% of bullying stops within 10 seconds.
- Make an appointment with the child's teacher and find out how the school deals with these situations. Discuss a plan of action with the teacher to help increase support for your child.

Besides the above suggestions, parents should listen to the child and not place any blame on him. Remain calm to support the child and plan a course of action. It helps to have your child understand the psychology of the bully by letting him know that deep down, the bully is unhappy, passive and insecure. Knowing this information helps your child get through the next encounter.

Contact the police should the bullying involve criminal behaviour such as sexual assault, use of a weapon or threats to safety. Seek professional help when the child cannot overcome fears and anxieties to the point where it interferes in daily activities.

What to do when your child is the Bully
- Model appropriate behaviour.
- Remove any violence in the home and explain that violence (whether verbal or physical) is not permissible or tolerable.
- Explain the concept of empathy and how hurting others is never acceptable.
- Seek professional help when your child continues to bully others.

TIP: Bullying on the Bus
- It is a common form of bullying among school age kids (outside of the school playground)
- It is difficult to combat because there is little adult supervision on the bus
- Parents need to look for any anxiety present in their child when it comes to riding the bus such as avoiding the bus, asking for rides, being late, or loss of interest in school, etc.
- Do not rely on the driver to discipline the bully
- Besides other measures already stated, encourage friendships with another child, suggest volunteers for the bus, and perhaps initiate with the bus driver or school a seating plan for the bus.

TIME OUT

GENERAL

Time out is when the child is removed from other people and his surroundings to a "quiet, empty" place where he has nothing to look at or do with no one to talk to or listen. It is an effective disciplinary technique that deals with a child's inappropriate behaviour. When used properly, time outs will teach children peaceful ways of solving problems; it will offer the time required to "cool down" and reflect on inappropriate behaviour.

Many toddlers feel that the only time parents pay any attention to them is when they are misbehaving. Often times, parents will try to reason with the child; however, reasoning is an ineffective technique with a child so young. Time outs work well with children beginning at 18-24 months (note that time outs are done differently for preschoolers and school-aged children). For 2-5 year old children, time out remains the best form of discipline.

Tip: Time Out - Not Always a Solution

Do not rely on time out for every single difficult behaviour. Use other techniques as well such as distractions, removal of toys, and so forth. Ignore harmless misbehaviours that you can live with. Examples of behaviours that you can discipline with time outs include hitting, temper tantrums, destruction of property, pushing, writing on walls, throwing food at the table, and so forth.

PURPOSE & ADVANTAGES OF TIME OUTS

The purposes and advantages of using time outs as a form of discipline include:

- Decreases undesirable and inappropriate behaviours
- Learns to discriminate among acceptable and non-acceptable forms of behavior
- Leaves your child feeling guilty (a little bit of guilt never hurt anyone)
- Beneficial for both child and parent; the child will stop and think while parents have time to "cool off" and not do anything they may regret later
- Eliminates the need for yelling and screaming
- Learns to accept responsibility for inappropriate behaviour
- Learns more self-control
- Less aversive than physical punishment (the worst form of correcting any behaviour)
- Guarantees that parents will be consistent in forms of discipline

EFFECTIVE TIME OUTS

Places for Time Outs

- Time outs should be in an area that is easily monitored and accessible (e.g. a chair in the corner of a room, though not the bedroom; a dining room is an excellent spot).

- Set your child quickly in a small chair facing a bare wall.
- The area of a time out should be a boring place for "quiet thinking" since time outs consist of immediately isolating the child.
- Time outs should be in a play pen for the younger toddler and corner for older toddlers and preschoolers.

Duration of Time Outs

- For a time out to be truly effective, it has to be for a short period of time.
- Children will find a way to use their imagination to turn a boring activity into an interesting one, given enough time.
- Children aged 2-5 years should have 2-5 minute time outs. A 6-8 year old child should receive 5-minute time outs. An 8-10 year old child can receive a 10-minute time out while children aged 10-14 years can receive 10-20 minutes.

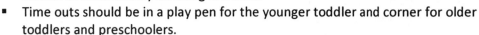

Comment: Children with ADHD should have shorter time out periods than the suggested above.

Behaviour During Time Outs

The child should not be permitted to speak and parents should not communicate with him in any way during a time out.

- No noises should be tolerated including mumbling or grumbling sounds.
- Playing with toys, listening to music or watching television should not be allowed.
- Any violations of time out rules should result in automatic resetting of the clock for another time out period.
- Do not worry if your child is not quiet during a time out. Ignore the tantrums, noise making and begging. In fact, a child who is not quiet during time out does not mean that this disciplinary technique is not working.
- If your child attempts to leave the corner, then without saying anything, gently return him to the chair with your hands.
- If your child screams, yells, kicks the wall, curses or says anything, do not respond as long as he is still sitting in his chair. If he moves, then gently place him back in the chair.

- Do not tell him how long he will be sitting there; this will give him too much power and proves to be counter-productive.
- **SECRET**: One of the secrets of time outs is ignoring the child altogether. This means no eye contact, no conversations and definitely not being in the same room as the child.

PROCEDURAL GUIDELINES

- Give your child **"3 times in"** for every 1 time out each day. This means that you offer some form of personal interaction with your child such as verbal praise, hugs, smiles, etc. This helps restore the positive relationship with your child. Note that children who are overly criticized or feel neglected will not care or want to please their parents.
- Remain **consistent** for the types of behaviours that constitute a time out.
- **Use time out frequently for targeted behaviours**. For the first few days, you may need to use time out more than 1-2 times per day to gain a difficult child's attention.
- If your child is about 3 years of age, you may need to **consider increasing the length of time** spent in time out to attain his attention and let him know that you mean business.
- **Never threaten** to use a time out by saying, "If you don't stop hitting, you are going into time out". In order for time out to be effective, there can be **no warnings or second chances**.
- **Never start any sentences with the word "if"**. For example, "If you are not good, then I will place you in a time out".
- A child is more likely to accept time out when disciplined properly (i.e. before the behaviour has escalated). Using **time out immediately** also keeps a parent from becoming too angry. The child then gains control when the parents should be in control.
- Ensure that your child stays in the **time out for the full allotted time**. Some toddlers may need to be held in the chair, so do not be discouraged. The child should not be the one deciding when time out is over, since this gives him too much power and is counter-productive.
- A portable **kitchen timer** can be set for the required time of a time out (see *Duration of Time Out* above).
- When the timer goes off, go to your child and tell him that he can get up now. Do not make any comments or remind him of what he did wrong.
- Once your child completed a time out session, praise him for good behaviour during his time out. Remember not to ask for any apologies or give any lectures about the bad behaviour.
- Be sure to give time out sessions to siblings as well, so that your child does not feel like he is the only one who receives negative attention.

RESISTANCE / REFUSAL

Some parents become discouraged with time outs, because the child repeats the misbehavior immediately after being released from a time out; other children seem to improve temporarily, but by the next day, they will repeat the same behaviour parents are trying to change; and finally, some children refuse to go to time out or will not stay there altogether. None of these reasons means that you should abandon time out. **Remember that you need to use time outs repeatedly, consistently and correctly for it to work.**

There are a number of ways to handle resistance or refusal. You may need to experiment to know which one works for your child since each child is unique. The following are some strategies for handling resistance or refusal for time outs.

- Tell your child that you will **count to 3** for them to get in the time out, otherwise the duration of time out will be doubled.
- The very difficult child (e.g. children with ADD) may need to be placed on a **short rewards program** (e.g. a chart with stickers each time so they do a time out).
- Use the **cost response method** where you select an activity or object that you can take away. Tell the child that until he completes the time out, he will not be able to use the object or engage in the activity (e.g. no television, no playing with favourite toys).

RESPONDING TO OUTBURSTS

Parent Concern: How do I respond to my child when she says "I hate you" or "I don't like you"?

GENERAL

- It is hard to hear the child you love tell you that she hates you and it is even more difficult to not take it personally.
- Many children know that by yelling mean statements such as "I hate you" or "I don't like you" is a quick and short way of getting a lot of attention and what they want.
- Your child outbursts is not a reflection of your parenting skills.

WHEN & WHY IT HAPPENS

Your child may yell at you:

- For not buying her something at the store or not giving her what she wants.
- During a fit of rage or a force of manipulation when she does not get her way.
- To express her frustration with not getting her way or for being misunderstood.
- To show you that she can fight with you at a grown-up level and feels secure enough to show you the full force of her fury.

WHAT TO DO

- **Resist your first impulse** to yell back at her or tell her that what she is saying hurts you. Instead, you should acknowledge your child's reasons for the statements she's making by stating "you sound pretty angry" or "I understand why you are mad".
- **Allow some time to pass** so that both of you will calm down.
- **Respond calmly and do not overreact**. Simply state that her language is unacceptable and focus on the emotions, not the words.
- **Be firm**. Let her know that if she continues to use this kind of expression, then she will be restricted to her room. The length of time spent in her room or the loss of privileges (e.g. watching television, playing with friends) will be determined by the intensity of her words. Once you have set limits, be calm and consistent when enforcing them.
- **Do not spend too much time responding** to your child's anger. Simply tell her that you love her and walk away, leaving the door open for a calmer discussion later. When she is calm at a later time, you can then say that "screaming and yelling 'I hate you' is not an acceptable thing to say to a parent".

- **Recognize your child's feelings by listening**. Anger does not simply disappear when you say "it is not nice to talk that way". Anger loses its intensity when you begin to recognize and accept that your child has feelings. Once the anger has reduced, you can then establish guidelines for the inappropriate behaviour.
- **Find the source** of her anger. Determine whether your child is hearing someone else talk in the same angry manner (e.g. friend, sibling). Talk about this person's behaviour and ask your child what she thinks of this behaviour. This is the time to talk about the meaning of words.
- Ask your child to share her feelings with words by **labelling her emotions** without judging them. Ask her to think of specific solutions to certain situations that make her angry, allowing her to decide and possess control of future situations.
- **End with love**. It is important for children to hear that we all have feelings of intense anger, even hatred. Explain that these feelings are rational and do not last very long and that you will always love her, no matter what.

Think About It!
When your child feels angry and powerless, she may resort to hurtful words to express her feelings. These outbursts should not be taken at face value (i.e. she does not really mean it when she says she hates you – it means she is extremely angry that she doesn't get her way and you are the one imposing the rules). Whatever the reason may be, it does not mean that you should tolerate the behaviour. Temper your own emotions so that you can take control of the situation.

TEACHING MANNERS

GENERAL

- Young children can be taught proper behaviour and appropriate manners when around others or out in public.

- Parents should remember that sitting still and being quiet does not come easily to most children who are, by nature, compulsive and self-centered.

- You do **not need to become angry or shame** your child if he cannot sit still. This will make him feel embarrassed and will not help matters.

- However, you can try the following suggestions to teach appropriate manners:

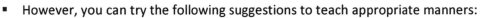

  - ✓ **Foster good table manners at home.** Children should understand that the table is a place to sit and eat, not misbehave. Explain the consequences of misbehaving at the table (e.g. removing toys, time out).
  - ✓ Encourage your child to say **"please" and "thank you".**
  - ✓ **Explain** the type of behaviour that is appropriate in public places (e.g. not talking too loud, no running around).
  - ✓ **Be firm and consistent** in your rules; do not back down, otherwise you are sending mixed messages.
  - ✓ Tell your child **what is expected** of him in advance of going out in public.
  - ✓ **Be prepared.** Bring things to the restaurant to keep him busy until the food arrives such as a toy or book.
  - ✓ Show your child a **video of proper etiquette** and how one should behave in public and watch it together.

DISCIPLINE STRATEGIES: AN AGE-BY- AGE GUIDE

GENERAL

- A natural struggle will always exist between children and parents.
- Discipline refers to teaching a child right from wrong, appropriate and inappropriate behaviours as well as protecting the child from harm.
- The biggest obstacle to effective discipline is "parents not being parents" due to various reasons including tiredness, too busy, unable to stand up to children, and so forth.

- The sooner parents begin setting limits, the better. Children raised without any reasonable limits will only demand attention and experience difficulties adjusting socially.
- Waiting to introduce discipline into a child's life later than 10 months of age could make the task much more difficult. Similarly, trying to discipline before memory even develops is futile.
- Every family is different and each situation is different. However, there are universal rules that apply to everyone at all times.
- The most effective discipline is neither uncompromisingly rigid nor overly permissive. Strict parents may seem evil or unloving while permissive parents may seem uncaring. As such, parents must find a balance between the two while teaching children appropriate behaviours and actions in the midst of loving them unconditionally.
- Parents must learn to discipline without resorting to yelling, threatening or falling apart.

TIP: Disciplining a Baby?
Parents should begin disciplining a baby to:
a) Instil the concept of right and wrong
b) Teach self-control and respect for others
c) Protect your baby, home and your sanity

SETTING RULES & APPLYING CONSEQUENCES

The following are some ways parents can effectively discipline children:

- Set reasonable and consistent limits.
- Always **explain** expectations at developmentally appropriate stages.
- **Realize** your child's limitations and set expectations accordingly.
- **Set** realistic consequences. For example, grounding a 3 week old baby may not be feasible.
- **Prioritize** rules, giving priority to safety and then behaviour (e.g. whining, temper tantrums and interruptions). Concentrate on 2-3 rules at first.
- **Ignore** unimportant and irrelevant behaviour (e.g. swinging legs while sitting).

- **Do not give in to tantrums.** This will only teach your child that tantrums are effective ways of getting what she wants.
- **Avoid nagging** and making threats without consequences. The latter may even encourage the undesired behaviour.
- **Structure the home environment** (e.g. place breakable objects out of reach).
- Reinforce desirable behaviours with **praises.**
- **State** acceptable and appropriate behaviours as alternatives to negative or unacceptable behaviours.
- Know and **accept age-appropriate behaviours.** For example, accidentally spilling a drink is normal for a toddler.
- **Develop a disciplinary plan.** Decide the consequences for particular incidences of misbehaviour ahead of time. Planning will lessen the anger and distress of the behaviour.
- Ensure that **communication is two-way** between parent and child and not simply a "do what I tell you!" Allow your child to have a say in family rules and responsibilities. This is a great ego boost for the child, allowing them to feel more useful within the family.
- **Explain** the goals of disciplinary actions. Be clear on what it is you are trying to achieve and what the discipline is meant to teach.
- **Be a role model** for your child. By doing so, your child will pay more attention to what you say.
- **Discussion** among family members is sometimes good to discuss changes in rules or the enforcement of rules.

The following are some helpful suggestions when applying disciplinary consequences:
- Whenever possible, make sure the disciplinary action is carried out **in private** and not in front of others.
- **Apply** consequences as soon as possible. Delaying discipline takes away from its effectiveness.
- **Do not enter into agreements** with your child during the disciplining process. As children get older and begin to question rules, it is ok to reason and ask them for ideas.
- Make sure the **consequences are brief** (e.g. time out should be 1-5 minutes depending on the child's age).
- Use **time outs** until the age of 5 years.
- Offer **natural and direct consequences** such as breaking a toy will automatically incur no longer playing with that toy.
- **Clearly explain** the misbehaviour and the rules.
- **No physical punishment** since it teaches aggressive behaviours are permissible.
- **No yelling or screaming** as it will teach your child to yell back.

- **Follow through with consequences with love**. Ensure that your child understands that the discipline is against behaviour and not the person.
- **Protect your child's self-esteem** by sometimes beginning your discipline by stating, "I am sorry, but I can't let you..."
- Recognize that **no reaction** is sometimes the best answer. No reaction is useful for non-aggressive behaviours such as whining or pestering.
- **Be sure you have your child's attention** when discussing the issue at hand. Take hold of his hand or wrist, look him in the eye and identify the issue.
- **Model** forgiveness and avoid bringing up past mistakes.
- **Guard** against humiliating the child.

TIP: Non-Effective Discipline
When parents plead, bargain, bribe, threaten, offer second chances or long explanations, they are wishing for and not expecting obedience. Regardless of how great a parent's explanation may be, most developing children only see one point of view (i.e. their own). Sometimes, it is better to simply say "because I said so" without any threats or apologies.

DISCIPLINE TECHNIQUES: AN AGE-BY-AGE GUIDE
Birth - 12 Months
- Birth to 4 months: No discipline necessary
- 4 to 8 months: Mild verbal disapproval
- 8 – 18 months: Structuring the home environment, ignoring, distracting, verbal and non-verbal disapproval

Early Toddler Years (1-2 years)
- Temper tantrums, contrariness and "no" answers are typically seen at this age.
- Disciplinary strategies in the early toddler years may include:
  - ✓ Limit aggression
  - ✓ Prevent destructive behaviour
  - ✓ Disciplinary intervention to ensure safety
  - ✓ Remove the child or object with a firm "no"
  - ✓ Brief verbal explanations (e.g. "you can't play with this, because it is hot")
  - ✓ Redirect to alternate activities
  - ✓ No time outs for early toddlers due to the susceptibility to fear of abandonment
- Babies enjoy the "no" game, so do not let it fall into a game or fit of laughter; babies will not take you seriously if you do so.

Late Toddler Years (2-3 years)
- During these years, children are frustrated at realizing their limitations and such struggles often lead to temper tantrums or outbursts.
- Have empathy and realize the meaning of these manifestations (i.e. find the triggers to prevent outbursts).
- Redirect and remove the child, especially from a public setting.
- Offer a simple verbal explanation and reassurance once the child regains control.

TIP: Always maintain eye contact to make sure you have the child's full attention.

Preschool Years (3-5 years)
- Memory and communication skills increase, particularly in understanding explanations and following instructions. Most children are able to accept limitations and act in a way that obtains others approval.
- Reliance on verbal rules increases, though the child still requires suspension to carry through direction and safety.
- Typical trouble areas for children at this age include whining and not listening (e.g. ignoring your repeated attempts when calling him for dinner).
- Disciplinary strategies for the preschooler include:
  - ✓ Time outs when the child loses control
  - ✓ Redirect to other activities
  - ✓ Small consequences related to and immediately following the misbehaviour
  - ✓ Lectures do not work
  - ✓ Restrict settings for misbehaviours
  - ✓ Natural consequences (e.g. not weaning mittens while playing in the snow will lead to cold hands)
  - ✓ Do not ask more than twice (e.g. "put your toy away"; ask a second time, but warn of negative consequences)
  - ✓ Avoid making unrealistic threats
  - ✓ Praise good behaviour
  - ✓ Model the behaviour you want to see

School-Aged Child (6-12 years)
- Children's increasing independence may lead to conflicts; they are now better at demonstrating self-control.
- Most problematic at this age is getting the child to do what he is supposed to (e.g. clean up, complete homework).
- For this age group, discipline strategies may include all of the above as well as the following:
  - ✓ Use logical and related consequences (i.e. cause and effect)
  - ✓ Offer a second chance when possible with an explanation of the behaviour you would like to see

- ✓ Negotiation and family conference
- ✓ Delay of privileges (e.g. "when you finish your homework, you can watch TV")
- ✓ Communicate your feelings (so that your child will listen and respond positively)

TIP: Disciplining Other People's Children
✓ If the parent is present, then it is inappropriate to step in and discipline a child who is misbehaving.
✓ If you are in charge and the parent is absent, it is necessary and appropriate to discipline.
✓ Firmly state the rules when the child is with you and the parents are absent and let the child know that he will go home if he continues to misbehave.
✓ Ensure that you are not favouring your child and that the guest (i.e. play date) has enough attention as well.

General Behavior
Issues

NIGHTMARES

GENERAL

- Nightmares are **frightening dreams** that occur late in the sleep cycle, causing a child to awaken with a sense of lingering fear or anxiety.
- Nightmares may occur during the night or day, also when napping.
- They affect 20-40% of children aged 3-12 years of age.
- The peak age for the occurrence is between 3-6 years of age.
- The frequency of nightmares decreases as the child ages.

CAUSES

- **Psychological stress/emotional conflict**: Periods of emotional tension, stress or conflict can induce a nightmare. A dream typically involves some threat or danger to the young child (e.g. physical danger- like being chased, psychological threat- like being teased).
- **Negative exposure**: Exposure to frightening images (typically found in television, movies, books, or video games) can induce common nightmares about real or fantastical creatures such as animals, insects, or monsters.
- **Febrile Illnesses** and some other medications (e.g. antidepressants, barbiturates) may cause nightmares.
- Nightmares are commonly seen in children with central nervous system damage and/or depression.
- **Post-traumatic Stress Disorder**: Nightmares may occur after a traumatic event and they may mimic aspects of the trauma. However, most nightmares do not recount actual events.
- **Family History** of nightmares is a cause for nightmares in about 7 % of cases.

SIGNS/SYMPTOMS

- Often times, a child's reaction to a nightmare might awaken the parents.
- Most children's nightmares occur early in the morning
- The child will wake up scared and upset. He is anxious and have feelings of impending harm.
- Vocalization and autonomic movements are minimal.

- There is a mild increase in heart rate, breathing rate, or sweating in the young child who just had a nightmare.
- Upon abrupt awakening from a nightmare, the child is usually alert and aware of present surroundings. He is slightly confused and disoriented, having immediate recall of frightening dreams. If he can talk, he would tell you what frightened him in the dream.

WHEN TO CONSULT A DOCTOR

- For most children, nightmares do not require medical investigation. Parents can easily identify when their child experiences a nightmare. While nightmares do not usually cause significant distress, it may cause disruption in daytime functioning in some cases. This is particularly true if nightmares are frequent and sleep is avoided.

- *Consult with your child's health professional, if you notice the following:*
    a. If it occurs more than twice a week over several months
    b. If it is extreme and persistent (may indicate psychological difficulty)
    c. If it interferes with waking or daily functioning

WHAT TO DO

- Since sporadic nightmares indicate an underlying disorder in children, most respond well to reassurance and support.
- To reassure your child, you may want to try the following:
    a. Minimize exposure to violence on television, movies, and video games
    b. Read, talk, and relax with your child
    c. Make bedtime a safe and comfortable time
    d. Reassure your frightened child that everything is okay and that you are near.
    e. Help your child imagine a happy and positive ending to a recurrent dream
    f. Encourage the older child to keep a dream journal

TIP: Helping with Nightmares
- One way to help a child who had a nightmare is to ask him to draw a picture of what frightened him (Ask to do this in the morning)
- Ask the child how he could defeat the monster next time. By talking and drawing about his fears, the child learns that he can master his fears.
- You can tell the child that dreaming is like watching television in your head. If you are scared by what you see, you can always change the channel.

NIGHT TERRORS

GENERAL

- Night terrors are frightening dreams that occur during the sleep cycle (at night or during the day) and cause a child to awaken.
- They are usually episodes that are short lived, but can occur over a period of several weeks.
- It affects 1-4% of children who are 3-12 years of age, with a median age of onset of 3 ½ years (equally affecting males and females).
- Night terrors may occur at least once per week in a child who is younger than 3 ½ years or 1-2 episodes per month in the older child.
- Most children outgrow night terrors as they mature neuro-psychologically or by adolescence.

TIP: Night terrors cause significant distress and may impair social relations. As such, you may need to avoid sending your child to a friend's house for a sleepover.

CAUSES

- Causes of night terrors are unknown; however, they are commonly associated with periods of emotional tension, stress or conflict (similar to nightmares).
- Generally, night terrors are preceded by the following:
  -Fever, pain (e.g. caused by ear infection)
  -Sleep deprivation/fatigue (most common for triggering night terrors)
  -Medication (e.g. sedatives) affecting the central nervous system
  -Family history; some studies indicate an increased likelihood of night terrors among people who have a close relative (parent, sibling, child) with night terrors or sleepwalking
  -Arousal disorders (i.e. disorder that causes a person to awaken during sleep)

SIGNS/SYMPTOMS

- Terrors typically occur early in the sleep cycle (about 30-90 minutes after falling asleep).
- Generally, a child will suddenly awaken from his sleep; sit up on the bed and scream or cry. He may thrash about or jump out of the bed, often fighting any form of restraint as if escaping from a trap.
- In most cases, a child awakens briefly after a night terror and then falls back to sleep. In addition, a child experiencing a night terror may run around and throw items.

- He does not realize that you are there, even though his eyes are wide open and staring at you. He is unresponsive to stimuli and difficult to arouse and console during the frightening time. The fighting and screaming may last as long as half an hour.
- When the child is awoken, he is disoriented for several minutes.
- During the episode, the child with night terrors often experiences signs of autonomic arousal (i.e. fast breathing, increased heart rate, sweaty).
- Most episodes last about 1-10 minutes, though the child remains inconsolable for about 5-30 minutes before relaxing and returning to a quiet sleep.
- In the morning, your child will have no recall of the event. He may have a vague sense of frightening images, but no specific recall of what happened. In fact, questioning him the next morning about what happened may only make him anxious. If your child was awake during a night terror, only fragmented pieces of the dream may be recalled.

DIAGNOSIS

- Night terrors are easily identifiable; however, it is important to differentiate night terrors from nightmares.
- In order to diagnose night terrors, the child must:

a. Have multiple abrupt awakenings usually beginning with a scream or a cry
b. Exhibit signs of intense fear or anxiety
c. Breathe fast and have rapid heart rate
d. Be difficult to awaken or comfort during the episode
e. Have a vague or no recollection of the episode when he wakes up later

WHAT TO DO

- There is a paradox in helping a child who has had night terrors. Since the child is asleep throughout the episode, trying to reassure him at the time is fruitless. All you can do is to restrain the child to prevent injury.
- Educate your family about night terrors to decrease anxiety. For example, let your family know that episodes are not harmful. Also, prepare any babysitters or caregivers for an episode.
- Educate your child about consistent bedtime routines and the importance of sleep.
- Avoid a late bedtime since this may trigger a night terror.
- Eliminate potential sources of sleep disturbances and maintain a consistent walking time every morning.
- Protect your child against injury. Parents should ensure that the child is in a safe environment and provide barriers that prevent him from impulsively leaving the room (e.g. to leave the house , break a window).

- Try to help your child return to a normal sleep. Your goal is to help your child relax after an episode and enjoy the rest of the night in a calm sleep state. You can help him relax by turning on the light (so that he is less confused by shadows), offer soothing comments (e.g. " You are safe"), and speak calmly and repetitively.

WHEN TO SEEK HELP

Consult your child's health professional when:
- Your older child experiences frequent night terrors within a few weeks or when terrors interferes with waking.
- You suspect that your child is experiencing seizures (e.g. drooling, jerking, and muscle stiffness).
- Episodes last longer than 30 minutes.
- Your child does something dangerous during an episode.
- Episodes occur during the second part of the night.

TOILET TRAINING

GENERAL

- Learning to use the toilet is an integral part of a child's development.
- A child will be emotionally and physically ready to use the toilet usually between the ages of 2 and 3 years (some earlier). Parents and caregivers can only help toilet train, but it is ultimately depends on the child (when he is ready).
- Toilet training is not a quick learning process or consistent and "accidents" do happen. Typically, training is completed anywhere between 2 weeks and 2 months. However, it usually takes between 3-6 months to be out of diapers for good.
- Parents should know that wetting at night is common for children until the age of 5 years.

Weaning from the Diaper

Readiness to wean from the diaper depends on physical and emotional factors.

(A) Physical readiness: Able to know when he needs to go to the toilet and is able to hold "it in" for a reasonable period of time; able to drop pants or lower clothing by himself.

(B) Emotional readiness: If you try to wean your child too early, then he may develop stress, anxiety, pressure, shame or the inability to withstand what is expected of him; it may affect him in the future. However, a child who is ready to be weaned can observe parents going to the bathroom and feel a sense of belonging to the "adult world".

- Maturity depends not only on age, but depends on the individual character of the child. Having said that, the best time to probably wean the child is when he is interested in weaning himself.
- If your child is interested in weaning, then you can allow him to go to the potty and bring down his diaper. Once he shows an ability to hold his urinary and bowel functions until he has reached the toilet, you can then remove the diaper altogether.
- Once a diaper has been removed, it cannot be returned. As such, you should always prepare for "special situations" (i.e. accidents).
- Weaning from the diaper at night requires a different level of maturity than weaning from the diaper in the day. It is better not to wake up your child to go to the bathroom since he does not learn to control his needs this way. Similarly, do not prevent him from drinking before sleep. He will eventually learn to control or wake up to use the toilet in the night.

WHEN TO START

A child may be ready to begin toilet training when he*:*

- Recognizes when the diaper is wet/soiled (i.e. he knows that he is "going to the bathroom")
- Uses consistent words to communicate (i.e. tells you that he needs to go)
- Demonstrates interest in the toilet
- Stands up and sits by himself
- Able to pull the pants up and down
- Understands simple instructions
- Stays dry for longer periods of time (e.g. wakes up with a dry diaper)
- Recognizes the feeling of a full bladder (e.g. paces, jumps and down, holds his genitals, pulls at his pants, squats down, "the potty dance")
- Summer is better because of less clothing but any season is ok, if the child is showing developmental readiness
- If your child does not learn to use the toilet after a couple of weeks of training, then he is not ready; stop and try again a few weeks later.

Steps for Toilet Training

- Tell your child to tell you when he needs to go.
- Show him to the potty.
- Stay with him while he sits on the potty.
- Do not make him sit on the potty if he does not want to.
- Empty dirty diapers into the potty or toilet to help your child understand what he is supposed to do.
- Make the child feel safer by having him sit on a special seat and/or by placing a secure stool or box under his feet while sitting on the toilet.

WHEN NOT TO START

- When travelling
- At the time of birth of a sibling
- When changing from crib to bed
- During a move to a new house
- When the child is sick

TIP: Disposable Training Pants

- The literature is contradictory on disposable training pants.
- Nighttimes control often lacks behind daytime achievement, so you can use them at night (especially when parents are out/absent for a period of time).
- Switch to regular underwear when training pants stay dry for a few days.

HELPING YOUR CHILD

The American Academy of Pediatrics (AAP) recommends that parents use a child-oriented approach to toilet training. This basically means that parents should follow the child's lead in knowing when he is ready to toilet train (i.e. when the child is behaviourally, developmentally and emotionally ready). In addition, the AAP asserts that the potty should be introduced slowly and parents should educate the child as soon as interest in the toilet appears. Parents are also advised not to push or force the child. *You can help your child learn to use the toilet by trying the following:*

✓ **Teach him words** that everyone understands (e.g. pee pee, BM for bowel movement, poop).
✓ Let him **watch you** use the toilet.
✓ **Read books** to your child about toilet training.
✓ Provide his **own potty**. He will be more secure and stable on the potty than on a regular toilet. If you do not use the potty, then you will need a toilet seat adapter and foot stool.
✓ **Be consistent!** Use the same words and routine for toilet learning at home as well as in the day care program. Talk to other caregivers and babysitters about how you toilet train to be consistent.
✓ Allow your child to sit on the potty fully clothed in the beginning (without weaning from the diaper) until he is **comfortable** using it.
✓ **Encourage practice** runs on the potty whenever your child gives a signal (e.g. holding genital area, facial expression, squatting) or after naps and meals.
✓ **Develop a routine** by having your child sit on the potty at specific times throughout the day (e.g. in the morning, after a nap, after snacks and meals, before bedtime).
✓ If your child wants to get up after one minute of encouragement, **let him get up.**
✓ Your child will get used to the idea of going to the potty several times throughout the day. Once he is comfortable sitting on the potty without a diaper, parents should **encourage** him to sit on it at set times of the day (e.g. in the morning, after a nap, before bedtime).
✓ **Never force** to sit on the toilet.
✓ **Do not get angry** if he has an "accident". Reassure him that accidents sometimes occur and, when they do, it is not a big deal. Be sure to respond sympathetically and avoid yelling or physical punishment.
✓ Ensure that you have enough **time and patience** to help your child learn to use the toilet everyday. Remember that toilet training does not happen overnight.
✓ **Do not worry about accidents** occurring since these are certainly bound to happen.
✓ **Praise** your child often (e.g. going to the potty on time) and be **patient, supportive and understanding**. Encouragement and verbal praise from parents and caregivers provides positive support. However, it is not a good idea to reward children with food or candy for going to the potty.

✓ When your child has used the potty successfully for at least a **week**, then suggest that he try cotton underpants or training pants. If and when he is ready for this, then be sure to make it a **special moment.**

✓ Once you start using training pants, use diapers only for naps and night-time.

TOILET TRAINING RESISTANCE

DEFINITION

▪ A child over the age of 2-3 years and is not toilet trained after several months of trying, can be assumed to be resistant to the process (even though he may seem to have bowel and bladder control).

▪ Sometimes due to toilet training resistance, children may hold back their bowel movements and become constipated.

▪ Other complications of resistance may include (a) late toilet training, (b) higher incidence of stool withholding, (c) more encopresis i.e. soiling, needing physician intervention.

CAUSES

The most common reason for toilet training resistance is that the child has been lectured or reminded too much (i.e. forced to sit on the toilet against his will or for long periods of time). Some children resist toilet training due to the fear of verbal or physical punishment. Reasons for refusing toilet training may also include fear of the toilet or being alone in the bathroom, immature child and wanting extra attention.

WHAT TO DO

▪ **Stop all reminders** about using the toilet. Allow him to decide for himself when he needs to go to the bathroom. Do not ask, probe, or remind him to go to the bathroom.

▪ **Do not accompany** your child to the bathroom or stand by him when he is on the potty. Your child needs to get the feeling of success that comes from doing something on his own and then allowing him to find you to tell you what he did.

▪ **Do not make your child sit** on the toilet against his will, because this will foster negative attitudes towards the entire process.

▪ **Transfer responsibility** to your child; he will decide when to use the toilet after he realizes that he has nothing left to resist.

▪ **Explain natural bodily functions** such as "pee" and "poop" to your child and that it belongs to him. Tell him that his "poop" wants to go in the toilet and his job is to help the "poop" get out. Once the "pee" or "poop" is out, explain that he will feel good.

▪ **Provide incentives** for using the toilet such as:

✓ Plenty of **positive feedback** (e.g. praise, smiles and hugs) if the child stays dry and clean.

✓ If the child soils or wets himself on some days and not others, this **recognition** should occur whenever he is clean for a complete day.

✓ On successful days, take the time to **play with** or take him for a walk to the playground.

- ✓ **Give stars** for using the toilet. You can use a calendar and place a star every time he uses the toilet. You could even give stars for simply sitting on the toilet.
- ✓ If you really want a breakthrough, make your child an offer he can't refuse.
- ✓ Sometimes, **special incentives** can be invaluable.

- ▪ If your child won't sit on the toilet, then try to **change his attitude**. Ask him if he wants to use the big toilet or the potty chair – give him a choice. If he chooses the potty, then get him to sit while watching television.
- ▪ **Don't punish or criticize your child for accidents**. Respond gently and do not allow any siblings to tease him.
- ▪ **Involve the day care** workers by telling them to allow your child to go to the bathroom anytime he wants to.
- ▪ **Comment:** If there is a refusal to toilet train and you have tried all of the above suggestions, then a 1-3 month break may be necessary to allow trust between parent and child to be re-established. Consult the box below for when to seek help if your child continues to resist the toilet training process.

TIP: Clothes for Toilet Training – Dress for Success
✓ Simple and easy to put on and off clothes
✓ Little girls can wear dresses or skirts and in cooler weather, wear tracksuit and pants
✓ Use clothes that can easily drop to the ankles or kick off completely
✓ Less is best
✓ Gradually expand the time wearing underwear

When to Seek Help
Consult your doctor when:
✓ Continues to wear diapers during the day at about 3 ½ years of age
✓ Continues to wet the bed at night after 5-6 years of age
✓ Toilet training takes longer than 6 months
✓ Child refuses the toilet after several tries
✓ Child is older than 4 years of age

NAIL BITING

GENERAL

- Nail biting is a common habit in young children and adults. While it is uncommon in children under the age of three years, the incidence increases as the child gets older (most commonly, 3 years and older).
- Typically, nail biting begins after the age of ten. Its occurrence is equal in boys and girls, though boys seem to bite nails more than girls.
- Nail biting causes ragged nails, damaged cuticles, broken skin, nail bleeding, bleeding near the skin, skin infection and transfer of infection from saliva. It can emotionally affect a child's self-esteem.

CAUSES

- The causes for nail biting have been universally attributed to **stress and anxiety**. As common as nail biting is, it has not been exhaustively studied to attribute further causes to its onset.
- Nail biting seems to relieve the intense tension and stress found within childhood that is both good and bad. Examples of stress in childhood include moving to a new home or neighbourhood, new bedtime routine, new sibling, learning in school, making new friends and feeling shy around others.
- If your child bites his nails primarily around stressful times, then it is his way of coping with stress.
- Biting one's nails can become a force of habit, whereby it may be difficult to stop once already started.
- They enjoy it
- It may guarantee attention from adults.

WHAT TO DO

- The best and most difficult way to help your child stop nail biting is to **find out the reason for it and resolve it.** As such, look out for situations that seem to facilitate your child's biting habits. Once these situations are identified, you can try to eliminate or modify it.
- If stress or anxiety is the main cause of your child's nail biting habit, then **talk** to your child about his worries and address these situations immediately. When dealing with stress and anxiety, a child must learn to cope in positive ways as early as possible, otherwise it becomes a habit.
- **Distract** your child by offering him something to fiddle with in his hands or redirecting his attention to a fun activity.

- If your child bites his nails out of boredom, then ensure that he is **occupied with a toy** or game such as a puzzle.
- **Do not scold** your child for his habit. Most of the time, nail biting is done unconsciously and without awareness. Instead, tell him that you will leave the room every time he bites his nails and will return when he has stopped.
- **Doing nothing and pretending to ignore**, seems the only sensible course of action. If you draw attention, it reinforces the behaviour as does putting nasty stuff on the nails and gloves.
- The less fuss you make **about your child's nail biting habits, the more likely he is to stop.** Drawing attention and/or putting gloves on his hands to prevent nail biting only reinforces the behaviour.
- A **physical solution** (e.g. polish on the nails) to help stop nail biting may be helpful for some children. A bitter-tasting bite averting solution is available in drug stores, but be sure to check the ingredients for safety and make sure he does not rub his eyes with the polish on.
- **Discourage** nail biting by trimming the child's nails regularly so that he does not have anything to bite.
- **Help your child become aware** of his own habit. Encourage the child to understand when he bites his nails. You can agree on a code that reminds the child to stop biting his nails and practice an alternative habit (e.g. placing his arms at the side of his body). Your child will be more likely to success in eliminating his habit if he feels like a partner in breaking his habit, so get him involved in your mission to stop nail biting.
- Remember, nail biting is a difficult habit to break so maintain an **empathetic attitude, offer lots of support and be creative** in your distraction techniques for stressful situations.
- In toddlerhood, sometimes it is best to leave nail biting alone since it may subside naturally.

WHEN TO CONSULT A HEALTH PROFESSIONAL
- Severe nail biting may indicate excessive stress and anxiety. Consult your child's health professional when the nail biting is severe or excessive or when other worrisome behaviours present such as picking the skin, pulling eyelashes or hair, changing sleep patterns, and so forth.

THUMB SUCKING

GENERAL

- It is normal for babies and young children to thumb suck. Between 75% and 95% of all infants suck their thumb for soothing purposes brought on by a natural sucking instinct.
- Thumb sucking often starts around the age of 3 months when the infant accidentally discovers his thumb, (and sometimes, even before the baby is born or soon after birth). It usually ends by the infancy stage or by his first birthday.

- In 30-45% of preschool children, the habit of putting the thumb in the mouth/thumb sucking can occur well into the toddler and preschool age.
- Most children will gradually stop on their own by about age 3-4 and more than 80% will give up thumb sucking by age 5.

WHY IT HAPPENS

- The reason thumb sucking happens is because the mouth acts as a **source of exploration** and pleasure. When a baby sucks his thumb, the brain produces endorphins which calm the body and provide pleasure.
- Many babies take anything and everything straight into their mouths. Babies quickly learn this pleasurable **sensation**, which it typically forms into a habit.
- Some babies who thumb suck do so to help them go to sleep, comfort in times of stress, and sometimes, solely for purposes of **oral gratification**. It is used for comfort when they feel hungry, afraid, restless, quiet, sleepy or bored.
- The little thumb is like a pacifier or blanket, acting as a source of **great security**. For your little one, the thumb comes especially handy when he is feeling stressed, tired or just out of it.
- There is **no evidence** to suggest that thumb sucking is a sign of **emotional neediness**.
- Also, it is not known why some children suck their thumbs longer than others.

CONCERNS

The only time thumb sucking may cause concern is if it continues beyond 6 years of age or affects the shape of the child's mouth and the position of teeth. Factors that affect damage include duration, frequency, intensity, and style of thumb sucking. During and after the eruption of the permanent teeth, such sucking may cause problems with the skeletal development of the mouth and the alignment of the teeth. It pushes the upper incisors out and the lower incisors in. Such malocclusion resolves spontaneously if sucking stops before permanent teeth erupt. More commonly, the thumb may develop calluses or an irritant eczema that can be infected (bacterial or fungal). It can cause transmission of germs from the fingers and facial rashes.

WHAT TO DO

- Before you start treatment for thumb sucking, make sure you are **comfortable and confident** with your plan and that other people will be consistent with your plan.
- Remember that the more you pester, scold or tease your baby, the more likely he is to suck his thumb.
- **Do not criticize the child**. Do not talk about your dissatisfaction of his habit in front of him as this will become a cause for more thumb sucking. Provide lots of extra hugs, kisses and attention to offer increased security and comfort.
- **Motivate with rewards**. Do not consider it as a bribe, but rather a prize for his good work to help motivate him not to suck his thumb. You can develop a reward system such as putting stickers on a calendar or record each day that he does not thumb suck. After a certain number of days, have a celebration for your child. At the age of 3, your child is old enough to understand the power of rewards (e.g. stars, stickers, toys, etc).
- **Decrease stress**. Try to stop doing those things your child does not like.
- **Find alternatives and provide distractions**. Try to engage him with some new toys or anything interesting such as a puzzle or an activity so that he forgets about the habit (e.g. teach your toddler how to make a fist with his thumb when he has the urge to suck).
- **Paint his thumb** with vinegar, or something he does not like, not as a punishment but just as a reminder not to suck the thumb. Use a non-toxic, bitter-tasting nail coating such as "thum"; apply it like finger nail polish to the thumb nail each morning, before bed, and whenever you see your child sucking on his thumb. It is most successful if it is combined with a reward system.
- **Call in a professional**. Ask your child's health professional or dentist to talk up the benefits of stopping to thumb suck to your baby. Sometimes children are more apt to listen to experts.

Helping your Child Stop!
✓ Do not remove your child's thumb from his mouth when he is awake.
✓ Do not punish or shame your child for thumb sucking.
✓ Select a time when your child is happy so that he can cooperate with you to the fullest when learning how to stop sucking his thumb.
✓ Do not be judgmental or allow other people to make fun of your child.
✓ If you are concerned and home treatment (or the above suggestions) do not work, talk to your child's health professional.
✓ If your child has recently undergone any sort of trauma such as experiencing a divorce, death of a pet or any family problems, then do not start any treatment for thumb sucking.

Thumb sucking is most often resolved with home treatment, however, when home treatments have not worked, other treatments may be necessary. **These include**:

- **Behavioral therapy:** Behavioral therapy helps a child avoid thumb sucking through various techniques, such as substituting tapping fingers together quietly.
- **Thumb devices:** Thumb devices, such as a thumb post, can be used for children with severe thumb-sucking problems. A thumb device is usually made of nontoxic plastic and is worn over the child's thumb. It is held in place with straps that go around the wrist. Thumb devices need to be fitted by a doctor.
- **Oral devices:** Oral devices (such as a palatal arch or crib that fits into the roof of the mouth) interfere with the pleasure a child gets from thumb sucking. It may take several months for the child to stop sucking the thumb (or fingers) when these devices are used.

ADDITIONAL COMMENTS
- Some children may be frustrated when you put gloves on their hands or remove a wrap around the thumb of the adhesive bandage. Explain to your child that gloves, bandage or a cloth is not punishment, but that it is only there to remind him not to suck his thumb.
- Some health professionals recommend not using any gloves or bandages since it may have the opposite effect of reminding the child to suck his thumb.
- If, after the all the efforts, you find it difficult to stop your child's behaviour, you can discuss the use of a thumb sucking guard with your health professional.
- Some experts believed that any treatment that does not include your child's cooperation may not work and make prolong the habit.
- Caregivers disagree about whether it is best for infants to suck their thumb or to use a pacifier. This seems largely an issue of preference (please see my book on feeding & nutrition for the chapter regarding pacifier use versus thumb sucking).

PACIFIER WEANING

WEANING

- The pacifier is probably one of children's most comforting and favourite possessions.
- No specific age applies to all children for weaning from the pacifier. Children can use the pacifier until the age of 4-5 years, before permanent teeth come in (unless there are dental, speech or language concerns).
- Many paediatricians recommend that the best time to wean is **18-24 months** of age.

- Most children give up the pacifier gradually on their own as they become busy exploring the world around them, and especially, when peer pressure begins.

- While it can be difficult to wean, try the following:
  - ✓ **Begin slowly**: Start encouraging your child not to use the pacifier during nap time, then slowly, less in the day. You can leave the pacifier initially at night.
  - ✓ **Choose a good time to begin weaning**: Do not wean in times of stress (e.g. moving, new day care, or a new baby). Give your child time to adjust.
  - ✓ **Be consistent**: Do not return the pacifier when you have taken it away already. This will confuse the child and promote more fits for the pacifier.
  - ✓ **Substitute the pacifier**: Trade the pacifier for a toy or other favourite object.
  - ✓ **Offer a reward**: Have a sticker chart where you place a sticker every time your child does not use the pacifier. Offer praise and extra hugs when your child decides not to use the pacifier on his own.
  - ✓ **Be safe**: Do not cut holes in the pacifier since this is considered a choking hazard.

BOREDOM

Parent Concern: How can I deal with my child when he tells me his is bored, especially when there seems to be so much stimulation going on around him?

GENERAL

- The definition for boredom means different things to different children at varying times. You can try to identify what he means, talk to a teacher (about school aspects, focussing in school, etc). Try to understand the reasons, instead of solving the problem and not running to do everything in order for the nagging to stop.
- Children are used to being entertained in our current society with various television and electronic games. While these games may sometimes be effective, they are passive activities that tend to limit creativity, resourcefulness and proper brain development.
- Sometimes, it is ok to allow your child to be really bored. Allow him to find a solution to his own boredom to allow his brain to be creative and imaginative. This will enhance his self-esteem by increasing his confidence with problem solving abilities.

WHAT THE CHILD MEANS

- **"I feel lonely"** – Maybe he wants more adult attention/spend more time with him and needs parent attention.
- **"Something is bothering me and it is hard for me point it"** – E.g. tired, hungry, etc
- **"I am anxious"** – something is scaring him and therefore, does not free himself to research.
- **"It is hard for me to persist on what I am doing"** – I am overwhelmed as it is not my ability and I am not successful.
- **"I am depressed or emotionally hurt"**
- **"I am accustomed to immediate satisfaction"** – the child is not taught to wait and he looks at the process not only the results.
- **If he says schools is boring,** maybe he has a non-challenging education class and has a bad school attitude which is part of negative thinking.

WHAT TO DO

- **Allow your child to feel bored.** It is important for parents not to run every time your child nags. If he gets used to you doing everything for him and solving all his problems, he will never learn to solve his own problems and obtain his own satisfaction. This may cause difficulties when he gets older.

- **Help your child choose** between stimulating activities, but do not choose for him.
- **Stimulate his curiosity** by allowing him to explore his surroundings and not stopping him (e.g. allow him to touch an object and explain what it is to him).
- **Gradually teach him to be alone**. Decrease the amount of time you spend playing with him, so that he can play alone for longer periods of time.
- **Plan events** and play dates with other children.
- **Don't suppress his interests**, but support them.
- **Limit** television use, computers and video games. It is important to find equilibrium between passive and active activities.
- **Stimulate imaginative games** (e.g. playing hide and seek, working tools).
- **Teach your child to identify emotions**, since boredom can mask emotional difficulties. Talk about emotions including anger, sadness and emptiness.
- **Allow your child to solve problems** by asking him what ideas he has to solve his boredom problem. Do not jump to offer him a quick solution.
- **Be empathetic** and mention that you feel bored sometimes too. You can explain that sometimes your body needs some quiet and alone time too.
- **Be a good role model** by letting your child feel your quiet time with you by reading, gardening, and so forth.

CROSS DRESSING IN CHILDREN

GENERAL
- Cross dressing is when a child wants to wear clothes that are usually worn by the other sex.
- It is not unusual for young children to try clothes of the opposite sex.
- Parents are often more worried when their sons want to wear dresses than when their daughters want to wear jeans.
- To the young child, it is all part of being a child and playing for fun. Parents should know that cross dressing is not any different than other play activities.

- Currently, there is no compelling research to address the relationship between cross dressing at a young age and identifying as a transsexual or transgendered later in life.
- By the time children are about 3 years of age, they are aware and know their sex that is, if they are a boy or girl). However, they do not understand that they will always be a boy or girl until the age of 6 years.

REASONS FOR CROSS DRESSING
- Children explore different parts of their personality and the gender roles they perceive.
- Reasons for cross dressing may include:
    - ✓ Enjoying colors or textures
    - ✓ Trying out different attitudes and behaviours (e.g. dresses like a fireman or ballerina)
    - ✓ Not knowing people of the same sex to copy clothing and behaviour (e.g. no dad)
    - ✓ Thinking the other sex has better clothes or toys (e.g. girls get all the pretty things)
    - ✓ Believing that parents wish for the child to be of the other sex
    - ✓ Child has an unhappy relationship with parent of the same sex and may feel unloved
    - ✓ Expressing warm, nurturing side (e.g. wants to be like sister, because he doesn't like the rough play of boys)

BEST WAYS TO RESPOND

- **Validate** your child's feelings. Do not discount his interests or tastes and do not tease him.
- **Encourage healthy exploration.** You can have a fun, dress-up box at home with a whole range of alternatives for both sexes.
- **Establish boundaries** for behaviour. You can tell your child that while he is in school, boys wear pants but that he can dress as he likes at home.
- **Reduce your child's stress** and make him feel more secure by spending quality time with him.

HOW LONG IT LASTS & WHEN IT IS A PROBLEM

- Typically, there is a decrease in cross dressing behaviour around the age of 5-7 years. This is a time when the child may be identifying with same-sex parents; has a better developed sense of self and is receiving messages from his peers, family and school about what is and is not appropriate.
- If your child's desire to be or dress as the other sex is causing inner conflicts, discuss this with your child and health professional.
- If you are worried that cross dressing is more than the play all children participate in, look for any stressors in the family that may cause your child to cross dress.
- After you answer the following questions, you can decide when to consult your child's health professional
    - ✓ How long is cross dressing going on?
    - ✓ How old is the child?
    - ✓ How important is cross dressing for him?
    - ✓ Does the child have opportunities to be with an adult of the same sex?

BREAKING ATTACHMENT TO THE BOTTLE

GENERAL

- A bottle is not only a source of nourishment, but of emotional gratification. It is similar to the favourite blanket, toy or teddy bear.
- Breaking an attachment to the bottle is very difficult for small toddlers.
- Improper use of the bottle past the age of one year may lead to health problems including dental issues and obesity.
- The ultimate goal of breaking an attachment to the bottle is helping your child feel comfortable without that bottle. Support your baby as she associates new objects with a feeling of satisfaction and enjoyment.

SUGGESTIONS TO HELP BREAK THE ATTACHMENT

- There are various ways for breaking an attachment to the bottle. It depends on numerous factors such as how many bottles are taken per day, the strength and severity of bottle attachment and your child's temperament.
- Each child is unique, so strategies suggested may not work the same for everyone.
- Try the following suggestions to help break an attachment to the bottle:
  - ✓ Provide your child with a **substitute container** for her beverage such as a cup. By the age of one year, many children are proficient in drinking from a cup; your job is already easier when your child knows how to use a cup.
  - ✓ **Make the cup a necessary part of weaning**, by using a Nubi cup (i.e. a sippy cup that has a soft nipple similar to a bottle). This will ensure that you are not simply ripping the bottle away from your child and expecting her to give up the bottle "cold turkey".
  - ✓ Have your **child become a part** in the process of weaning to a cup by having her join you at the store to pick out her new cup.
  - ✓ Show **enthusiasm and praise** when she uses the cup, so that she will continue to use it more often.
  - ✓ **Offer plenty of hugs and kisses** during the weaning process to make up for the lost comfort she is no longer receiving from the bottle.

METHODS OF BREAKING THE ATTACHMENT
Stopping "Cold Turkey"

When your toddler is not too dependent on the bottle (i.e. one bottle per day), you can make the transition to a cup more smoothly; actually, you can stop the use of a bottle altogether when your child is already proficient in using a cup, without much of a fuss.

Gradual Withdrawal

It may be difficult for your child to stop using the bottle, especially when she is taking 8 ounces 3-4 times per day.

- While giving up the bottle will be difficult for the child, try **gradually reducing** the number of bottles she has per day or the amount in the bottle. For example, if your child usually drinks 8 ounces in the bottle each time, begin adding only 6 ounces for a few days, then reduce to 4 ounces, and so on, until it is zero altogether.

- **Get rid** of the bottle that is least interesting or what may be least difficult to break and then wait about 5 days before getting rid of another bottle. Typically, the most difficult bottle to break an attachment to is the one right before bed. You should try to help your child find another way to settle down and fall asleep without the bottle (e.g. offering milk in a cup).

- Be **firm and consistent**. If she insists on drinking juice or milk from the bottle, then calmly and firmly state that she will begin drinking these fluids from a cup (saying "they are only available in a cup from now on").

- Help **transfer your toddler's attachment** from the bottle to another comfort item; encourage the use of a doll, a stuffed animal or toy.

- Keep the bottle **out of sight**, so that it may be **out of mind**.

- Offer plenty of **hugs and cuddles** to your child to provide that extra comfort during the difficult time of weaning.

- Keep your child away from thinking about the bottle and changes in her routine that phase out the bottle by **engaging her in fun activities** during the times she would normally have a bottle (e.g. bottle usually given at nap time; rock her to sleep instead or sing). Or, be in a place that is not likely to remind her about a bottle.

- Allow the bottle **only at mealtimes** to help break the attachment more easily between your child and the bottle.

- Make drinking from the bottle less appealing. You can try changing the nipples on the bottle to ones that have very small holes. This makes it more difficult for the child to suck on the bottle and receive fluids, making it more likely to abandon the bottle voluntarily.

- You can also insist that she take the bottle while sitting in a particular chair, instead when she plays or explores. If she gets up, tell her it is the end of the bottle session.

FREQUENT FALLS

GENERAL

- It is rare that frequent falls are symptoms of a major medical condition.
- In the young toddler (e.g. 13-15 months), part of the problem is because:
  - ✓ Lack of experience with balance and coordination which takes a lot of practice to perfect (until somewhere around the 3ʳᵈ birthday)
  - ✓ Most children at this age cannot clearly see what is under their nose. They are somewhat far-sighted and possesses limited depth perception. So, judging distance can be tricky. (By age 2, the vision improves to 20-60, and age 3, 20-40, and age 10, 20-20).
  - ✓ Preoccupation with what is going on around than where she is going.
- Meanwhile, prevent falls and prevent injuries (e.g. use carpet if possible, keep off hard surfaces, check sharp corners, make stairs inaccessible, footwear, use non-slip socks or slippers).
- Toddlers have to take some falls in order to master staying on their feet. Do not over protect or over react when she falls. **This may inhibit natural drive to explore.**
- **Some contributing factors to frequent falls may include the following:**

Neuromuscular
- Seizures (e.g. Petit Mal Seizure)
- Recurrent fainting or dizziness
- Somatosensory dyspraxia (i.e. frequent tripping and falling)
- Charcot Marie Tooth (weakness, frequent tripping and falling)
- Cerebral Palsy
- Muscle weakness (e.g. Duschene Muscular Dystrophy)
- Spinocerebellar ataxia
- Brain disorders

Musculoskeletal
- Gait disorders and joint instability
- Intoeing gait or joint stiffness
- Osteoporosis (a contributing factor to falling)

Eyes
- Impaired vision
- Poor coordination and clumsiness

Other Reasons
- Fragile X Syndrome
- Medications that cause dizziness or drowsiness
- Paroxysmal vertigo
- Postural hypotension
- Menier's disease (affects the middle ear)
- Poorly controlled diabetes
- Thyroid problems
- Unsuitable footwear

Environmental factors
- Loose mats or rugs
- Uneven walking or slippery surfaces
- No handrails on stairs
- Poor lighting

SLEEP

GENERAL

- Some babies will sleep through the night by the age of 2-3 months while others will sleep through the night by 1 year.
- It is important to realize that most babies cannot sustain a sleep period of 6-8 hours until they are about 6 months old.
- Some children are more affected by sleep patterns than others. As parents, you will know whether your child will be able to handle the occasional late night or missed nap.
- Falling asleep is similar to separation (i.e. separation from the awake state, from the world of toys and from parents). The world of sleep involves darkness, the unknown, dreams and fears. Teaching self-soothing methods to help your child fall asleep is the key to a good night's sleep for both parents and children.
- Successfully establishing healthy sleep habits lies in the parent's attitude as well as the child.

TIP: Factors Affecting Sleep
Illness (e.g. ear infections), snoring, GER (gastroesophageal reflux) sometimes disrupts sleep patterns. It can take weeks to get your child back on track, though sleep disturbances are normal when your child is sick or undergoing changes (e.g. moving the child to a big bed, moving to a new home or any new transitions that require adjustment).

BEDTIME ROUTINE

- After the newborn period, it is possible to get your baby in the habit of going to sleep around the same time every night. **Babies love routines and rituals**, so you can ensure that the same ritual is completed every night before bed – stay committed!
- Try to impose the **same bedtime routine** every night, even when you are not there. Ensure that the babysitter or family members who are caring for the child while you are away are familiar with the bedtime routine.
- Allow enough time in the evening for a relaxed dinner, quiet play, bath and story before bed. Be sure to give your child **plenty of attention** during this time.
- Your toddler should be sleeping in a **room of her own**. Decide upon a suitable time for her to go to bed and after the final goodnight kiss, leave decisively.
- **Bath before bedtime**: You may want to try bath soaps enriched with lavender and chamomile, since these are known to soothe and relax.
- **Sleep induced environment**: Dim the lights, turn the television and music off, keep distractions to a minimum and keep a night-light to keep the scared child company. You can leave the door slightly open if your child is afraid of being alone or afraid of the dark.

- **Stories, songs and cuddles**: Read a story in a soft monotone voice. Sing lullabies or play soft music while massaging your baby's stomach as she falls asleep.
- **Rock** your baby in a cradle or stroller. However, only use the stroller when your baby is awake and then move her to the bed.
- **Goodbyes**: Share goodnight kisses and make your departure. Keep the time short but positive when you leave.

TIP: "Monsters" Under the Bed

- Fear can keep the most tired child awake.
- A child's imagination develops as she grows older and can cause problems in sleeping habits.
- The key is not to reinforce your child's fears.
- You can lie down with her until she falls asleep and repeatedly assure her that there are no "monsters" under her bed. Take a look under the bed with her and show her that nothing is in there.
- You can even use a "monster spray" to get rid of the "monster" by filling up a spray bottle with water and spraying it under the bed every night.

FALLING ASLEEP

- Some babies fall asleep on their own and may or may not wake up many times throughout the night. Others need help learning how to fall asleep on their own.
- Before trying the soothing methods below, ask yourself these questions: Is she taking many naps throughout the day? Is she hungry? Is she too cold or too warm? Are there many distractions?
- Keep the following soothing methods at a minimum since you can postpone the learning process of falling asleep (especially since the child can become dependent on these).
  - ✓ Do not put your baby to sleep when she is hungry. Ensure that she is **fed well** in the evening to help her sleep better.
  - ✓ **Comment**: During the first few weeks of life, your baby may have fallen asleep at the breast or bottle in a feeding session. When your baby is a little older, you can **feed her when she is not too tired** and then put her in the bed (while awake) about a half-hour later when she is tired and full. After 6 months of age, some experts claim that babies do not need to eat at night. This depends on your baby; discuss this with your health professional.
  - ✓ **Massage her stomach** to help her fall asleep. Do not change the rhythm of the massage since you may disturb her.
  - ✓ It may be easier for your baby to fall asleep on her own with a **pacifier** (better than falling asleep with a bottle).

- ✓ Try carrying your baby around in an **infant carrier** to help settle her to sleep.
- ✓ **Rock** your baby in your arms to lull her to sleep. While she may wake up every time you try to place her in the bed, it eventually helps send her to sleep.
- ✓ You can push your baby in the **stroller** in a soothing rhythmic motion to help her fall asleep. Keep going until she closes her eyes, but do not place her in the bed immediately after. Give her some time to sink into a deep sleep.
- ✓ Some babies sleep better with their **arms tucked** into their blankets. Also, placing a stuffed animal or blanket that smells like you will help your child fall back asleep should she awaken during the night. Ensure that the blanket does not cover her face, but is close to her body to feel your presence or warmth.

> **Myth: Formula helps babies sleep better.**
>
> **Fact:** There is no evidence that proves that formula helps babies sleep better (including babies who are breastfed and supplemented with formula). If it were true, many formula-fed infants would sleep through the night in the first few weeks of life and this is certainly not the case!

NIGHT WAKING

If your infant or toddler is *in the crib***, the following are reassuring ways to calm her:**

- Do not rush to your child when she wakes up at night. Give her a few minutes to see if she goes back to sleep on her own.
- If she has difficulty falling back asleep, use the methods discussed above (e.g. soothing, calming, cuddling) found in the section on *Falling Asleep*.
- If she cries and continues crying, then reassuringly calm her from your bed (if you are near enough to be heard). Wait a few minutes before rushing to her side.
- If she still continues to cry, then go to the door of her room and reassure her for 2-3 minutes before leaving.
- Continue going back and forth every 2-5 minutes or for as long as it takes for her to fall asleep. You can go close to her bed, reassure her and then leave. If she continues crying, then return every 2-5 minutes, reassuring her by rubbing her back or patting and holding her until she stops crying.
- If your child feeds at night, then gradually decrease the amount of feeding. You can try to switch to water (usually after the age of 6-7 months and then decrease the amount to discontinue).
- If you put your child to sleep very early, then you may need to shorten napping times and delay the last one so that she will be able to go to sleep later in the night. This will help her sleep through the night and reduce night-time awakenings. (see section of napping time)

If your child sleeps *in the bed,* **then the following are reassuring ways to calm her:**

- If your child comes to your door crying, then reassure her and put her back in bed. Leave the room.
- When the child returns to your door again, talk to her briefly saying, "I understand you are upset and I don't mind if you cry at the door. When you are ready, go to your bed."
- Reassure your child that you are nearby and leave.
- You can continue in this way until she goes back to bed or goes to sleep by the door or unless you can put her to bed without waking her up.

- You can also get a chair and sit next to the bed. The next day, remove the chair a little further away and stay there until she falls asleep. Repeat this at every nap and bedtime, increasing the distance each time. Gradually remove the chair over a period of 2 weeks until your child learns to sleep independently.
- If you put your child to sleep very early, you may need to delay the time you put her to bed. This is to help her sleep longer and without night awakenings. You may also need to shorten the duration of her naps.
- You are still teaching your child to fall asleep on her own without being nursed, but you are there to support her.

TIP: Psychological Damage of Children Left Crying
There are no studies that demonstrate harm (i.e. emotional or psychological) to the child when left crying. You can let your child cry without worrying about psychological damage. Remember that the more attention you give, the longer the crying will continue. However, when 1-2 weeks pass with no improvements in crying, then you should rethink the reasons for your baby's cries including: lack of support or confidence, risks or fears, child-rearing philosophy, or inadequate timing or planning.

NIGHT FEEDINGS

After the age of 6 months, you may want to wean your child off of night-time feedings. To help her settle into a pattern of not waking to be fed, you can try the following:

- **Reduce** the feedings at night gradually (e.g. replace with water and decrease gradually until altogether stopping).
- If your baby is crying for a feeding at night, wait a few minutes and then go pat and rub her back to **reassure** her. If you are confident that she is not hungry, then you can be there for support and comfort for as long as she cries.
- If you hold your child, then put her back in the crib asleep or not, **kiss her and leave**.

- **Visit** your baby every few minutes when she is in her bed and crying. The crying will eventually subside, though you may have to persevere through a couple of hours in the beginning.
- For the next few nights, **stop offering feedings**. Instead, adopt the tactics for night waking for as long as it takes to teach your baby to sleep through the night.

NAPTIME

- Many toddlers are able to get by with one afternoon nap.
- A toddler of 18 months typically requires about 1-2 ½ hours of nap time per day; however, naps should be early in the day so that they do not interfere with night-time sleep.
- It is a good idea to move lunchtime so that your child can take an afternoon nap earlier and sleep better at night. This allows some evening time for parents since your child will probably go to bed earlier.
- Late naps are generally not too popular with parents, especially since late naps tend to result in late dinners.

- **To adjust the best time for your child to take a nap, try the following**:
  - ✓ Begin a calming pre-nap ritual about 10-15 minutes earlier than usual in the afternoon. Once your child is accustomed to an earlier nap time, move nap time another 10-15 back and continue this process until you have reached the desirable time.
  - ✓ Wake your child up after 1 hour.
  - ✓ You can try to wean the morning by pushing it later and later until it becomes an early afternoon nap. This will probably eliminate the need for a late nap.
- Toddlers who have late napping schedules tend to be late risers. To change it, begin waking up your child 10-15 minutes earlier each morning until you have reached a desirable time.
- Remember that a late morning nap could push back your child's afternoon nap. In this case, you should try moving the morning nap earlier.

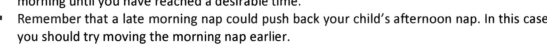

TIP: Early Risers
Studies suggest infants who are late to bed and are consequently overtired, are sleeping more poorly than infants who are not overtired. Some babies wake up very early, especially if they go to sleep early. To help your baby sleep later in the morning, try the following:

- Keep your baby up later at night. You can do this by slowly increasing bedtime by about 10 minutes until you have delayed bedtime by 1-2 hours. At the same time, you will have to alter her naps and meals. Limit daytime naps and shorten their duration.
- Ensure that all the blinds and curtains are closed so that the sun's early light does not wake your baby. Make sure there is not too much noise in the house that could wake your baby.
- Wait until your child wakes up in the morning and do not rush as soon as she does. Give a few minutes in the crib until your attention is needed.
- Postpone breakfast. Do not feed your baby as soon as she wakes up so that she will not get used to waking up early for breakfast.

DIFFICULTIES FALLING ASLEEP

GENERAL
- Trouble falling or staying asleep is a common parent concern.
- Various medical illnesses should be ruled out before stating that difficulties falling asleep are a behavioural or emotional problem.
- Organic causes that need to be ruled out include snoring, sleep apnea (due to large tonsils), rashes (e.g. eczema), URI (Upper Respiratory Infection) with stuffy nose, neurological conditions or asthma.

- *Others causes for difficulties falling asleep may include:*
  - ✓ Side effects of drugs or stimulants
  - ✓ Restless Leg Syndrome
  - ✓ Poor sleep habits
  - ✓ Stress / anxiety
  - ✓ Going to bed too late (too wired to fall asleep or over-stimulated during the day)
  - ✓ Family issues (e.g. divorce, death)

- **Comment**: Children with ADHD or Autism often have difficulties falling or staying asleep. Consult with your health professional should this be the case.

WHAT TO DO
- Ensure a **good sleeping environment**.
- Maintain a **consistent bedtime routine** (e.g. snack, bath, story time, hugs).
- Give your child a **warm bath**, using products that contain lavender or chamomile designed to induce relaxation.
- Play **soft music** in the child's room, ensuring a slow tempo and low volume.
- **Read a story** to help your child relax before bed.
- Place a **night light** in the child's room, so that he does not feel uncomfortable about being left alone in the room.
- **No stimulating activities** should be completed before bed (e.g. video games, TV, exercise).

- **Reduce drinks and examine dietary habits**. Change eating habits, if required, and cut all caffeinated beverages with no sugary desserts.
- For older children, teach **relaxation techniques** to help quiet their mind before bed.
- If appropriate, **maintain naptime routines**.
- **Do not stay in bed too long** to fall asleep; lying around hoping to fall asleep is unpleasant and makes the child more anxious. If he does not fall asleep within 20 minutes, then he needs to go to another room or do something quiet without bothering others. When he feels good and tired, then he can go back to the room. This can be repeated as many times as required.
- If the child comes to the parent's bed, then **set a firm and uncompromised limit** that he must go back and stay on his bed.
- **No drugs or sedatives** should be used on children to help put them to sleep.
- Cognitive behaviour therapy is the best treatment for insomnia. However, a referral to a sleep specialist may be required should difficulties persist.

TIP: Consequences of Insomnia
Children can be irritable, hyperactive, lethargic, depressed, aggressive, mood swings, decreased attention span, difficulties at home and in school, due to a lack of sleep.

SLEEP IN THE NEWBORN

GENERAL

- Flexibility is key when it comes to sleeping routines as each baby is unique in respect to sleeping patterns.
- Newborns can sleep 12 – 22 hours spread over a 6-7 hour sleep period.

- It is quite normal for a baby to seem like she is hardly sleeping in the first month. While some need to sleep more, others need to sleep less. The average baby who do everything by the book do exist, but are the minority. As long as your baby seems healthy, happy, and gaining weight, no need to worry about his wakefulness.
- It is important that you do not allow your newborn baby to sleep longer than 4 hours at one time, since she will need to feed. At this stage, the liver is not yet mature enough to handle sugar needs.
- If your child has any weight gain problems, then wake your baby up to feed. Feed more frequently, including at night upon consultation with your health professional.
- The following table outlines age and associated sleep duration:

Age	Sleep Duration
The Newborn (first few weeks of life)	✓ Your baby is not yet mature enough to benefit from being awake for a long period of time. ✓ Sleep time allows your baby to develop.
End of 1st month of life	✓ Most babies are alert about 2-3 hours, though most alertness is found in one long stretch.
4 – 6 Months of life	✓ Babies begin to lengthen out periods of both waking and sleeping.

FACTORS AFFECTING SLEEP

- **Sleep Cycle**: Babies spend more time in REM (rapid eye movement) sleep where they are more likely to be woken more frequently (to ensure nourishment required for sustained growth) than adults who tend to fall rapidly into a deep sleep state and stay there for a longer period of time.
- **Temperament**: An infant's temperament may allow her to be awake and alert most of the time with difficulty falling asleep, while another may fall asleep rather quickly.
- **Type of Feeding**: Breastfed infants typically require nourishment more frequently than formula-fed infants.

- **Location of Sleep**: Where your baby sleeps is important in determining how well or how long she sleeps. For example, when a baby sleeps next to her mother, she tends to wake up more often than a baby who sleeps alone. At the same time though, the baby who sleeps next to his mother will usually fall back asleep quicker than the baby who sleeps alone.
- **Illness/Ear Infection**: This may affect your child's sleep patterns, especially in older infants or young children rather than newborns.
- **Wrapping**: Hugging your newborn in a lightweight cotton or muslin material can help settle your baby to sleep. There is evidence to show that wrapping your baby reduces crying and waking by allowing your baby to sleep stably on her back by reducing flapping arms. Consult your health professional in respect to wrapping, baby sleep, and the risk of SIDS (Sudden Infant Death Syndrome).
- **Temperature**: Ensure that your baby is not too hot or too cold by room temperature.
- **Hunger**: I noticed that some babies who do not adequately gain weight and are hungry all the time stay more awake than others.

HANDLING EXPENSIVE REQUESTS

> **Parent Concern:** How can I handle my child's constant requests for expensive products that other classmates have (e.g. brand name shoes, electronics)?

GENERAL

- Envy and jealousy are natural feelings your child may express. She may want something that someone else has and wants to have what everyone else has; this is a normal feeling.
- Parents should explain the difference between wants and needs. At the age of 6 and 8 years, children are at a developmental stage where they are able to appreciate different perspectives and life experiences.

WHAT TO DO

You have to decide on a budget that you are comfortable with when spending on your child. **If your child exceeds the budget, say "no" and then do the following**:

- **Find out why she wants what she wants** by asking her what she likes about it so much. You can possibly redirect her to her own interests by asking her questions until she realizes that she does not want what her friend has.
- Tell your child you **love her and acknowledge her feelings** about what she wants, so that she does not feel like you are dismissing her completely. Explain that you simply cannot afford what she is asking for, because you have to buy other things such as food. Explain that some families are able to afford more and there are those who are not able to afford as much.
- **Set realistic expectations** of what she can get and when.
- **Allow her to cry** when she cannot get what she wants, so that she is able to work through her emotions.
- Encourage her to **earn her own money** and save up (if she is old enough). She can do chores around the house for a small pay so that she learns the value of money. This way, she will prioritize what she really wants and appreciate it that much more.
- You can ask her to make a **wants and needs list** and show her many chores she would need to complete to save the money for these items.

TRANSITIONAL OBJECTS

GENERAL

- **Security objects** are items that are usually soft and easily held or carried by a young child. These objects are also referred to as **transitional objects** since they help the toddler make the emotional transition from dependence to independence.

- Examples of security objects include a soft blanket or a corner of it that the child rubs against his nose, a cuddly stuffed animal, bottle, pacifier, and almost anything with a soft and pleasing texture.
- Object attachment often develops towards the end of the first year of life, although attachment to pacifiers occurs at an earlier age. For example, a strong attachment to a favourite blanket peaks at 18-24 months of age and then diminishes steadily after 39 months of age. By 5 ½ years of age, fewer than 8% of children are attached to blankets.
- There is no evidence to suggest that children who are attached to a security/transitional object are abnormal, overanxious, maladjusted or insecure than other children. Moreover, it does not reflect an unhealthy relationship between parent and child.
- Hanging onto a comfort object for a long period of time is not associated with any difficulties later in life. Children can hold onto their objects for as long as they need to.
- Parents may become frustrated when the security object falls/misplaced/lost and they need to keep track of it to soothe their child.
- **Safety and Security Objects:** Ensure that your child's security object is safe and does not pose a safety or choking risk. Objects can become dirty and spread germs. Pacifiers can cause dental problems if prolonged. Bottles used excessively can cause dental carries.

CAUSES/WHY

- The causes for security objects is **not clear** since some children engage in this comfort-seeking behaviour while others do not.
- The incidence of attachment to transitional objects is varied among cultures. For example, Korean-born children living in the United States may show fewer attachments to blankets than American children.
- Transitional objects help a young child make the emotional transition from **dependence to independence**. Toddlers are at a stage where they discover themselves as **separate beings** and not extensions of their parents. This discovery is exciting and frightening all at once, so a security object offers comfort during this phase.

- Attachment to a security object can be beneficial to a child. Security objects may serve as a substitute for the parent in his/her absence and may assist parent/child separation. These objects provide the comfort of something familiar, a portable source of reassurance. In particular, security objects provide a way of maintaining a connection with parents whenever they may be away.

WHEN SECURITY OBJECTS ARE USED

- Although most children form a bond with a security object before the end of the first year of life, dependence does not peak until the second year.
- Most children leave their transitional objects behind by the age of 3-5 years or only turn to these objects during stressful times.
- Children often like to have their security objects with them at **bedtime** to help soothe and settle them for sleep.
- Security objects are often used when the child is **frustrated, tired** or making any sort of **transition** (e.g. moving homes, new sibling, a night away from home). Sometimes, children who do not become attached to a security object at an earlier age will suddenly become attached when confronted with an unsettling or frightening situation such as a new transition.

WHAT NOT TO DO

- **Do not tease or scold** your child for using a security object.
- **Do not say** that he is a big boy now and take the security object away. It will be difficult for children to lose their security objects before they are ready.
- **Do not talk** about the security object or about giving it up all the time; the less talk, the better.
- **Do not** run out and buy many of the same object since the transitional item is unique and special to your child – there is only one for him.

WHAT TO DO

There are measures you can take to ensure the use of security objects as less pervasive and to help the child give it up easily when he is ready.

- If possible, **limit the use** of security objects to the home or car especially when the habit is in the early stage; explain that the object can be stolen elsewhere or when taken outside the home. If the attachment is already formed, then do not worry about setting any limits.
- Ensure that you have a **duplicate** of the security object in case it is lost or stolen. If the attachment is mild, then you may not have a duplicate ready; your child will shed a few tears for the lost object, and move on.

- **Wash** the security object regularly, since objects can become dirty and spread germs. You can wash the object while your child is sleeping or explain that your child's favourite friend needs a bath or swim in the washing machine. You can even let your child help you hand wash the object of attachment in the sink.
- To help lessen the need for a security object, make sure you offer your child lots of **love and comfort**. This can be in the form of hugs and kisses, but also play sessions, talking, and having fun in different activities together.
- **Divert** your child's attention from the security object by offering fun activities for him to do with his hands such as puzzles, arts and crafts, car toys, etc.
- Sometimes, external factors may divert your child's attention or rear him away from the security object such as a day care teacher (who limits the use of the object during specific hours).

WATCHING TELEVISION

GENERAL

- Exposing your infant to various mediums of television (e.g. shows, games, DVD) will not cause lasting harm when television viewing is moderated. For example, watching 1-2 favourite television programs per day will not cause irreparable harm.

- It is certainly not recommended to leave your child in front of the television all day long.

- The American Academy of Paediatrics (AAP) does not recommend television viewing for children under the age of two years. The benefit of interacting with your child directly (in the form of singing, talking, reading, listening to music) is more important to development than any television program.

- Too much television for young infants and children has been proven to effect brain development and decrease important person-to-person interaction; these are central to a child's social, emotional and intellectual development.

- Some research found that there is a relationship between watching television at a young age and attention problems as well as increased risks for obesity, poor social development and aggressive behaviour.

- Children under the age of 2 years rarely understand the content of a television program and often confuse imaginative or pretend play (seen on television) with reality at a time when they are still developing cognitive skills.

- In very young infants, a little television is fine. A recent study by Boston's Children's Hospital and Harvard Medical School found that the effects of television viewing on cognitive development in babies (measured by language and visual motor skills at age 3) between birth and two years was neutral. This study has provided some relief for parents who know that they will not be taking away early stimulation when placing infants in front of the television while making a meal, answering emails or other short-time chores.

- Although prior research had connected television viewing to cognitive delays, these studies were lacking control for socio-demographic and environmental factors. Infants who watch large amounts of television are more likely to come from families with lower incomes and lower parent education where parents score lower on language and vocabulary tests.

- A variety of technological tools are currently available to help parents monitor television program such as blocks and filters.

> **TIP: Audiotapes & CD's**
> An educational medium that is better than the television is an audiotape or CD where the child is required to visually imagine what is stated. Stimulating your child's creativity provides opportunities for self-expression and learning.

HEALTHY TELEVISION HABITS

Every now and then, parents need a break and typically find a DVD or television program to occupy their child while they relax, take a shower or prepare a meal. When you need to relax, be creative with the activities your child can engage in. For example, you can play an audiotape or CD in the stereo system to allow your child to visually stimulate his imagination. Overall, parents should resist the temptation to turn the television on until the child is at least 2 years of age. In addition, parents should attempt to instil the following healthy television habits.

- ✓ **Interactive television** (i.e. games that involve the viewer) can be a great source of education for children; however, too much can be unhealthy.
- ✓ **Limit** the number of hours your child watches television. The AAP recommends that children older than the age of 2 years should not watch more than 1-2 hours of quality programming per day.
- ✓ **Establish rules** for watching television. For example, your child earns the right to see one hour of television after completing all his chores or homework.
- ✓ **Be consistent** with television rules to avoid conflict.
- ✓ Keep the television **out of the bedroom**.
- ✓ **Do not allow** the child to watch television while he is eating or doing homework, especially since research shows a possible link between eating while watching television and obesity.
- ✓ **Read reviews** and ratings of television shows before your child watches any to ensure that the program is developmentally appropriate and reinforces family values.
- ✓ **Watch television with your child** when possible. If you cannot watch the whole program, then try to watch the first few minutes to assess the appropriateness of the program.
- ✓ Offer a variety of **home activities** such as reading, play dates, playing board games or playing outside, starting a game of hide and seek and sports to develop healthy habits.
- ✓ **Talk** to your child about what he watches on the television and share your own beliefs, values and opinions. You can also use the television to explain
- ✓ confusing situations and express feelings about various topics such as love, drugs, smoking, work and family life.

HEALTHY HABITS: INTERNET SAFETY & VIDEO GAMES

Internet Safety
- **Share email accounts** so you can monitor messages.
- **Bookmark** your child's favourite sites.
- Monitor your child's use of any chat room. **Be aware** that posting messages in chat rooms reveals email addresses to others.
- Keep the computer in a **common family area** where you can monitor its use.
- **Avoid** a computer in the bedroom!

Video Games
- **Review ratings** for violence, strong language, mature sexual content or inappropriate content for children.
- **You can play video games** to truly assess appropriateness.
- **Assess your child's behaviour** after playing games for aggressiveness. Help him understand how violence or anything played in a video game is "different" in the real world.

Social-Emotional Related Behaviour

SHYNESS

GENERAL

- Shyness can involve a reluctance to join in social interactions or group play at school. Feeling shy can make a child feel more embarrassed by public attention, even it is good attention.
- There is a wide range of shyness among preschoolers. While some children feel comfortable speaking in front of others or being the center of attention, others feel uncomfortable with people outside of the family.
- About one-half of children continue to be shy until the age of six years with half of these children becoming more outgoing and less shy by their teenage years.
- Children with extreme shyness may grow out of it when they mature or may grow to be shy adults.
- It is important to remember that shyness is typically a character trait than evidence of pathology.

PRESENTATION

Shyness can be manifested as a child who:

- May be slow to warm-up to a group or situation
- Clings to you when unfamiliar children or adults are present
- Stands away from other children while playing or does not take part in social activities/games
- Refuses to speak to others (even when asked direct questions)
- Will not go to places like the school playground unless accompanied by a parent or close friend

There can be an overlap between shyness, anxiety and social phobia. Shyness may begin as a normal trait, but can become exacerbated by external influences (e.g. trauma, illness, death in the family, child abuse or neglect) to become pathological with a high degree of anxiety, worry, social withdrawal and other habits. Ironically, it can sometimes be the parents who attempt to help the shy child, but only worsen the problem instead.

CAUSES & CONSEQUENCES

Causes

- **Genetics:** The cause for a shy child is mostly a **personality inborn temperament** rather than any developmental causes. Shyness arises in part from the area of the brain that controls how we respond to new and unfamiliar things. It can also be a fundamental trait of certain personalities and such children may tend to be quiet throughout much of their lives. It is essential to remember that normal temperament covers a wide spectrum and the quiet or lively child may be quite normal.

- **Environmental and family relationships**: The tendency towards shyness can be reinforced by environmental (home) conditions (e.g. inconsistent parenting, family conflicts, harsh criticisms, dominating siblings, shy parents teaching shy behaviours, overprotective parents who inhibit the child). Some studies show that a shy child has at least one shy parent.

Consequences
- **Shyness, particularly severe shyness, can reduce your child's quality of life in various ways including**:
  - ✓ Reduced opportunities for social play and interaction
  - ✓ Reduced self-esteem
  - ✓ Feelings of loneliness
  - ✓ High anxiety levels
  - ✓ Reduced ability to reach full potential due to fears of being judged or criticized
  - ✓ Reduced feelings and involvement in rewarding activities

- Positive aspects of shyness include succeeding academically, listening attentively to others, being less aggressive, properly behaving and not getting into trouble. Generally, these children are easy to look after and are to have stronger and closer parent/child relationships.

> **TIP: Shyness = Unhappiness?**
> Shy individuals can be just as happy as more extraverted types. Shyness is not necessarily correlated and does not signify unhappiness.

HOW TO HELP
- Learn the type of situation that makes your child shy (e.g. when in groups, when presenting in front of others, when unfamiliar children are around). **Support** your child in any new or fearful situation.
- **Look for ways to help your child feel good** about herself and the interactions she is engaged in. For example, you can comment on how well she spoke with friends or family members and that you are so proud of her.

- Help ease your child's anxiety and stress by **preparing her for unfamiliar people and situations**. Let her know that you are, for example, taking her to a new day care where she will meet new playmates and teachers that are excited to meet her. By knowing what to expect (e.g. noise level, activities and new people), she will feel more prepared and less anxious in an otherwise uncomfortable situation.
- When meeting a new adult, you can **prepare her on how to greet**. For example, you can tell her that she will have to say "hello" or maintain eye contact, smile or give a high-five. **Do not tell other adults or children that your child is shy** since she may see this as an excuse not to socially engage with others.

- **Do not over-prepare** your child since this may have the opposite effect of increasing anxiety rather than decreasing it. To ensure that you do not over-prepare her for an upcoming situation, be sure to only spend a couple of minutes going over what she can expect. Parents may rehearse what will happen which may effectively help gain mastery of a new situation.
- **Take your child to school or an event earlier** than the other children since everyone's heads turn when a child comes in late. This may be embarrassing for her and may increase her level of anxiety.
- When arranging play groups, **have her show the other children how to play** an activity she has already mastered. This will help boost her confidence and increase her comfort level with the other children. You can also arrange for one-on-one time for her and a friendly peer.
- Arrange as **many small play groups** as possible and have adults sit in the group to provide comfort ability.
- **Avoid** very large play groups whenever possible.
- **Choose playmates** that are laid back rather than aggressive for your child to feel comfortable.
- **Encourage** her to find toys for other children to show them how to play (e.g. how to build blocks, play with a fire truck) to build her confidence.
- **Competitive music, arts or sports clubs** are often wonderful experiences for shy children, allowing them to have a sense of mastery and camaraderie without feelings "less" when not winning.
- **Never push** to step up or move forward towards a group when she is not ready. Instead, you can say things like, "why don't you go and show them your new doll?" You can even accompany her to a group play session and volunteer to participate along with her until she is comfortable enough to be left alone. Stay as long as she needs you and retreat as soon as she is comfortable.
- **Encourage to participate in activities with other children and help "break the ice" when necessary**. Identify activities that take advantage of the child's strength. Positive reinforcement is particularly effective when she succeeds in certain activities.
- Your child may feel comfortable stepping into a situation with a **security item**. Equip her with a security blanket or favourite stuffed animal. This may also be an "in" for her to enter a play group or have something to show the other children.
- **Start talking** to other children so that she can see that it is not scary starting up conversations with others.
- Try **goal setting** in unfamiliar situations. Aim for small incremental steps and praise her for any progress (e.g. saying "hello" to another child may be an important first step).
- **Do not criticize** for being shy and do not mention your child's shyness to anyone since labels can perpetuate shyness.

- **Do not draw comparisons** between your child and other children at the risk of hurting her feelings or self-esteem, only exacerbating her shyness.
- **Be outgoing yourself.** Model confident and outgoing behaviour to lead by example.
- **Accept** your child's shyness as part of her personality. Express appreciation for who she is.
- **Talk to your child's teachers** about her fears. Listen to how she feels in situations that make her nervous or anxious. Since children can be left behind in school, teachers can help draw her out of quietness and shyness.

TIP: How Teachers can Help
<ul><li>The teacher has to accept the child no matter who she is.</li><li>The teacher should step in to help the child who is uncomfortable or lost.</li><li>For specific types of work, a teacher can pair the shy child with a friendly and more outgoing child.</li><li>Comment when the shy child is successful and have positive comments for her in front of the group.</li><li>Teach children how to appreciate others and their differences.</li><li>If the child continues to be shy, withdrawn, or unhappy, or shyness is an obstacle to learning and making friends, discuss with parents and the child's counsellor.</li></ul>

WHEN TO SEEK PROFESSIONAL HELP

Seek professional help when:
- It takes much longer than one would expect to ease a child into a situation.
- Extreme shyness seems to go on for an extended period of time.
- Shyness prevents your child from doing age-appropriate activities (e.g. having friends, going to parties or play groups, playing in the park).
- It blocks her from forming relationships with individuals outside the family.
- Your child seems disinterested in interacting with others or does not make consistent eye contact with people.
- She is alone most of the time and has difficulty making friends (may indicate a social phobia).
- There is a fear of embarrassment or being criticized by others.
- Your child has tantrums with uncontrollable crying around others, particularly strangers.
- Speech difficulties present when talking with other people.
- School refusal due to feelings of rejections.

For some children with extreme shyness, a formal professional desensitization program involving cognitive-behavioural techniques may be necessary.

ESTABLISHING FRIENDSHIPS

GENERAL

- Social development begins when your child's life begins. Providing your child with his first positive social experience (i.e. with you) begins the foundation for healthy social development. However, babies are unique and born with different temperaments where some are more sociable than others.

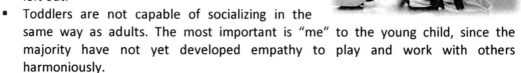

- It is important for a child's socio-emotional development to make friends. Having a child that struggles socially may be worrying for parents. The child himself may feel rejected, lonely and left out.
- Toddlers are not capable of socializing in the same way as adults. The most important is "me" to the young child, since the majority have not yet developed empathy to play and work with others harmoniously.
- Young children are typically devoid of social graces and unable to control many impulses (e.g. sharing toys, offering to play with another child). However, they will grow and learn over time to share and cooperate with others, be sensitive to others' feelings and work on expressing their own thoughts through words rather than aggressive action.

SOCIAL SKILLS: DEVELOPMENT AND AGE

First year of life:

- An infant is a social being from birth, loving other babies and often is very tolerant of toy sharing. While you can try to get your infant to play with others, you should not force it.

Between 1 – 2 years of life:

- It is not until 15-18 months of age that toddlers begin to understand the difference between themselves and others.
- This is the age where they can become truly sociable. For example, your child may reach out to another child who is crying or laughing; though, he may not understand the reasons for crying or laughter, he does understand that someone is hurt or something funny happened.
- Children less than the age of two years do not make real friends or play together with children of their own age; however, they tend to sit side-by-side doing the same activity. While they enjoy playing with other children (or rather next to other children), they do not yet know how to launch a friendship.
- By about 18-24 months of age, toddlers typically enjoy being around other children. While they engage in parallel play (i.e. playing next to or near other children), they may not necessarily play with them. This is normal since they are still learning many social cues from being in the company of other children.

Between 2 – 3 years of age:
- Social skills develop at this age; however children may still be more attracted by the games other children are playing with than by particular children.

3 years+:
- Children at this age are more likely to select activities, because they want to be with a particular child. As children approach the age of three, they learn to be sympathetic and generous with others. They also develop real friendships. It becomes clear now that boys are more assertive while girls are more communicative.

HELPING YOUR CHILD BECOME SOCIABLE
- Social skills are learned and you are the best person to **teach your child** how to become more sociable and how to make friends.
- Provide plenty of **opportunities to socialize** with others. Exposure to other children in a large family, play group or day care will help socialize your little one sooner.
- **Do not pressure** your child to socialize from an early age since it usually does not help; allow him to socialize at his own pace.
- **Model appropriate social behaviour** by socializing with your child. (e.g. at the dinner table, on an outing, at the playground, reading, playing games).
- **Encourage sharing**, social graces (e.g. please, thank you) and help develop conversational skills by consistently talking to him.
- **Praise and do not criticize.** Make him feel good about playing with others.
- **Show affection** since the child who is more open and affectionate will be more likely to have friends.
- **Encourage helping out** around the house in doing chores and caring for others to develop better social skills.
- **Register him for sports or other activities** that he enjoys where he has the opportunities to meet other children who have similar interests.
- **Start playgroups** beginning with one-on-one time, since it is easier to socialize with one other child at a time. Select a child that he seems to get along with the most. Later, set up larger play dates and play groups so that he feels more comfortable around more children.

- **Encourage cooperative games** such as playing ball, hide and seek, arts and crafts, etc.

Additional Suggestions

- In early socializing, supervision is important even when everything seems to be fine.
- Stay nearby, neutral and do not get personally involved since this may disrupt your child's social skill development.
- Do not let your friendship with other parents embarrass your child or get in the way of his friendships.
- Build your child's confidence since he needs to feel good about himself first before reaching out to others.
- Assess why it is difficult for your child to make friends such as aggression issues, shyness, self-containment, etc. Deal with it accordingly.
- Remember that it is normal for a child to be shy since this may be his personality and temperament. It is okay for your child to engage in quieter activities and not be a "social butterfly".
- Praise for participation and encourage responsiveness when he does engage in play activities with other children.

SOCIAL REJECTION

GENERAL

It is difficult for parents to witness their child being rejected by peers. Social rejection often reminds parents of their own childhood experiences of isolation and rejection. However, parents must separate their own past experiences from their child's since this will only serve to enhance the child's difficulties.

To help your child cope and respond to social rejection, parents can try the following:

- Sometimes, rejection is due to difficult behaviours (e.g. whiny or aggressive acts). Try to **understand** when rejection occurs to help your child improve these behaviours.
- **Listen** and understand your child's emotions. Let him know that you understand that he is hurt and that it is not nice to be socially outcast.
- **Explain** that rejection is a normal situation and is certainly not because he is worthless or unloved. Help your child understand that sometimes there will be situations where peers do not want to play with him and that this is normal and happens to everyone. This will help maintain or enhance his self-esteem.
- **Offer other possibilities** by reminding your child that he has other friends or other activities that he likes to do.

There may be times where your child will continually want to play with a specific individual who consistently rejects him. In these cases, it is better to teach your child to learn how to **"stop/leave"** the situation. He must learn to understand that sometimes, it is better to leave or stop wanting something when it is not possible.

If your child seems to be rejected by many of his peers and almost has no friends, then parents should assess causes with a health professional. The child may suffer from emotional problems or he may be unable to "read" social situations properly. Discuss these concerns with your child's teacher, school psychologist or health professional.

WHINING

GENERAL

- Whining is a type of low-grade crying that is steady and unrelenting. It is a form of expression and desire, even when the child is rested, healthy and happy.
- It occurs in toddlers and preschoolers, peaking between the ages of 3-6 years. Whining usually begins in infancy with the "fussy" infant.
- Children generally know who they can whine to and get away with it when the behaviour is successful. They may whine with parents and not with other adults and adults who may be less tolerant to it.

CAUSES

- Children may whine for **attention** and may be triggered by a parent saying "no" to something.
- An **inborn temperament** may be to blame for whining. Some early infants who are irritable may become chronic whiners.
- Children are more prone to whining when they are **tired, hungry, bored, over-stimulated, sick or frustrated**.
- Whining may occur when the child feels **out of control, overwhelmed and has a lack of vocabulary to express frustration and anger**.
- Whining is more likely to occur when she **cannot play with a particular toy** that she covets at the moment or when she is **unable to complete a certain task**.
- Sometimes, there is **no reason** for whining other than the fact that parents allow it. The child will continue to whine as long as she think it is an acceptable form of behaviour.

WHAT TO DO

- To **eliminate triggers** of whining, make sure that:
    - ✓ She is fed when she is hungry.
    - ✓ She naps or rests when she is tired.
    - ✓ She is involved in activities when she is bored.
    - ✓ You change her diaper when she is wet.
    - ✓ She is not coming down with something (i.e. sickness).
- **Do not label** your child as a whiner since she will live up to that label or expectation.
- **Pay attention** to her since many children often whine to seek attention. Set aside some time when you can give her your undivided attention. Also, try not to take too long in answering her questions or offering help when she asks for it.

- **Do not push her** past a certain level of performance that she may not be able to complete. Frustration is a necessary part of growing up and should be within limits.
- **Be a role model** and do not whine yourself. Without realizing it, parents often make requests of their kids in a nagging and whiny tone. Try to always use a "regular" tone.
- If your child begins to whine and you could not prevent it, then try the following:
  - ✓ **Do not yell** to stop the whining. This will often perpetuate it, so be patient.
  - ✓ Try to be as **calm** as you can be.
  - ✓ **Distract** her when reasoning does not work. Overlook her request and offer a diversion that will take her mind off what she is whining about (e.g. toy).
  - ✓ **Whine together** since you sometimes end up laughing together.
  - ✓ **Encourage her to be verbal** about what she is whining about.
  - ✓ Use **reverse psychology** by telling her that you don't think she is whining enough. If your child moves from whining to a full-blown tantrum, however, then do not try this again.
  - ✓ **Ask her questions** about what she is whining about. Ask things like "are you tired", "are you hungry", and "do you want to play?"
  - ✓ Tell her you will only listen when she uses her **"regular" voice.**
  - ✓ **Avoid eye contact** and do not respond to her as long as the whining continues. Do not say "yes" to something after having said "no", because you want her to stop; it will reinforce the behaviour.
- When your child stops whining, **try your best to fulfill her request**. If you cannot give her what she wants, then explain why you can't and offer other options.
- **Play a tape** to show her what she sounds like when she whines and play another tape to show her what her "regular" voice is like.
- **Praise** her when she accepts a "no" answer without whining.
- **Do not remove privileges** or punish her for whining (it is a form of attention and may reinforce the whining).
- **Be persistent, firm and consistent.**

Comment: Talk to your doctor if your child whines all the time, seems generally unhappy and none of the above suggestions seem to work.

THE SENSITIVE BABY/CHILD

Parent Concern: My 3 ½ year old son is sensitive at the slightest provocation or challenge. He cries for a long time, almost as though something terrible just happened. What should I do?

GENERAL

- Babies begin learning to calm themselves in the first few months of life while remaining interested and engaged in the environment. They learn to relate to people in a warm and trusting way by studying their parents' faces and gestures. Particularly gratifying is the growing ability to vocalize and express thoughts and feelings with words and gestures. However, these goals may be elusive for the overly sensitive child. New people, sights, sounds and smells may be easily overwhelming for some children and can make them cry.
- As a toddler, the very sensitive child continues to be demanding and clingy. He may throw awful tantrums, especially when parents leave him at the day care. New situations may upset him and he may avoid playing with other children in the new day care setting. He may even act aggressively by moving out of fear, biting or hitting.
- Sometimes, even the slightest challenge or provocation for trivial events can cause the sensitive child to collapse weeping or crumbling to the floor in tears. He may cry longer than warranted, show dramatic emotional responses (e.g. anger, crying) causing parents to be embarrassed and peers discerned.
- For the young child, crying is a method of communication that allow expression of feelings and frustration. Typically, this method is reduced as vocabulary increases; however, the sensitive child may continue to cry as he gets older.

CAUSES/TRIGGERS

- **Genetics:** The extreme emotional sensitivity is a personality trait (often inborn) that appears to be partly genetic. In many cases, it can be seen soon after birth. For example, these babies may seem uncomfortable in certain types of diapers and may startle easily.
- **Feeling emotionally overwhelmed:** A sensitive child may become upset when he goes to a new and potentially threatening situation (e.g. visiting the doctor, barber, friend's home), where he feels emotionally overwhelmed.
- **Parental behaviour:** A parent's behaviour may trigger or perpetuate an emotional outburst. Remember that young children are especially attuned to parental emotions. For example, a preschooler who senses that his mother is upset may react by crying for what may seem like no apparent reason. Some children may cry more easily when parents unconsciously encourage it by, for example, overreacting to an emotional or physical injury.

HOW TO REDUCE SENSITIVITY

To reduce crying to a more bearable level, you can try the following:

- **Be sensitive**. Try not to get angry with your child since knowing that you are upset with him will only reinforce his belief that there is something wrong with him. Your child wants your approval and love.
- Respond with **understanding and empathy**. For example, do not insist that he "toughs it out" as it can make him feel more isolated and vulnerable.
- **Do not make fun** of your child's feelings. Keep teasing to a minimum. Allow him to witness joking between siblings and family so that he may learn not to let it hurt his feelings so easily.
- **Do not be over-protective or over-cuddle** the sensitive child. Cuddling the child every time he cries will only serve to reinforce his sensitivity. This will do more harm in the future than good. Moreover, cuddling teaches him that getting emotional will get him out of unpleasant situations.
- **Do not reinforce crying.** Some children may think this is the only way to gain attention, so pay extra attention when he is behaving appropriately. Crying should not be rewarded nor punished. The parental response to crying should be neutral, when possible.
- **Do not discourage crying**. Crying is a sign that he is overwhelmed and discouraging crying may only upset him even further.
- **Use distractions and alternatives**, whenever possible. If these do not work, then offer a small dose of comfort. Teach him to say "I am sad/hurt" when something is bothering him to replace crying (i.e. teach expression).
- **Increase self-esteem with praise.** Low self-esteem can increase crying, so boost self-esteem every chance you get by acknowledging good behaviour and accomplishments and using criticism sparingly.
- **Discipline with a light touch or communicating disapproval.** Punishments such as yelling out or time outs are not necessary. When the child makes a mistake, try to focus on the positive first. For example, if your child spills juice, then tell him you are happy he finished the juice but that he was supposed to spill the juice in the cup.
- **Do not label your child as "sensitive".** If you need to explain your child's sensitivity to others, do so when he is not around.
- **Do not always assume that there is nothing to cry about.** Investigate the cause first and remember that a sensitive baby may even cry over a small scratch. It is important to respond with at least a look to every cry.

Comment: The Positive Side of a Sensitive Child

According to some researchers, many sensitive children are also more understanding and empathetic to the feelings of others. They also tend to laugh more than others. In addition, a highly sensitive child is often bright, articulate, creative and insightful.

THE CLINGY CHILD

GENERAL

- It can be quite unsettling and burdensome to have a young child attached to you at all times, particularly when you are trying to get things done.
- Clinginess is a common phase in the early years of life including the preschool age. It typically presents around the age of nine months, peaking at 18 months and becomes less intense over time.

WHY IT HAPPENS

- The causes for clinginess are unique to each child since children handle stress differently. **However, common causes may include**:
    - Illness (e.g. ear infections)
    - Temperament (i.e. impulsive desires to be attached to the caregiver)
    - Late walker (may be a cause for excessive clinginess)
    - Traumatic experiences (e.g. parental divorce, hospitalization, illness or death of a parent, natural disaster)
    - Distressing separation or threats of abandonment
    - Sudden transitions (e.g. arrival of a new baby, moving to a new home, new day care center)

WHAT TO DO

- In the beginning, you should try to **ignore** as much of the clinging behaviour as you can.
- Provide great amounts of **physical attention** (e.g. hugs, kisses, physical contact, and reading books) that will help your child be more secure.
- Allow your child to **play independently**, but ensure times of social interaction with you and others as well.
- **Play hide-and-seek games**. Gradually extend the time that you are hidden from view and use the same phrases when you leave and come back from hiding. This helps your child understand that you will always return to him.

- **If you need to separate from your child**:
    - ✓ **Prepare** your child for separation. For example, when he goes to the day care, make sure you introduce him to the teacher before leaving him there on the first school day to help ease the transition.
    - ✓ **Create goodbye rituals** like offering a kiss or hug before you leave. You can also try giving your child a small, special stone that he can leave in his pocket as a symbol that you are always there. This can help build your child's confidence.

- ✓ **Always be consistent and leave**. Do not communicate your own anxiety about leaving since this will certainly not help your child's anxiety. Reassure your child that you will see him later, say goodbye and leave.
- ✓ **Find a potential substitute** that your child likes and trusts such as a babysitter, friend or sibling.
- **When at home, tell your child to play with toys or games to keep him interested in an area in the room while you are in the same room doing something else**. This will offer similar support, but not exactly following you everywhere you go in the home. Be sure to talk to your child while you are doing your own activity to encourage moral support. Maintain comforting contact when you are out of view (talk or sing to him).
- Also when at home, **be consistent in telling your child that he cannot come with you into the shower or bathroom**. Let him know in a firm tone that you will not be long and tell him he can play by himself in his room or your room or with other family members while you are in there. Offer rewards for the first few times until he lets you go without a fuss.
- **Be patient** with your child. Offer love and support, especially since he will eventually outgrow it.

WHAT NOT TO DO

- Make sure you are not dependent on your child's dependence, unconsciously encouraging it. Become aware of your own role and the part you play in your child's dependence and clinginess.
- Do not rob your child of confidence by being overprotective or offering too much reassurance. Try to find the balance between allowing your child to grow independently while using your help and guidance.
- Do not share your anxiety with your child since he will feel it and become anxious himself.

Additional Concern:
If my child still clings onto me despite all my efforts, what should I do?

- ✓ Conduct your day calmly with your child by your side. Let him hold onto you so that he can see that his efforts to gain attention by this manner fail; he is likely to then give it up.
- ✓ Remember that some degree of clinginess is common well into the preschool years.
- ✓ Excessive clinginess can be a sign of separation anxiety disorder or other disorders. Consult a health professional should you have any further concerns.

TALKATIVENESS

Parent Concern: What can I do when my child chats all the time while I am trying to do something? (e.g. When I am on the phone or trying to prepare dinner?)

GENERAL

- Talkativeness typically begins between 3-4 years of age when the brain is maturing in language-related areas and tends to occur more in girls than boys.
- Language skills are new and exciting for your little one and she wants to speak as much as possible. The lack of inhibition combined with new language skills means that she will often say what is on her mind.

- Talkativeness is a function of child personality, confidence level and environment. Children tend to speak excessively when they are placed in safe and comfortable situations (e.g. home) or when they are anxious. Incessant talking can be a way of getting attention. Non stop talking is also a way to say (look at me, listen to me, etc).
- The amount of chatting by the child does not indicate long-term intelligence; however these talkative children do tend to do better when beginning school.

GETTING A MOMENT OF PEACE

- **Do not tell your child not to talk** too much since it can set her back. Instead, you can say that you cannot talk at the present time, but that you will be able to talk later.
- **Ask** your child to be quiet without discouraging her to speak.
- **Remind** her that it is impolite to interrupt and tell her to wait until you are finished doing what you are doing.
- You can say such things:
    - ✓ "I know you have something to share, but it is not your turn to speak right now."
    - ✓ "Sometimes, I need quiet time and right now is one of those times."
    - ✓ "As soon as I am finished what I am doing, I would love to listen to you."
- Do not say the following things:
    - ✓ "You talk too much!"
    - ✓ "We have heard enough out of you!"
    - ✓ "Can't you be quiet for a change?"
- If children hear the above messages repeatedly, they will feel inhibited to share their thoughts later in life. Negative messages can impact a child's sense of worth and self-confidence.
- **Teach your child appropriate talking behaviours**, especially when among other peers and teachers, etc. Teach socially acceptable behaviour such as waiting turn to speak and not interrupting others, who also has something really exciting to say or share but cannot get a chance because someone else is always talking.

ENDLESS QUESTIONS

Parent Concern: Why does my child ask so many questions?

GENERAL

- Shortly after a child learns to talk, many questions arise. Asking questions is the way a child learns about the world and a way of practicing language skills. It can also be due to attention seeking or the child insatiable needs to figure out how things work and what goes with that.
- The most common word used by toddlers is "why" and these questions can be repetitive and endless.
- Young children want to learn the "how" and "why" of everything around them to understand how the world works, so offer valuable and informative answers (depending on the child's age).
- From the age of 4-6 years, the child begins to ask numerous questions. The age of 5 years is when children tend to attempt solving their own questions before asking others.
- Do not discourage your child from asking questions and make sure that you respond as honestly as possible, even if it means answering "I don't know". If you cannot answer the question at the time it is asked, then you can say that you will explain it later (instead of dropping what you are doing).
- When you believe your child is asking many questions for attention-seeking purposes, then pretend to ignore the questions. If it is related to a disciplinary matter, avoid getting into any conversation with him and know that "because I said so" is a good enough response (especially to a "but why?"). It is fairly obvious when questions are for genuine curiosity purposes or attention-seeking.
- Relentless questions can sometimes make parents anxious, but parents should be aware that children ask more questions as they expand their language skills.

TIP: Knowing My Name

In the first few months of life, the name of the child is used continuously; however, this does not mean that he understands that the name is designed for him and not for other toys, persons or objects. It is between the ages of 12-15 months that he understands that his name is designed only for him.

SHARING

THE CONCEPT OF SHARING

Sharing is an important aspect of socialization; however it needs to be taught, nurtured gradually and appropriately. We value sharing tremendously in our culture. We associate it with maturity, empathy and social competence. Parents talk about it repeatedly while preschool teachers constantly remind children to share. Yet, many children find the concept of sharing difficult and confusing to understand.

- Think about sharing from a young child's point of view. They just mastered the concept of ownership and they see little reason to relinquish anything. They do not understand that something given away may be returned to them.
- Although confusing and upsetting to a toddler, many find the concept of sharing fascinating.
- Every child is unique and each will learn the various characteristics of generosity, kindness and self-sacrifice at different paces and to a varying degree. However, it is essential that children be introduced to these concepts at an acceptable and appropriate age.
- Young children are especially comfortable sharing toys when it is highly valued. It is easier to share a stuffed animal or a puzzle, if he can still keep an eye on it or play with it alongside the borrower. Quantity also plays a role; a child is more likely to share a crayon or a toy car if there are others in a box.
- Before the age of three years, the concept of sharing does not seem to make any sense to the young child. He does not yet understand that objects can and do belong to other individuals and not just him.
- He will continue to believe that all objects belong to him until about 2 ½ - 3 years of age. Your son is at an age commonly referred to as the "terrible twos". This age group exhibits more self-awareness and feelings of autonomy; particularly over many things they call their own.

HOW TO TEACH & PROMOTE SHARING

- **Do not expect too much too soon.** If you push too hard, all you are teaching your child is to comply with authority.
- **Occasionally he may refuse to share.** It is normal to go through periods of possessiveness, especially when he is feeling stressed.
- **Social interactions** with other children are great opportunities for you to teach how to share with friends (e.g. play dates or play groups)

- Play **imitating games** that involve giving things to others. This way, children will learn to share with one another and enjoy playing games that foster teamwork and cooperation.
- **Establish sharing activities at home** such as buying toys and books to share between siblings and/or parents. Encourage children to swap toys every once in a while and plan family activities together (e.g. working together in the yard). You can also ask to borrow something of your child's on occasion while explaining why it is important to share. Another example would be to share a magazine or book with your child, presenting the concept of sharing. You can say, "David would like a turn" (give the child a choice about giving it up. The child is more apt to do so). If he is not finished with the toy, you can tell him he can have a turn soon.
- **Model appropriate sharing behaviour.** Give your child the opportunity to work it out with the other individual he is fighting with. If things are not working out between the two, then you can step in and show them how to share a toy or they will not be able to play with it anymore. You can also encourage your child to offer a favourite play toy to a visiting guest.
- **Put your child's favourite toys away.** Every parent knows that your child's favourite toys cause major problems. As such, be sure to put your child's favourite toys away when play dates come over. Do not allow your child to take his favourite toy to play groups or any others socialization groups as well.
- **Provide numerous, various and similar toys** during group play. It will allow you to offer another toy or similar toy to one of the children fighting and allows children to understand that not everything is their own.
- Allow sharing **selected toys**. Note that it is unfair to expect your child to share absolutely everything.
- **Always praise** for sharing or helping out. You can say things like: "what a good sharer you are"; "nice manners"; etc. Similarly, you can withdraw privileges of playing if your child refuses to share until he agrees to. Explain the discomfort and unhappiness it causes others when one does not share.
- Explain that **friendship with others is more important** than objects or toys.
- **Maintain a calm and neutral tone** always when talking to your child about sharing. You can use positive words by telling your children what they should do rather than telling them what they should not do (e.g. do not say "don't take that toy away from him"; instead, you can say "please give your friend the toy").
- Try **distracting your child** to other activities, diverting attention away from the disrupting toy to another. This usually does the trick in resolving any sharing disputes.

DEVELOPING SELF-ESTEEM

GENERAL

- Self-esteem is an individual's evaluation of his own worth. It is how we feel about ourselves and our behaviour is a direct reflection of these feelings.
- Part of being a parent is providing your child with **encouragement** and the development of a healthy self-esteem.
- A child with high self-esteem will be able to take responsibility for his own actions, tolerate frustration, accept criticism, act independently, handle positive and negative emotions in a healthy manner, prides in accomplishments and attempts new tasks and challenges.
- A child with low self-esteem may avoid trying new things, feel unloved or unwanted, frustrates easily, ignores own talents and abilities, easily influenced and may feel emotionally indifferent.

PROMOTING SELF-ESTEEM

Be generous with praise and recognition	<ul><li>**Let your child know** that he is doing something well.</li><li>Offer praise, even in front of other family members & friends (e.g. "You are very kind; I like the way you arranged your room; you tried your best").</li><li>Remember to **offer praise for attempts**, even though these attempts may not always be successful.</li><li>**Encourage** your child to attempt new and challenging tasks.</li></ul>
Avoid criticism	<ul><li>Criticism should be used to teach and build self-esteem, not tear it down. Be sure not to offer criticism that is in the form of ridicule or shame.</li><li>While it is necessary to criticize your child's actions, you should **offer constructive criticism** that outlines what he did well and what he needs to work on. For example, rather than saying "why are you such a lazy and disorganized boy?" you can say "I would like you to keep your clothes in the closet and not all over the room".</li><li>**Keep criticism under control.** Do not repeat the same criticisms over and over again, because that may serve to lower your child's self-esteem.</li></ul>

Making Decisions	<ul><li>Help encourage your child to **make good, conscious decisions**.</li><li>You can help by clarifying the problem, offering solutions or discussing possible solutions.</li><li>Allow your child to make the decision and **solve the problem on his own,** after you have taught him to carefully consider the consequences.</li><li>Provide plenty of space. Do not hover over him or always offer assistance as this will decrease his confidence.</li><li>A child's decisions should make him feel good about himself, so stand by him when he makes bad decisions. Nobody is perfect and your little one will make mistakes.</li></ul>
Love & comfort	<ul><li>Be sure to tell your child that you love him, hug him and smile (e.g. "I love you no matter what").</li><li>**Offer a consistent amount of attention** so that your child feels worthwhile by talking and listening to him when he talks. Avoid saying "I'm busy".</li><li>Be fair by **not comparing** your child with other children including siblings, playmates or peers. Do not make any comparisons, whether positive or negative since you may ultimately weaken his self-esteem.</li><li>Make your child **feel like a valued member of the family** by offering equal consideration.</li><li>Simply be there for your child.</li><li>Offer empathy.</li></ul>
Modeling & expectations	<ul><li>Inspire your little one to think well of himself by being a role model for him to look up to.</li><li>Model self-respect and self-confidence; avoid doubting yourself.</li><li>**Watch your language**. Do not say things like "you are fat" or "you always...you never" and so forth.</li><li>**Avoid stirring up guilt** by saying things like "it's because of you that we can't go out".</li><li>Balance expectations from your child. Remember your child's age and ability in all situations.</li><li>Set reasonable limits and **provide expectations** that are **clear and consistent** so there is no confusion; knowing what to expect can make a child feel more comfortable and secure.</li><li>Put him to work by assigning tasks around the house. Express your confidence in his abilities to complete the chores or help out. You may even offer assistance during a task.</li><li>**Accept your child's feelings**, even if it includes negative and difficult emotions.</li><li>Teach him to express and communicate his emotions.</li></ul>

EMOTIONAL HEALTH

RAISING AN EMOTIONALLY HEALTHY CHILD

- Emotionally healthy children tend to perform better in academics, possess effective coping strategies during stressful times and experience mutually respectful relationships.
- **Spending quality time** with your child is the most valuable contribution parents can make towards developing the child's emotional health.
- **Talk and listen** to your child to allow communication and the expression of feelings, wants and needs.
- Show **respect and value** each child for her unique and special qualities.
- **Be prepared** as parents by knowing the behaviours and development of your child at each age to help better identify any real problems.
- **Praise** for good behaviour and positive actions; you can even offer small rewards.
- **Be clear and consistent** about rules, education and expectations.
- **Punish with caution**. Excessive yelling, threats or physical strikes teaches a child how to respond when they are upset and can lead to emotionally unhealthy perception and response situations.
- **Demonstrate appreciation** for others.

TIP: Emotionally Healthy Parents – How to Deal with Guilty Feelings

- Feelings of guilt include: "I don't hold her enough"; "I screamed at him today"; or "I had no patience and was irritated with her all day".
- Parenting is one of the hardest jobs in life, so it is common that parents will sometimes lose their patience or exercise discipline or punishment, and later feel guilty about doing so. As such, it is important for parents' emotional health to deal with guilty feelings.
- Some parents have a difficult time simply saying "no" to their child while others say "no" all the time and later feel guilty about it.
- Remember that children feel what you are feeling. If you are experiencing guilty feelings, then children will know that and use it to their advantage. This provides the child with power that can be strong and destructive.
- Children need parents who are strong, confident and act in a firm, consistent manner. So, if you acted a certain way you are feeling guilty about, then make it a point not to say or do it again the following day. BUT, do not show your guilty feelings or "make-up" for your guilt.

TIP: Infancy & Childhood Emotional Attachment

(A) Infancy

- Formation of attachments between child and parents/caregivers is of vital importance for emotional health. It is important for parents to be warm and affectionate as well as sensitive and responsive to child's needs.
- It is important to have a goodness-of-fit whereby interactions between parents and child demonstrate being in-tune through turn taking in expressing emotions e.g. Parent smiles and then child smiles in response.
- If parents express emotions freely, children will model this.

(B) Childhood

- The best parenting style is "authoritative" (according to Baumrind). These parents set limits in a loving manner (no harsh punishment) while guiding the child.

ANXIETY

GENERAL

- Anxiety is a mood state characterized by strong negative emotions, fear, distress, worry and bodily symptoms where the child apprehensively anticipates future danger or misfortune.
- It is important to distinguish between normal levels of anxiety and unhealthy or pathologic levels of anxiety.
- Anxiety disorder is considered when the child experiences excessive and debilitating anxiety.
- The frequency of anxiety in children is unknown, though seems to be under-reported and under-diagnosed. It is often overlooked in children, because some children hide the anxiety or mask it in angry tantrums or defiant behaviour.
- An anxious child can impact the family since he can be overly demanding and very emotional in certain situations. As such, early identification and therapy is necessary to maintain a healthy and happy child and family.

TIP: Generalized Anxiety Disorder

A child with generalized anxiety disorder (GAD) may be chronically anxious and appears restless, nervous and tense. If the child experiences severe anxiety, he may experience feelings of helplessness, feeling inferior to others and loss of realism. He may be afraid to engage in new behaviours that may threaten his security, thus become a "homebody" and depressed.

SOURCES OF ANXIETY

- **Temperament**: Some children are born with anxious temperaments and seem to be concerned about many situations right from birth.
- **Genetics**: Studies show that 50% of children with panic disorder present with family histories of the disorder.
- **Developmental aspects:** Throughout childhood, fear and worries are part of normal development. Fears of the dark, monsters, parental separation, animals and strangers are often seen.
- **Psychological factors**: When internal or external stresses overwhelm children, normal coping abilities are lessened for unknown reasons.
- **Environmental changes** that may predispose to anxiety include the birth of a new sibling, changing to a new school or neighbourhood, moving to a new home, etc.

- **Traumatic events**: Examples of traumatic events that contribute to anxiety include parental conflicts and separation, illness or injury, unexpected deaths, family or community violence, natural disasters, and so forth.
- **Medical causes**: Cardiovascular diseases, arrhythmias, hyperthyroidism, infections and certain rare tumours may contribute to anxiety.

IDENTIFYING THE ANXIOUS CHILD

Children who struggle with excessive anxiety may present the following:
- **Physical signs:** Stomachaches, headaches, fatigue, dizziness, dry mouth, vomiting, decreased appetite, nausea, fainting, increased heart rate, blurred vision, muscle tension and numbness.

- **Behavioral symptoms:**
  - ✓ Withdrawal from peers, social activities and family interaction
  - ✓ Sleep difficulties (e.g. difficulties falling asleep, staying asleep, nightmares, night terrors)
  - ✓ Excessive fears (e.g. thunderstorms, elevators, worried about something bad happening)
  - ✓ Avoiding peers
  - ✓ Difficulties initiating conversation with peers or speaking in class
  - ✓ Difficulties concentrating
  - ✓ Eating disturbances
  - ✓ Crying or screaming
  - ✓ Fidgeting and avoiding eye contact
  - ✓ Anger, aggression, irritability/hyperactivity and tantrums
  - ✓ Excessive clinginess and separation anxiety
  - ✓ Bedwetting
  - ✓ Separation anxiety from parents

- **Cognitive symptoms:**
  - ✓ Thoughts of incompetence and inadequacy
  - ✓ Being scared, hurt or sad
  - ✓ Intrusive thoughts about wild animals or monsters
  - ✓ Obsession with perfectionism
  - ✓ Pessimism and negative thinking patterns such as imagining the worst, over-exaggeration and guilty thoughts

HOW TO HELP

Environment	<ul><li>Reduce stressors at home and school (since anxiety may result in decreased school performance).</li><li>Avoid or minimize stimulants such as caffeine and drugs.</li><li>Avoid over-scheduling and extracurricular activities.</li><li>Establish daily routines and structure to reduce anxieties.</li><li>Provide opportunities for the child to communicate (e.g. at mealtime or during play).</li><li>Provide opportunities for exercise to relieve stress or other</li></ul>

	activities to help the child feel good (i.e. playing with friends, reading books). ▪ Offer comfort (verbal reassurance of safety) and distraction. ▪ Set limits and consequences for breaking limits. ▪ Reward when the child tries to approach a feared situation and praise coping efforts. ▪ Teach problem solving strategies and do not jump in right away to solve problems.

TREATMENT & WHEN TO CONSULT THE HEALTH PROFESSIONAL

When your child presents with excessive anxiety to anticipated future events that prevents him and the family from enjoying normal life experiences, a health professional should be consulted. While some fears can be expected and typical for young children, others are inappropriate and excessive. Consult with your child health professional when the child seems to be displaying the previously mentioned symptoms of anxiety.

▪ Typically, the main form of treatment for anxiety is to directly deal with the anxieties and fears by exposing young children to objects, events and situations that produce the anxiety in the first place. A form of therapy often used with young children who present with anxiety is cognitive-behavioral therapy. Cognitive behavioural therapy is most effective for treating anxiety in children. Behavioural therapy focuses on techniques such as progressive desensitization, relaxation training, guided imagery and flooding to reduce anxious responses or eliminate specific phobias. This type of therapy teaches children the following:

⇒ To understand how thoughts and feelings contribute to anxiety and how to modify negative thoughts to decrease symptoms. Discuss unhealthy thoughts and show the child how to turn them into positive and productive feelings.

⇒ How to change maladaptive thoughts to decrease symptoms (e.g. by replacing thinking patterns such as "I'm going to die" turns into "I can handle a little bit of dizziness")

⇒ How to cope with anxieties and fears (other than escaping or avoiding situations, persons or places)

⇒ Social reinforcement can sometimes be used to encourage and reward the child for successful coping with anxiety

⇒ Teach positive self-talk.

$\Rightarrow$ Encourage the child to share his emotions and thoughts.

$\Rightarrow$ Help him identify feelings and show your feelings as well.

$\Rightarrow$ Listen to your child and do not dismiss his feelings or negative thoughts.

Medications are not always used for anxiety disorders in young children since it may be ineffective in treating the actual source of anxiety. However, it may help in some children such as those with OCD (obsessive-compulsive disorder). Anti-anxiety medications are sometimes used in cases of severe anxiety in consultation with your health professional and psychologist.

SEPARATION ANXIETY

GENERAL

- Separation anxiety is when your child fears being away from you or other family members he feels most attached to. It is different than stranger anxiety (which is normal for children) since it is a fear attached to the people the child knows.

- Separation anxiety affects most babies and toddlers to varying degrees with some children having more pronounced anxiety than others.
- Separation anxiety is to be expected to some degree in all children under the age of 5 or 6 years.

WHEN IT STARTS & IT'S DURATION

- Separation anxiety can begin as early as 7 months of age. It is especially difficult during the first year of life. However, it usually peaks around 12-18 months.
- While some babies and toddlers may never experience separation anxiety, others suffer it much later (sometimes around 3-4 years of age).
- Unfortunately, separation anxiety can last as long as a few months or can be on and off for a period of time. In severe cases, the anxiety may continue for a few years.
- In most cases, separation anxiety fades during the last half of the second year of life or, at least, becomes less frequent and intense.

CAUSES & PREDISPOSING FACTORS

There is a diversity of opinions among health professionals regarding the reasons for separation anxiety. Most believe that children grow to feel a strong attachment to the parents and caregivers and when left alone, they are scared. The desire to be with the parent or caregiver is a sign of attachment to the child's first great love – YOU!

Yet, the following are some reasons to help explain separation anxiety:

a) **Maturity**: Separation anxiety is a sign that your child is maturing. His cognitive skills have expanded to the point where he understands the difference between places and people, comparing and judging them. With the increasing independence that accompanies exploration, the child takes comfort knowing that you are close to him (should he need you).

b) **Object permanence**: When your child is at a young age, he does not yet understand the concept of object permanence (i.e. even if someone or something is not visible, it still exists). As such, your child feels that if you are out of sight, you are out of mind (not knowing if and when you are coming back). He cannot grasp the fact that he will see you later. However, at an older age, he understands object permanence and knows that just because he cannot see you, you are there or will return.

c) **Improved memory**: The young child will remember you saying goodbye, though he is not sure if and when you are returning; thus making him incredibly anxious and causing separation anxiety. This is similar to object permanence; however, as your child's memory improves with age, he will remember all the times you return after leaving.
d) **Temperament** may play a strong role in how your child reacts to situations.
e) **Genetics**: Some health professionals believe that genetics play a role in the development of separation anxiety. According to these experts, anxious parents tend to have anxious children and some children are "born" with higher levels of "alarm hormones".

TRIGGERS & SYMPTOMS
Possible Triggers
- Leaving your child with another caregiver or at a daycare center
- Placing your baby to bed at night
- New siblings, family members or caregivers
- Changes in the home environment (e.g. moving homes, changing rooms) or family dynamics (e.g. family death, step-parents)
- Children who experience/ predisposed to extreme or intolerable separation anxiety typically come from close-knit families, in which strangers or anything new is mistrusted.
- Other children who seem particularly prone to separation anxiety are those with developmental disorders in learning or attention (ADHD).

Symptoms
- Inconsolable crying
- Clinging and/or resisting all attempts to calm the child
- Wanting to be carried or held all the time
- Wary of other people
- Regresses in some areas
- Difficulty going to bed
- Night waking or nightmares
- Temper tantrums

WHAT TO DO
To minimize anxiety and guilt, maintain a good sense of humor and try the following. However, you should remember that each child is unique and will respond differently.

Before Leaving	✓ Ensure that the caregiver is reliable, understanding, supportive and responsive.
	✓ Caregivers should arrive 15-30 minutes before you plan to leave.
	✓ Try to schedule leaving after naps and mealtime since tiredness and hunger may increase the risk of a separation anxiety episode.
	✓ Notify your child in advance that you are leaving.
	✓ Do not leave when your child is sleeping since he may panic when he wakes up and finds you not there.
	✓ Offer your child something to look forward to (e.g. reading a book together or playing together) upon your return.
	✓ *TIP:* Help your child cope with separation anxiety through short practice sessions at home. You can leave the room while he is there supervised. Return a short while later and reassure your child that you will always return.
During the Leave	✓ Offer a comforting hug and kiss to make your departure a happy ritual.
	✓ Do not prolong goodbyes or make them overly sentimental (even when your child is tearful).
	✓ Do not show him any stress or anxiety that you may be experiencing yourself.
	✓ Reassure him that you will return and say something like, "see you later alligator".
	✓ When you take your child to the day care, do not drag him in there and then "ditch" him. Spend a few minutes playing with him in this new and exciting environment and then say you will return. This will allow him some time to get comfortable before you leave.
Once you Leave	✓ Repeated appearances will make it harder on you and the child, so when you leave – LEAVE!
	✓ When possible, leave only for a short period of time.
	✓ Limit outings for 1-2 hours until your child is comfortable with you leaving. At that point, you can lengthen the time spent apart.
	✓ Have the caregiver create a playful and fun distraction for your child to enjoy when you leave, so that he will not miss you or cry.
	✓ Some babies can cry for hours on end when the parent is gone. In these cases, you may have to limit the time away from your child until the "missing mom" phase is gone.
	✓ If your baby is truly inconsolable when left with another caregiver, then you should re-evaluate your child care situation. It is possible that the caregiver is not providing your child with the attention he needs or it may simply be that he is experiencing a severe case of separation anxiety.

WHEN TO BE CONCERNED

- When worries or fears are developmentally inappropriate, separation anxiety disorder may be present.
- Separation anxiety disorder is defined as an excessive worry or fear about being apart from certain individuals or family members.
- This disorder usually occurs around the 3rd or 4th grade.
- Symptoms of separation anxiety disorder may be different in each child, though may include:
  - ✓ Excessive worries about getting lost or away from the family
  - ✓ Excessive distress when separated from the home
  - ✓ Refusal to sleep alone
  - ✓ Repeated nightmares with the reoccurring theme of separation
  - ✓ Refusal to go to school
  - ✓ Frequent stomach aches, headaches, muscle aches and tension
  - ✓ Excessive clinginess
- A child's psychologist or mental health professional typically diagnoses anxiety disorders in children or adolescents.
- Treatment will depend on your child's age, overall health and medical history, extent of symptoms, expectations, tolerance to medications or therapies.
- Effective treatment depends on a comprehensive evaluation of the child and family (e.g. cognitive behavioural therapy, anti-anxiety medication, consultation with the child's school).
- Early detection and intervention will help reduce the severity of the disorder.

IMAGINARY FRIENDS

GENERAL

- It is common for young children between the ages of 3-8 years to have an imaginary friend (i.e. a pretend buddy).
- Often, imaginary friends appear between the ages of 2-3 years and stay for a couple of years (usually until the preschool years of 5-6).
- Imaginary friends come in all shapes and sizes and can have different personalities and behaviours. Sometimes, the make-believe friend is someone your child knows, a storybook character, or purely made up from your child's imagination. In some cases, imaginary friends can be stuffed animals.
- Some children may have more than one imaginary friend that appear alone or together. Others have a new pretend friend every week or one that lasts for years.
- There is a feeling that imaginary friends occur more frequently to an **only** child, the eldest in the family, abused or neglected children as it is more likely to provided them with needed company, relieve distress and loneliness that indicates pathology.

- Imaginary friends are companions for your child. They are under his control and desires and pose no threat or harm.
- As the child grows and attends school, imaginary friends quickly disappear around the age of 8 years and are replaced with real friends.
- Do not worry about your child being anti-social or shy simply because he has an imaginary friend. In fact, studies show that children with imaginary friends are less shy, more creative and more popular than those without.

THE ROLE OF THE IMAGINARY FRIEND

Imaginary friends help your child in various ways including the following:
- Being an ideal companion (especially when lonely or bored)
- Playmate (kids talk, read and play with them)
- Listens and supports your child (e.g. helps your child deal with fears and anger)
- Belongs only to your child (i.e. special friends)
- Passes no judgment or faults against your child
- Exploration of a make-believe world
- Protector and provider of comfort in a scary world
- A way to practice social skills
- A private life that no one else is a part of

- Helps children work through real-life issues
- Children are able to vent anxiety and feel more acceptable
- Enables the child to differentiate between good and bad behaviours
- Creates a healthy conscience

RESPONDING TO IMAGINARY FRIENDS
- **Accept and welcome** your child's imaginary friends and imagination. For example, you can go along with the imaginary friend by adding a pillow beside him when he goes to sleep.
- **Respect** your child's privacy.
- **Allow** your child to take the lead in how you respond. You will usually be asked to make room for the imaginary friend in different ways (e.g. providing a car seat, table setting). Do not offer an extra plate or kiss unless your child asks you to do so.
- **Do not allow the child to place blame** on his imaginary friend. Tell him that his friend could not have said or done anything to be blamed for and provide an appropriate disciplinary action (e.g. cleaning up the mess).
- **Do not allow the imaginary friend to become your child's personal voice**. Some children will not respond to a question or comment until they speak with their imaginary friends. Tell the child that you are only interested in hearing what he has to say or do himself.
- Some parents seem to use the imaginary friend to help the toddler learn skills including brushing teeth or putting on a jacket. This may not work since, in some children, it may resent the loss of control over their friend; thus, the child becomes uncooperative. Only use this technique if your child allows for it.
- **Encourage your child to do things himself** (e.g. opening doors, cleaning up). Do not do these things for his friend and try not to take away opportunities for your child to learn key skills.
- **Allow him to figure out what is real** and what is not.
- **Encourage the use of other outlets** to explore the imagination (e.g. dolls, stuffed animals, puppets, books, movie characters).
- **Provide play dates with real children** so that the imaginary friends gradually disappear.

TIP: Your Child's Mind
Often times, your child's imaginary friend can offer you plenty of insight into your child's own thoughts. You can find out about your child's likes, dislikes, tastes, favourites and so forth.

WHEN TO SEEK HELP

Imaginary friends can sometimes indicate signs of serious difficulties requiring professional consultation in the following:

a) Imaginary companions still present by 9-10 years of age.

b) Imaginary friends are not usually warm, friendly or helpful; rather they are frightening or make your child do "bad" or self-destructive behaviours.

c) The imaginary friend that seems to take over the child. Usually this occurs with neglected or abused children and can be a precursor to dissociative identity disorder (formerly called multiple personality disorder). However, this is very rare and should not concern the majority of parents of children with imaginary friends.

CHILDERN FEARS

GENERAL
- A fear is being scared of something or someone. It is a normal reaction in childhood and an important part of normal development.
- In some cases, fears can interfere with daily functioning and cause significant stress. As such, understanding child fears and knowing how to respond will help your child reduce the anxiety of fears or eliminate them altogether.

CAUSES
- Children may experience difficulties distinguishing between imagination and reality until the ages of 5-6 years.
- Some parents, caregivers or friends may instill or enhance fears unintentionally by saying such things as "you're so cute, I'm going to eat you" or "I'm going to take you with me".
- Children often imitate individuals around them and may imitate a fear seen in another individual (especially a parent or caregiver).
- Certain events may be realistically scary and threatening such as sitting next to a growling or barking dog. It is a normal response to be afraid in some situations, however it sometimes becomes an exaggerated and consistent response.
- Basic evolution asserts a natural, in-born tendency to be afraid of some things including snakes, heights, airplanes, and so forth. It is a natural response that is a drive to survive.

WHAT TO DO
The following are general suggestions of what to do with child fears:

- **First try to understand** the child's fear and what he experiences. Do not rush to assume that you know what he is afraid of. For example, a child who does not like to be left alone in a room may appear afraid of the dark when going to bed. Instead, ask your child to explain his fears and express his feelings; this helps translate his fears into words.
- In many cases, **talking** about the fear itself reduces anxiety surrounding it. When a child describes his fear, the intensity of it reduces and the feelings become more realistic.
- **Do not tell** your child that his fears are "nonsense". This will certainly not help the situation.
- **Respond** to the child's fears seriously, even though they may be irrational. Tell him that you will all help fight his fear with him. This will give him a feeling of control and may help him succeed in conquering his fear.

- **Teach** him to fight against his fear with his imagination by coming up with an imaginative solution.
- **Do not panic** or react with fear yourself since this will only confirm his fears.
- **Do not get angry** at him for being scared, making it more difficult for him to tell you the cause of his fear.
- **Do not force** him to confront the source of his fear immediately. Most fears disappear on their own. Give your child a chance to calm down and reason himself out of the fear.
- **Reassure** your child that all fears are normal and let him know that you too have fears.
- **Praise** him for talking about his fears and trying to resolve them. You can provide positive reinforcement as well.

FEAR FACTORS: LOUD NOISES, COSTUMES & CHARACTERS

- Some toddlers may be afraid of various noises such as vacuums, sirens from police cars or firefighters. Some are afraid of costumes and characters, as it does not make sense in their human world.
- Do not force him to get up close to their fears (e.g. a clown). In case of fears of appliances or such things as sirens, explain to him that a big noise is coming and acknowledge the fear. You can say something like "it may sound scary, but we are safe". If your child still seems uncomfortable, then ask him to cover his ears or sing a song.

SEEK HELP WHEN

- ✓ Fears interfere with daily life.
- ✓ Content of fears and intensity are seen everyday.

FEAR OF STRANGERS

GENERAL

Most babies begin expressing a fear of strangers around 6-9 months of age (sometimes earlier), particularly when they see someone they do not know (a stranger) or a family member (e.g. grandparents, babysitters) that they have not seen for quite some time. This is known as stranger anxiety or fear of strangers. It may disappear quickly or not peak at all until after your child reaches one year of age.

In approximately two out of every ten babies, stranger anxiety is not an issue at all. This could be due to the fact that some babies adjust more easily to new situations or that these situations pass so quickly, that it is not even noticeable.

WHY IT OCCURS

It is believed that children get better at knowing the difference between familiar and unfamiliar faces and that they may actually become more fearful of the unfamiliar faces. At about six months of age, the baby is developing a strong attachment to you and other caregivers who regularly take care of him. He associates you and his caregivers with his well-being and can certainly distinguish you from others. Many babies naturally assume that unfamiliar faces or situations indicate danger. Thus, it is part of a survival strategy for babies to be fearful of strangers. Regardless of the reasons for stranger anxiety, it is a normal stage of development. It is a transitory phase that will subside with time.

WHAT TO DO

Helpful measures to relieve/reduce the fearfulness babies experience with strangers:

- ✓ **Do not pressure** your baby to be sociable. When he feels like being sociable, then let him be.
- ✓ Most babies experience a phase known as "showmanship" where they will be sociable with almost everyone they meet. Take advantage of this stage by **introducing him** to present and future caregivers.

- ✓ **Reassure and comfort** that everything is ok by staying around him when he experiences stranger anxiety, particularly when you want him to adjust to a new person such as a babysitter or family member. Let him know that this stranger is approved by you. You may also greet this person in a friendly manner so that your baby is less likely to be afraid.

✓ When taking him to unfamiliar places, **take a familiar toy** or favorite object with you for helping him feel comforted.

TIP: *What Can Strangers Do?*

When there is a "stranger" you would like your child to feel comfortable with for whatever reason (e.g. care giving, family member), you may try the following to help ease your child's comfort:

- Warn this person not to take it personally and explain the phase your child is experiencing. This will help the stranger better understand and be more comforting to your child.
- Rather than allowing the "stranger" to pick up or play with your child immediately, you can help break the resistance gradually by smiling, having eye contact, talking, and eventually offering toys and building up confidence from there.

FEAR OF ANIMALS

Parent Concern: My 3 ½ year old boy is scared and screams and runs away every time he sees any animals that flies or make noises. Sometimes he's so scared that he doesn't want to go out.

GENERAL
- Fears are considered normal at various parts of childhood.
- A common fear in childhood (and, actually well into adulthood) is the fear of animals.
- Some children are more fearful than others, depending on temperament.
- The following are common types of fears related to age:

  - ✓ **Toddlers:** Separations, noises, animals-insects, baths, potty, and bedtime.
  - ✓ **Preschool-age**: Animals-insects, ghosts, monsters, divorce, getting lost, and bedtime.
  - ✓ **School-age**: Separation, noises, falling, social rejection, bedtime, and new situations.

CAUSES
- Toddlers do not yet seem to possess the ability to understand that furry animals are pets rather than scary creatures.
- Some experts suggest that children who are afraid of animals (e.g. dogs) have not been introduced properly to the animal.
- There are factors that might increase the risk for fears such as an episode of risk for drowning – he will be scared to swim after that, or a scary interaction with a pet (e.g. biting, barking, being chased by a dog) can all lead to trauma/fear that lasts into adulthood.

COPING WITH FEAR
- **Do not overreact** to your child's fears, otherwise fears are reinforced.
- Reassure and comfort her while not encouraging her to avoid her fears.
- As your child learns to master her fears, support her and remind her that everything is ok.
- Do not be over-protective and do not force her to do things she is afraid of.
- Ask her to explain her fear (i.e. why is she afraid) so that you may potentially offer a positive explanation of a triggering event (e.g. explain that dog's barking is its way of talking).
- **Respect your child's feelings**. Do not ignore her fears or belittle her for them.

- Show your child **books and movies** with fun-loving animals (e.g. animal stories that make her laugh, movies that show kids loving dogs).
- Take a trip to the toy store and let her pick up her favourite stuffed animal.
- Take a trip to the pet store and encourage her to hold a pet (e.g. kittens or puppies).
- Help her fears and anxieties by offering her a security object when faced with her fear.
- Expose to domesticated and docile animals and ask her if she would like to pet one; though, you should not force her to pet or come close to an animal if she is uncomfortable doing so.
- In small segments, your child may become accustomed to the small animal that she constantly sees until she is able to reduce her anxiety and feel comfortable around it.
- Do not allow her to stay with an animal when she is terrified since this will increase her fears.
- Plan ahead – if you know there will be a situation where an animal is present, then let her know and be prepared (it is better than upsetting your child).

TIP: When the fear is abnormal
A fear is abnormal when it is: 1. Persistent 2. Occupies the child's mind to the point of interfering with daily activities. 3. When it is an irrational fear for the child's age and developmental level. You may need to consult with a psychologist to help your child with her fears.

FEAR OF DOCTOR

GENERAL

- A common problem seen in the paediatric clinic are children who fear or experience discomfort when visiting the doctor.
- It is normal for children to be wary of doctor's.
- Some toddlers and preschoolers are afraid or truly terrified of the doctor. Typically, these children tear, squirm, fight and make the visits uncomfortable and traumatic for themselves as well as for the parents and the doctor.

CAUSES

- At the age of 3-5 years, there are two levels of child development – **big imaginations and a belief in animism** (i.e. thinking that everything is alive). These can lead children to imagine the worst-case scenario when visiting the doctor.
- **Maturity level, emotional susceptibility and the child's temperament** are contributing factors. No matter what you do, some children will cry upon entering the doctor's building or office.
- A child's **memory** may contribute to anxiety related to visiting the doctor, particularly when the child remembers bad experiences (e.g. vaccinations, throat swabs).
- Some children **cannot handle** seeing a drop of blood or do not want the doctor to touch a scraped knee or bruise and may insist to have a bandage (they pay attention to their body integrity).
- Young children may simply be afraid of the examination room, especially if it is **not child-friendly** (e.g. no fun characters posted on the wall, murals, and toys).

WHAT TO DO

Before the Visit	<ul><li>**Act excited** about visiting the doctor.</li><li>**Be relaxed & confident**. Do not show any of your own anxieties or fears.</li><li>Instead of saying *"you have to go to the doctor"*, say *"it is time to visit the doctor"*.</li><li>**Prepare the child & be honest about the visit**. Honesty is key for a healthy parent-child relationship. For example, when your child is going to receive a vaccination, let her know that it may hurt for only a second and then she will feel better.</li><li>**Do not over-explain** the doctor's visits and **do not focus on painful procedures** since this can make her more anxious.</li><li>**Reassure** her that you will be with her at the doctor's office the whole time.</li></ul>

	- **Do not make promises you cannot keep.** For example, if you promise you will buy her a cookie after visiting the doctor, then make sure you do. - **Educate** your child about doctor's visits and let her practice being a doctor on her toys. The more your child knows about the visits, the less anxious and fearsome she will be. Tell her that the doctor helps children from being sick. - **Time the doctor's visit** so that it is not a time when she is hungry or tired.
During Visit	- **Show courage** when you are at the doctor's office, especially if your child is going through a painful experience (e.g. receiving a vaccination). - You can have the doctor check your ear or throat first and then your child's. This will **show the child that there is nothing to be afraid of**. - **Make her comfortable & allow her to express her emotions.** You can bring a comfort item from home to help her feel secure. - Provide **endless kisses** if she needs them. - If she cries during the visit, then let her know that it is **ok to cry**. - Allow her to **sit on your lap** (if possible) during an examination to help her feel safer and secure. - **Do not make threats** like "if you don't stop crying, then you will not go to the ice cream store". Threats are counter-productive.
After Visit	- Allow your child to **play with the toys,** especially if she continues to cry when leaving the exam room so that she knows the doctor's office is not "all bad". - **Plan a treat** for when you leave the doctor's office such as going to the playground or the ice cream store. Follow through with the treat, regardless of her behavior during the visit. This may help your child associate the doctor's visits with something pleasant. - **Praise your child** for visiting the doctor and being brave, even if she cried a little. - **You can talk about the visit** a few days afterward to give your child a chance to talk about what happened. She may be freer to talk about her emotions after it is over. - **Note:** After the ages of 5-6 years, you are able to reason with your child more.

ADDITIONAL COMMENTS
- For emergency visits to the doctor, you will not have time to prepare your child for the visit.
- The less frequent the visits and the longer gaps in between visits, the more anxious some children may be when visiting the doctor.
- Sometimes, the examination may be difficult regardless of what you do to help your child relax and feel comfortable. You may just have to visit the doctor as quickly as possible!
- If the visit is for the first time, you can have a brief visit to the office simply for fun (play with a tongue depressor, have a sticker, meet with the nurse, etc).

FEAR OF THE BATH

GENERAL

- Fear of the bath is a common childhood phobia, usually occurring between the age of one and four years.
- Reasons to fear the bath may include fear of the water pouring in, looming shower heads that may spout water, tub plugs and fear of being sucked down the drain, fear of soap in the eyes, or bad experiences (e.g. slipping, falling, water too hot or cold).

WHAT TO DO

It is first important to understand why your child is afraid of the bath since it is different for every child.

GENERAL SUGGESTIONS

- **Do not force** your child to enter the bath since it can be counterproductive. Rather, be gentle, understanding and encouraging to show how pleasant a bath can be.
- Give your child a **warning** or advanced notice for when he will be taking a bath to reduce the chances of him getting upset about taking a bath.
- **Avoid long conversations** about your child's bath habits in front of other family members or friends.
- Offer **bath toys** to play with in the bath. Keep these toys exclusive to bath time to create an incentive to take a bath. You can even take your child to the store and get him to pick out his bath toys.
- Allow him to play with water toys and have **fun with water** so that he is not afraid of it.
- Offer a variety of **character-inspired shampoos and soaps**, so that he can choose which one he would like to use when he is taking a bath.
- You can use **color bath tablets** that change the color of the water in the bath. This can be exciting and more fun!

SPECIFIC SUGGESTIONS TO SUSPECTED CAUSES

- If he is **afraid of the bath being filled with water and pouring out,** then you can fill the tub before your child enters the bathroom. Make sure you do not turn the water on when your child is in the tub. When washing his hair, use the water that is in the tub or fill a cup or bowl ahead of time.
- If he is **afraid of water, shampoo or soap irritating his eye,** then you can eliminate the fear of soap by using a very gentle shampoo. Although many shampoos and soaps do not hurt the eyes, some children hate the feeling of water or soap in their eyes. In this case, you can use a retractable showerhead and gently rinse the soap

out of his hair (this will work for the child who is not afraid of water pouring out of the showerhead). You can also offer your child goggles to cover his eyes.

- If he is **afraid of the showerhead itself**, you can detach the showerhead and remove it from the bathroom. This will remove your child's fear of water spouting out of the showerhead at any given moment. If this is not possible or does not work, show your child that there is no way water can come out without you turning it on; allow him to turn the showerhead on and off.

- If your child's fear seems to be that **he thinks he may be sucked down the drain,** (it may be difficult as a parent to know if your child has this fear), then explain to him that it is impossible to be drained along with the water. To help explain this impossibility to your child, you can unplug the bathtub after you take your child out and show him how the water is being sucked out very slow and little by little.

SUGGESTIONS WHEN NOTHING WORKS
- You can try using a **smaller bath tub** by placing the small one in the large tub. Sometimes, children feel more secure and safe in a smaller tub. You can add a small amount of water instead of filling it up to the top.

- Give the child a **sponge bath** (using a loofa) until he builds the courage to take a proper bath.

- You can **take a bath with him** to help him feel more safe and secure.

TIP: Bath & Bedtime

Do not give your child a bath right before bedtime since he may associate taking a bath with going to bed, prolonging bedtime. Give your child a bath in the morning or early evening to provide a gap between bath and bedtime.

FEAR OF HAIR WASHING

Toddlers feel strongly about their likes and dislikes. Hair washing is a common dislike among young children, often giving up a struggle. **The following are suggestions for washing your child's hair with minimal struggle:**

- Have the **bathtub ready** before bringing your child in and check that the temperature is good.
- **Prepare the rinsing water in a jug** nearby since running water from the faucet may scare her.
- **Prepare the shampoo and towel nearby**, so that neither of you need to endure the bath longer than necessary.
- **Explain** what you will be doing before you place your child in the bath and begin hair washing.
- **Use a 1-step shampoo and conditioner** to reduce the number of hair washing steps. Also, use a shampoo that is gentle, fragrance-free and non-irritating to the eyes.
- **Cover** your child's eyes with swimming goggles.
- **Use your hands** to rinse a little bit of hair at a time rather than pouring a large amount of water over her head. You can even use a hand-held spray for better control and less risk of misdirection.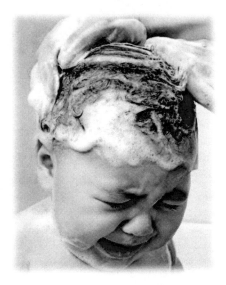
- Try the **reclining method** of shampooing and rinsing. By leaning backwards in the tub or over the sink, there is less of a risk of getting water in the eyes while rinsing.
- Turn washing into a **game** by allowing your child to shampoo someone else such as a doll or yourself even.
- **Avoid making hair washing an issue**. If your child refuses or becomes agitated, then back off and try again later.

Behavior with Family and Friends

PARENT-CHILD COMMUNICATION

GENERAL

- Parent-child or child-parent communication is an important parenting skill.
- Parenting will be more enjoyable when there is positive parent/child interaction.
- Whether you are parenting a toddler or a teenager, good communication is the key to building self-esteem as well as mutual respect.

PRINCIPLES OF GOOD COMMUNICATION

- Show your child that you **accept him** for who he is, regardless of his behaviour.
- Let him know that you are **interested** in his life and that you are always there to help.
- **Listen and offer attention** to your child. Turn off the television or put the newspaper down when your child wants to converse with you. If you are very tired, you may need to make the effort of being an active listener. Listen carefully and do not interrupt your child when he is trying to tell you a story.
- **Do not embarrass** him or put them on the spot in front of others since this can lead to hostility.
- **Do not use any belittling (i.e. put-down) words or statements** such as lazy, stupid or "what do you know – you're just a child!"
- **Don't tower over your child.** Physically bend down and get to his level.
- If an incident occurs, **always ask your child what happened first** so that he understands that you care about his thoughts and feelings.
- When you are angry about an incident or behaviour, **stay calm** and attempt to communicate with him. You can even talk with your child later, if you need some time to cool down.
- When having a conversation with your child about an incident or behaviour, do so in **private** (unless others are meant to be included). The best communication occurs when others are not around.
- **Do not preach and keep lectures to a minimum**.
- Reinforce open communication by **praising his efforts** to communicate with you.

WORDS OF ENCOURAGEMENT & PRAISE

- Children thrive on positive attention as well as the need to feel loved and appreciated.
- Most parents find that it is easier to provide negative feedback rather than positive.
- Using and selecting some of the words and phrases below on a daily basis will promote positive and open communication with your child:

  ✓ Good
  ✓ Excellent

  ✓ Wonderful
  ✓ That's right

- ✓ I'm proud of you
- ✓ I like the way you do that
- ✓ Much better
- ✓ Good for you
- ✓ You are doing better

- ✓ That is a great idea
- ✓ I'm so glad you are my son/daughter
- ✓ I love you
- ✓ You are the best

- You can show your child your feelings by smiling, gesturing, hugs, kisses, pats on the back and high-fives.

Tip: How to Encourage Child's Independence -"I can do it myself"
- Break down the task the child is trying to master into small parts (You can start your preschooler's coat zipper and let him finish the job)
- Let the child finish by himself even if it is not perfect – don't undermine his effort.
- Praise for accomplishments (child should be doing it because he is interested and not because of the praise).
- Let the child try independently no matter how long it takes. Be patient and wait. Reset the urge to help hurry them along (if you are in a rush, remind he has a few minutes to finish it)

SIBLING RIVALRY

GENERAL

- The birth of a new baby is filled with new emotions. Young children seldom express mixed feelings about a new sibling. They think they will be replaced, abandoned or forgotten.
- Often times, parents expect their child to become more independent with the arrival of a new sibling; however, the opposite is true. In fact, it is normal to expect more crying and emotional outbursts with your child becoming more dependent than independent.
- Young siblings (less than 3 years of age) are more likely to be jealous when the new baby arrives. It is especially true when the older child is the only child.

CAUSES

In young children:

The age difference between the 2 children (especially a young child with the new birth of a baby) can have an effect on how much regressive or aggressive behaviour is displayed.

- ✓ **Regressive behaviour** may include thumb sucking, wetting or soiling.
- ✓ **Aggressive behaviour** may include clinging, handling the baby in a rough manner and so on.
- ✓ Your child may be demanding attention by wanting to be held, especially when the mother is holding the new baby.

In older siblings:

- ✓ **Boredom and stress**: Under stress, children will take it out on an easy target (i.e. a sibling). For example, when the child has a rough day in school, he may pick a fight when he gets home. Similarly, when the child is bored, he may begin to rough play and pick on a sibling.
- ✓ **Wanting attention**: Kids need to know that parents care and they measure that via attention. This is particularly true for older siblings who remember life without a little brother or sister. It begins with fears of losing the hugs, attention and love.
- ✓ **Inequality**: If the child senses that he is not treated the same as a sibling, resentment can grow and conflict ensues.
- ✓ **Circumstances**: Various situations play a role in how much children fight include age gaps, birth order, gender and personality. Some kids view a younger sibling as more competitive and a threat rather than someone they can learn from.

PREPARING THE CHILD FOR A SIBLING

Before Delivery

- Let your child know that a new sibling will be arriving shortly and that he/she is going to be a big brother or sister.
- Reassure your child that he/she will continue to be your pride and joy.
- When setting up the rooms for your new arrival, do not tell your child that you are moving rooms "because of the baby". This will undermine everything you explained to him/her. You can, however, ask your preschooler to help in the preparation of the baby's room.
- If you are planning to enrol your child in school, then you should do so well in advance of delivery. This way, your child does not think that you are getting "rid" of him "because of the baby".

In the Hospital

- Call daily from the hospital and ask your child to visit you and the baby.
- If your child cannot visit you, then send him a picture of his new sibling.

Coming Home with the Baby

- You can give your child a small gift "from the new baby" when you are coming home. Do not say that the new baby is a present for him.
- Congratulate your child on being a new big brother or sister.
- Refer to the new baby as "our baby".
- Upon arriving home, spend a few moments with your older child.
- Encourage your older child to play with his new sibling in your presence.
- Set general rules with respect to the newborn. Explain that the new baby is not like a doll that you can play with and so forth. Tell the older child what he is and is not allowed to do (e.g. allowed to touch the newborn's head gently, give her kisses, touch her hands and not allowed to hold her while standing without your presence).

WHAT TO DO: EXTRA HELPFUL SUGGESTIONS

- **Listen** to any concerns your child may have about a baby on the way and address his/her concerns.
- **Help** your preschooler cope by adding extra hugs and cuddles, playing games or reading books together. You can spend time with the older child while your baby naps.
- Be sure to **focus on each child singly** sometimes by spending some quality time with each.
- **Incorporate your child** in helping activities such as asking to help change the diaper, entertain the new baby and so forth. This will help him feel like he is part of the expanding family while still allowing him (the older child) to feel special.

- If your child behaves aggressively, do not leave your baby and the older child alone for the next few weeks. **Intervene promptly and use time outs**.
- **Encourage your child to talk** (if possible) about his mixed feelings for the new baby. Explain that it is ok to feel angry, but never ok to hurt the baby.
- **Do not criticize** your child for regressive behaviour; be patient instead.
- **Do not relate** any behaviours of the older child to the behaviour of the little one.
- Make sure **each child is an active member of the family** including the newborn, so that he feels that he is your partner and not in competition for your attention with a newborn.
- **Keep family rituals** the same to help the older child feel more secure.
- **Do not tell** the older child that you love him and the baby the same, more or less. You can say that you love each child differently but equally as much.
- **Do not tell** your child that he needs to love the new baby.
- Ensure that all children are getting **praise and positive attention** (e.g. do not only provide negative attention that comes with acting out).

WHAT TO DO WHEN OLDER KIDS FIGHT
Offer attention on a regular basis with each parent.
- ✓ Give each child special one-on-one time to prevent sibling conflicts.
- ✓ Spend time alone with each child and focus your full attention.
- ✓ Children need space too, not just attention.
- ✓ Allot each child a corner of a bedroom or a basket of sacred toys to lessen the stress of sharing a room.
- ✓ Listen to your child's needs and wants.

Never compare and do not unwittingly favour one child over the other.
- ✓ Respect the uniqueness of each child in the family. Realize that he is an individual with strengths and weaknesses.
- ✓ Try to avoid comparing siblings to one another.
- ✓ When you say things like, "your brother already finished his homework and cleaned his room", you are inadvertently setting up siblings to resent each other. Note that your child who is being compared may also feel a pressure to stay perfect.
- ✓ Whenever your child complains of unfair treatment, skip the debate and simply ask him what he wants. Focus on needs as opposed comparisons.
- ✓ No one likes to be compared unfavourably to another. Excessive use of negative comparisons between siblings can have a powerful impact on their relationship and can harm both parties. The unfavourably compared child may suffer from low self-esteem and direct his anger towards both the parents and the praised child.

Family meetings

- ✓ Some conflicts can drag on, particularly older children who share clothes, bathrooms and computers.
- ✓ Regular family meetings help everyone feel like they have a voice and leads to things like household rules with everyone's input.

Do not overreact; stay calm.

- ✓ Sibling rivalry is often provoked by a minor disagreement (e.g. which television show to watch) and is sometimes a result of jealous feelings. However, rivalry is more often a result of the amount of time they share together and the endless pursuit of negotiating and compromising in their homes.
- ✓ Resist yelling, "stop it you two!" It is better to say, "you two seem so angry at each other" and then listen.
- ✓ Place children apart if they are about to hit one another.
- ✓ If you witness bitter and intense rivalry over extended periods of time, then look at yourself and your child-rearing techniques. Your relationship with your spouse may offer a better understanding of causes for your children's bickering.

Do not intercede if you don't have to.

- ✓ Let older children resolve their own disputes.
- ✓ Young children may need suggestions, but final decisions should be coming from them.
- ✓ Sometimes the best choice is to ignore the situation.
- ✓ Do not be too quick to criticize.

Never allow victimization or physical abuse.

- ✓ Do not allow one child to be injured or consistently beaten down by another.
- ✓ You must intercede when you witness physical abuse or when one child is constantly manipulating the other.
- ✓ Punishing a hitter with a long lecture and time out actually gives him what he wants: attention.

Reach your child's feelings to see what is really going on.

- ✓ We need to focus on the emotions that cause the fights and not just the fight itself.
- ✓ Allow children to tell you both sides of the conflict and express their feelings one at a time. Listen without judgment.
- ✓ Giving empathy is really powerful and works quickly on children.

Pull out the mediation tricks.
    ✓ Use some sharing techniques that feel fair (e.g. toss a coin to make a decision).

TIP: How to deal with fights
➢ Choose the best possible intervention that is appropriate to the type of fight. For some situations, you may need to separate the siblings while it may be better not to interfere in other situations.
➢ Ensure that you are not always agreeing with one sibling more than the other.
➢ Teach your children how to effectively resolve conflicts. Rather than being a judge and interfering, teach them how to express and communicate with one another to find the best possible solution.
➢ In any case, do not allow aggression (e.g. pulling hair, biting).

COMMENT: SIBLING RELATIONS
- In many areas, children learn from their siblings more than anyone else.
- Sometimes, fighting with a sibling is healthy for emotional development and future successful confrontations in the social world.
- Note that siblings who do not fight may not necessarily be closer than siblings who do fight and vice versa.

SPOILING

GENERAL

- Babies less than 9-10 months cannot be spoiled. Younger infants simply do not recognize cause and effect relationships yet; as such, they cannot intentionally manipulate or annoy you, and therefore should not be disciplined.
- Older infants and young children can be spoiled and require limits. Parents must differentiate between responding to the child's needs (i.e. responding appropriately) and simply doing what your child wants(i.e. responding inappropriately).
- Parents often have difficulties setting limits and confuse a child's needs with wants or whims, contributing to the spoiled child. Typically, these parents tend to alleviate a child's normal

frustrations (e.g. sharing, waiting) and do not want to hurt the child's feelings or cause crying. Sometimes, these parents also give the child excess attention (often at the wrong time).
- Parents should observe their babies or young children and trust their instincts.

TIP: Behaviours of the Spoiled Child

Some of the following behaviours are manifestations of a spoiled child (when they are excessive): manipulative, unpleasant, undisciplined, no rule following or responding to commands, needs and wants are intermixed, excessive demands, constant complaints (especially when bored) and frequently whines or throws a tantrum.

RESPONDING TO YOUR BABY IN THE FIRST YEAR

0 – 9 Months

- Babies cry to communicate needs (e.g. diaper changes, feeding).
- If your baby cries, the chances are great that he is feeling miserable. You check him to find out the problem and care for him.
- Sometimes, warm pressure on the abdomen, the motion and distraction will soothe your infant and allow him to forget about any pain or tension (at least temporarily).

9 – 12 MONTHS

- The older your baby is, the longer you can delay the response (though only for a brief time).
- Ensure that your child is not ill or unsafe when briefly delaying a response.
- Allow some time to solve the problem on his own. If he continues crying, then step in and reassure or caress him.
- Once you approach him, observe and hold him (if necessary).

ADDITIONAL COMMENTS: CARING FOR EVERY CRY AND PICKING UP AND CARRYING THE BABY

- Psychologists refer to the term secure attachment to explain basic trust. Attachment differs from dependency on parents. Rather, attachment enhances development while prolonged dependency hinders it.
- Some studies show that young infants who are held often and have their cries responded to promptly grow to be more independent as preschoolers compared to infants who were left crying alone. Also, the reassured infants are happier, more secure, less anxious, less likely to cry for no apparent reason, less clingy, less demanding and learn a basic sense of trust.
- Although it is difficult to spoil a baby at a very young age, there may be times where you may want to slow down your prompt responses and allow him to learn to solve problems on his own. This is due to the following reasons:
  - ✓ Prompt responses can prevent you and the child from getting things done and allows for fewer opportunities for him to practice his skills.
  - ✓ Allowing him to solve his own problems will allow him to learn to self-entertain and enjoy his own company (important for future self-esteem).
  - ✓ Your child may conclude that being carried around in your arms (though not stimulating) is preferable to no attention. As such, he will be raised to believe that his needs come before others.
- To ensure that your child learns the above skills and differentiates between his wants and needs and those of others, you can help by:
  - ✓ Ensuring that he has enough toys and new items that he likes
  - ✓ Offering distractions
  - ✓ Engage in an activity with him without picking him up
  - ✓ Leave him for a little longer periods each time and gradually lengthen the time between pick-ups (without making him feel ignored)
  - ✓ Chat or sing to him if it helps
- Do not feel guilty about letting your baby spend a little time on his own. However, do not forget that he is still a baby who needs plenty of love.

RESPONDING TO THE YOUNG CHILD

The older spoiled child is going to make your life miserable until he gets everything he wants. At the older ages, children know how to manipulate parents. You can try the following to prevent or deal with the spoiled child.

- Parents should **set age-appropriate limits** and boundaries. These limits should begin when the child begins to crawl.
- **Saying "no"** occasionally is good for children.
- Some crying is expected, though you should **distinguish between crying** related to needs and those related to wants.
- **Teach** the child to wait and do not feel guilty if you make him wait sometimes.
- **Do not give in to temper tantrums**, though you should stop tantrums when they are too disruptive or harmful.

- Begin **reasoning** with children around the ages of 4-5 years. In grade school, show a willingness to discuss the rules.
- **Praise** for good behaviour and for following the rules.

GRANDPARENTS SPOILING: WHAT TO DO

- Problems with grandparents can be related to sleep time, junk food, watching television (length of time), missing a nap or receiving gifts.
- It is important to make some sensible guidelines agreed by all and ensure that certain parental rules are not violated.
- Since parents are the ones who live with the child 24 hours a day, they will provide the rules about important issues. Grandparents living in the same house or close by should abide by these rules since it is easy to spoil the child in this case (leading to a confused and unhappy young one).
- If the grandparents see the child infrequently (once per year), then the child cannot be spoiled.
- If boundaries are ignored by the grandparents, then try having an open discussion. Discuss the boundaries and how grandparents cannot interfere with certain rules. If the grandparents refuse to abide by the rules, then refuse to let them be with their grandchildren until they are ready to listen and follow.

Myths
Myth 1: You will spoil your baby if you handle her too much. **Fact**: You can hold your baby as often as you like. You cannot spoil a young infant! **Myth 2**: Spoiled children exist. **Fact**: There is no such as a spoiled child. Of course, there are children who whine until parents arrive or pout when they do not get their way. However, these children are not spoiled. They are simply trying out new behaviours and attempts to get what they want. These are children who choose inappropriate behaviours that need to be redirected and replaced with other choices. Children need to be taught more effective ways of interacting and expressing their emotions and feelings.

DISRUPTION

GENERAL

- Children do not understand that parents can be tied up with other matters until about the age of 5 years when cognitive skills are more refined.
- Children tend to disrupt parents conversations out of boredom, bad manners or as an attention-seeking behaviour.
- Parents should help the child understand that he will not always be the center of attention, though he is always loved.

WHAT TO DO

- **Be kind and firm** at the same time. Explain that it is not polite to interrupt someone when they are talking on the phone. For example, you can say that "mom needs to talk to grandma and I can't talk to 2 people at the same time".
- Tell your child that **you love him no matter what**, but that he must behave in a respectful manner by not disrupting you when you are tied up.
- **Do not stop and give your child attention** when he is interrupting you. However, you can rub his back or hold his hand so that he knows you are aware of his presence. The message you want to relay is that you are there, but that you need to finish your phone conversation.
- **Exercise patience and set an example** of how to handle interruptions.
- **Do not react with rage** when your child interrupts your phone conversation since this will only compound his need for security and intensify the behaviour. Explain that he can be near you, but not to interrupt you.
- **Do not blast** your child for interrupting you when you get off the phone. It may take a few tries for him to learn not to interrupt you.
- Have a **busy box** ready to pull out when you are on the phone, so that your child's attention can be redirected. Explain that when you are on the phone and he does not know what to do, he can find something in the busy box. When your conversation ends, put the busy box away. Change the items in the box often.
- There may be times when you will need to attend to your child and you will have to tell the caller that your **child needs you**. If it is a call that you have been waiting for, then you can say that "I have been waiting for this call, but I will get back to you as soon as I can".

- **Do not use the phone** when you know there are certain times in the day that your child needs you most.
- **Set agreed-upon touch signals** so that your child can tell you what he needs while you are on the phone without disrupting you. For example, he can squeeze your arm to let you know that he needs help.
- When you know you will have to be on the phone, **let your child know ahead of time**. This way, he can let you know if he needs anything before you get on the phone.
- **Take the call in another room** when the behaviour is consistent and repetitive. He has to learn that when you are not available, you mean it. Set a later time to talk to him about his behaviour.
- **Practice** the behaviour with 2 pretend phones, one for you and one for him. This may teach him how to behave while you are on the phone. Tell your child that this is how you talk on the phone and show him how to play when you are on the phone. You may then swap roles where you play while your child talks on the phone.

- Use an **answering machine** to screen which calls are important to take and use a cordless phone to continue supervising your child's movements. You can also add **another phone** so that your child can talk with you and the caller (if it is a family member or friend).
- **Praise** the child's efforts when he behaves while you are on the phone.
- Make lengthy phone calls when your **toddler is asleep or not around.**

IGNORANCE

GENERAL

- Sometimes children deliberately ignore parents, pretending not to hear their requests.
- It is natural for you to be frustrated when your child ignores you or others.
- Children may ignore you to obtain a sense of power and control. It may make him feel like a "big boy" by pretending not to hear you.
- Essentially, your child is practicing his assertive skills with you.
- You should ensure that your child is not ignoring you due to hearing difficulties or developmental disabilities. These causes should be ruled out with your child's health professional.

WHAT TO DO

Suggestions for the Young Child's Ignorance	Suggestions for the Older Child's Ignorance
• **Be realistic**, clear, and age-appropriate. Make sure your requests are specific and realistic (i.e. doable). Saying "tidy up your room" is too vague for a 2 year old; saying "put your shoes in the closet" is more realistic at this age. • If you want your child to do something in a specific way, then you may need to **show him.** • **Simplify Your Request**: Young children need instructions of 1-2 steps at a time (e.g. "please come to mommy and bring your shoes"). • **Follow through on your request**: If you ask a 2 year old to bring you a book he is holding and refuses, then go and take the book from him. If you ask him to get off the table and he refuses, then physically take him off the table. • **Motivate** with compliments and praise. You can say that you are proud of him for getting his shoes for example. • You can also **provide incentives** to do	• **Homework**: If your child ignores your request to do homework, then **establish a clear time** when homework begins and all distractions (e.g. electronics, playtime) are off or away. • **Chores**: Rather than telling the child to "do the chores now", you will be more effective if you **set up a target time** for when chores have to be completed with consequences if they are not done. • **Do not argue or fight** with your child; simply state the rules and put your foot down. • When your child is ignoring guests in your home or refuses to comply with reasonable requests, it is time for you to remind him of the family rules. Explain who the guest is or why a particular request is important; if he still refuses, then **lay down the consequences.** Be clear and don't argue about it. • If your child ignores you with headphones and music, then this is

things. For example, "when you put the doll away, I will read your favourite story to you". You can also try the sticker & chart approach; one sticker for every time he responds to your requests.

- **Try not to use the word "no" too much**. Instead, of saying "no", you can **offer alternatives**. For example, instead of saying "no, do not throw the ball in the house", you can say "let's go throw the ball outside".
- When you **give your child a choice**, you allow him to assert himself in an acceptable way.

blatant disrespect. At this point, everything else should stop until he takes the earphones out of his ears. Do not try to communicate with him until his headphones are off.

- **Be consistent with your rules.**

GRATEFUL CHILD

- Being thankful or grateful can be a difficult lesson for children to learn in this day, when the environment tells them to expect things and not appreciate everything they have.
- It is the parent's responsibility and their job to teach the child to be grateful.
- **To raise a grateful child, you can**:

    o Set an example by saying please and thank you
    o Make a habit of addressing appreciation, even for the smallest things.
    o Write thank you letters and have your child write them with you (e.g. for a birthday present).
    o Talk to your child and ask her what and why she is thankful for.
    o Build the concept of giving into everyday life. For example, teach her to give clothes she has outgrown to a shelter.

PREFERRING ONE PARENT OVER THE OTHER

GENERAL

- At times, a child may prefer spending time with one parent to the other.

- Preference for one parent is most common between the ages of 18 months and 4 years, changing from moment to moment or month to month.
- Do not take parent preference personally since it is only a phase. Remember that your child loves both of you, even though it seems he has a favourite at times.
- Sometimes, parent preferences become exaggerated and may cause difficulty (especially when the child refuses to be left with one parent or may not want to eat or sleep with the unfavoured parent).

CAUSES

- **Personality**: Your child may wind up preferring one parent over another, simply because of personality matches.

> **TIP: Dealing with the Hurt**
> - It is ok to let your child know that he hurt your feelings, but do not convey the message in anger.
> - Try not to let your child's comments and/or actions be taken to heart.
> - Ensure that your child knows you love him, regardless of anything said or done.

- **Parental roles**: One parent may be the primary disciplinarian in the household while the other is all fun and games, causing preference for the "fun" parent.
- **"Familiarity breeds contempt"**: This is an old saying that may be true in the case of parental preference. If one parent is at home with the child all day long, then the child may get more excited upon seeing the other parent.
- **Emotional desires**: Depending on what needs the child has at the time, he may prefer the quiet or the nurturing parent.
- **Changes in appearance**: A sudden change in appearance (e.g. cutting hair, changing hair color, removing or growing a beard) may direct the child's attention and preference to the other or more familiar parent.
- **Parental overreaction**: A child may prefer one parent over the other when that parent rewards certain behaviours or overreacts to them.

WHAT TO DO

- **Do not make a big deal** over the fact that your child may prefer one parent over another at any given time. **Stay calm**, especially when you are not the favourite at the time.
- Ensure that you and your partner **alternate parental roles** in the household. Share the disciplinarian and "fun" role (e.g. arrange play dates for your child that both of you can participate in).
- **Do not say vengeful comments** such as "if you don't love me, then I won't read the book to you" or "I will not give you a kiss since you don't love me". These types of emotional responses will not help at all.
- **Do not say** that he should love mom and dad the same since it is not possible to love two people "exactly the same".
- If you changed your appearance lately, then **allow your child time to adjust**.
- Simply **play alongside** your child if you are not the preferred parent at the time. Show him that you are interested in what he is doing and continue **expressing your love** for him.
- **Respect your child's preference**, but place limits (to behaviours, not emotions) when necessary.
- **Respect each other**. Never use your child's preference as a weapon against your partner (e.g. "he doesn't love you because you are not home").
- **Check yourself**, when one of you (the less preferred parent) is hardly ever home or has not spent much time with him.

WHAT NOT TO DO

- **Do not reinforce the preference** by saying your son is a "mama's boy" or "I know I am not your favourite person". This information will eventually become a truth and you do not want that to happen! Instead, you can say things like "we are all so lucky to be a family" and "we both love you very much".
- **Do not give in** to all your child's demands and likes simply because you want him to like you more, if you are not the preferred parent. Your child may not show that he needs you as much as the preferred parent, but he does need you. Remember, it is only a phase!

DRESSING YOUR TODDLER

GENERAL

- Dressing is a common concern of parent-child struggles and a source of frustration for both.
- Many children enjoy some self-dressing by the age of two years. Many dress themselves by ages 4-5. Your child's readiness for learning (and wanting to learn) to dress herself will depend on development, behaviour and mood. Keep in mind that the ability to undress usually precedes the ability to dress; so you want to help your child first learn how to undress, but you cannot expect quick results.

- Parents need to realize that independent dressing is a learning experience and that the child will make choices and mistakes. Your child may (a) refuse to dress; (b) insist on dressing herself; and (c) take off clothes when starting to dress or a combination of these.

WHY IS DRESSING DIFFICULT?

- **Freedom and independence** are a part of growing up. As your child is growing from a dependent baby to a confident toddler who is ready to take on the world, she will naturally want as much control as possible over her life and will express a desire to dress herself.
- **Self-awareness is growing** and she will have favourite outfits to wear by the age of 4-5.
- When she knows you want her to do something urgently, she will resist the most.

WHAT TO DO

- If you have enough time, **let your child try to dress herself**.
- Ask her if she needs any help.
- Give your toddler plenty of time to do what she needs to do to get ready. You can pick out clothes ahead of time on the night before, if a particular outfit is the source of conflict. Wake her up earlier if you need to, since toddlers do not respond well to being hurried.
- **Provide a selection of two outfits**. This will empower your little one with choice and gives her a sense of control while allowing you to set your boundaries at the same time. This provides your toddler with independence and the chance to learn how to make appropriate choices. While offering two choices, say "you can wear either overalls or sweater and pants".
- If you do end up being in a rush, then you can **explain your position**: "Mommy needs to leave early today for a meeting" and then say "would you like help getting dressed just this morning?" This shows your child that she needs to get ready quickly

(maybe she can dress herself another morning). Wake up earlier if you need to, since toddlers do not respond well to being hurried.

- If your toddler takes off as soon as dressing time begins, then turn it into a **peek-a-boo game**. Put your face through his shirt to peak-a-boo or you can try to sing a song to get him in the mood of playing.
- **Make dressing a fun activity** by playing games rather than running away. Power struggles usually dissolve with laughter.
- **Do not express a bad attitude** when it comes to dressing your toddler. Children may cry as a result of their parents' behaviour.
- **Use tact**; do not say that a shirt's tag is on the front instead of the back when she puts it on for the first time.
- **Encourage team work**. Allow your child to take over and let her participate in choosing outfits and getting dressed. Maybe she refuses to dress because she does not like the clothes, you are picking out for her; let her choose (within reason).
- **Make your child's clothes accessible**. Place clothes in the lower drawer so that she can reach and help herself to feel more independent. Place clothes in the higher drawers when clothes are inappropriate, so that they are not easily accessible.
- **Acknowledge sensitivity**. Some children with sensory problems absolutely refuse some clothes; some get irritated over a scratchy tag. Hypersensitivity to labels, seams or socks are common. Luckily, this sensitivity is outgrown by age 6.

- Do not let your struggles get to the point of anger. Sometimes, you just have to get her going and dressed; **take charge before you lose your patience**.

TIP: Practice Dressing
You can give your child some extra hands or experience by providing specifically designed dolls or fabric books that allow her to practice zipping, buttoning, snapping and tying.

PARENT CONCERNS: Any recommendations for clothing?
- Since toddlers are incredibly active, use clothes that do not restrict movements or clothes that your child can easily get tangled in or trip during play.
- Make sure the clothes are not too small or too big.
- Comfort is important, so offer pants or jeans with elastics waists.
- The easiest clothes to put on or off include t-shirts, track suits, dresses, and so forth.
- Look for clothes with big buttons that are easy for your little one to grasp.

TUMMY TIME

WHAT IS TUMMY TIME?

- **Tummy time** is the time your baby spends lying on his stomach while he is awake. Tummy time is important for baby's development.

- An early 1990s recommendation stated that babies should sleep on their backs to reduce the risk of Sudden Infant Death Syndrome (SIDS). Babies spend about 12 hours of each day on their back and as such may develop flat spots on the back of the head, abnormal head shapes (see chapter on abnormal head shapes).
- Tummy time is especially important in the first six months of life. It will provide strength and help babies learn motor skills so they can lift their heads and push up on their arms.
- **Tummy time is important for the following reasons**:
    - **Prevents the development of flat head** resulting from spending too much time in one position on the back or in an infant carrier.
    - **Promotes physical motor skill development** in preparation for rolling over (from the stomach to the back and vice versa), lifting the head and holding it up, sitting, balancing, crawling and walking. There is no direct link between insufficient tummy time and gross motor delays . The child without early tummy time catches up just fine and by age one there is no measurable differences .
    - Necessary for the **development of the spine curvature**.
    - Provides your baby with **confidence and independence** while helping him become motivated to explore his surroundings as he learns to control his body and respond to certain situations.

Tummy Time: Ages

NEWBORNS

- Start tummy time as early as possible to make it easier for him to accept this position. Stop at the first sign of discomfort.
- Place him on tummy time for a couple of minutes several times a day.
- Babies can be given tummy time after a nap or diaper change
- Some recommend to put the baby on your chest or your partners chest - this is enough to start with. You can sing and talk with your baby while in this position.

2-3 Months

- Slowly increase the amount of tummy time in short spurts throughout the day. There is no reason to rush development in a healthy child. Wait until your baby begins to control his head and neck. Always stop at the sign of discomfort.

3-6 Months

- When the baby is able to lift his head and chest almost vertically to a flat surface, it is the best time for tummy time. Your baby is now mature enough and enjoys it because lifting up a heavy head is not such a chore (neurologically and psychologically ready).

By 6 Months of Age

- Many babies are able to roll over from their back to their sides, yet keep your baby sleeping on his back to reduce the risk of SIDS.
- There is not much you can do to keep an older infant on his back the entire time he is asleep.

TUMMY TIME: WHERE?

- Tummy time can take place on any flat, firm and clean surface that is covered by a non-fuzzy fabric such as a crib, playpen mat or on the floor, where the baby cannot roll off from any height.
- Hold your baby **on your lap**, slanted slightly upright. You can also lay your baby **across your lap** to settle him down instead of holding him upright.
- Have your baby **roll on a big exercise ball** and while he is on his stomach, you gently rock the ball back and forth.
- When you **carry** your baby around the house, do it so his stomach is facing down instead of upright. Your arm should support him under the chest (younger infants will need support for their head and chest; as your baby gains strength in the neck and trunk muscles, less support will be needed).
- In the newborn period, your baby can be on your partner's chest or on you, especially if you are lying on your back.

Important to Know: Be careful with blankets and quilts since these can block your baby's breathing and prevent him from moving freely.

TIPS: Expectations, Dressing, Bathing, Diapering & Feeding

✓ It is easy to remember to offer tummy time at certain times of the day. Your baby may even expect tummy time after a diaper change or nap.

✓ **Dressing & bathing**: Towel dry and change your baby on his tummy. Gently roll him from side to side as you dress him.

✓ **Diapering**: Roll your baby from side to side as you fasten the diaper tabs. After a diaper change, you can roll your baby on his tummy before picking him up. Allow him to play for a few minutes on his tummy while supervising him.

✓ **Feeding**: Change the arm you hold your baby in for feedings. Also, try placing him over your lap when burping.

PARENT CONCERN

What if my baby hates tummy time?

✓ Do what works for your baby, depending on his age and development.

✓ Remember that any amount of tummy time is better than none.

✓ Look out for good timing to provide tummy time (e.g. calm, diaper change).

✓ Start with short, frequent sessions. Build up the time gradually and do not feel guilty if you can only get a few minutes in the beginning.

✓ Use interesting props since no one will get excited by staring at a boring floor (e.g. use a mirror, colourful toys, music, and lights).

✓ Place your baby on his tummy on your stomach.

✓ Use a big exercise ball and rock your baby gently on it.

▪ Offer tummy time when your baby is **awake and supervised**. If your baby gets tired, you can roll him gently onto his back for sleeping purposes.

▪ It would be ideal to place the baby in tummy time **after a nap or diaper change** .

▪ **Offer company** during tummy time. Join him on the floor and shake a rattle or make facial expressions.

▪ **Provide entertainment and distractions** such as placing favourite toys within reach, play music or offer a squeaky toy to play with. You can also have the baby's siblings play alongside him.

▪ **Prop your baby up** on a rolled towel or nursing pillow to provide him with a new perspective of tummy time. Place the towel or pillow (3-4 months) under his chest and armpit with his arms out front . Stay close by or hold a security hand on your little's one bottom or back to protect him .

▪ Ensure that the baby is **not distressed** by a slippery or cold floor, scrunched blanket, and so forth.

Tip: When is it not a good time for tummy time

▪ Do not have your baby on the tummy when he is tired, fussy or hungry .

▪ Do not provide tummy time right after feeding, since this may lead to regurgitation (the less time is in your baby's tummy, the lower the chance of spitting up).

APPROPRIATE TOYS: AN AGE-BY-AGE GUIDE

Newborns (0 – 1 Month)	▪ At this age, toys should be light and easy to grasp. Although your baby cannot yet hold a toy, bathe her with a **soft washable doll or cloth** to stimulate her sense of touch. Look for handheld toys with a variety of textures. ▪ Choose **black and white mobiles** that play music and hang to the side or over the diaper change table. Mountable toys should have safety features. ▪ To stimulate vision (the least developed sense in the initial month), use black and white **books, stuffed animals or flash cards** made specifically for infants (high contrast patterns and bright colors are easiest to see). ▪ Babies love **soft music**, so play a tape player or music box (e.g. baby Mozart) in a place where she can watch it move and listen to the sound. This helps build neural bridges and stimulate alpha waves in the brain. ▪ **Comment: The best toy is the parent!** Talking while holding your baby 12-18 inches from your face is the best and most interesting toy. Parents responding to early cooing sounds with smiles, responsive talk and head nodding helps brain development.
2 – 6 Months	▪ Babies at this age begin to show a growing interest in touching, holding, shaking or kicking. ▪ **A lightweight baby rattle** shaped for your baby's hand will allow her to appreciate rhythm and music. ▪ **Overhead mobiles and toys the baby can kick** with her feet (around 4 months) are great. Ensure that these toys make soft and slow noises, rather than loud or sudden ones. ▪ **Activity bars** hung with dangling, squeaky or tuggable features fit across infant seats, car seats or strollers. Babies can explore all the interesting, noisy or gripping objects. ▪ Any squeaky or **noisy toys** the baby can hold, grip and squeeze are fun. ▪ **Activity quilts** the baby can play on are fun to play on with a parent or playmate. ▪ Babies can form attachments to **soft stuffed animals**, though you should pick ones that do not cause risk for choking. ▪ **Colourful teething rings** are helpful at this age.

6 – 12 Months	<ul><li>**Toys with shapes** allow the baby to have fun interacting with them, especially moving toys, wooden or soft blocks.</li><li>**Busy boards** with elements are good for her to learn how to press the buttons and produce sounds.</li><li>**Soft dolls, stuffed animals and books** are great.</li></ul>
1 – 2 Years	<ul><li>**Vehicle toys** (cars, trucks, tractors) that she can wheel or ride to help develop strong legs and muscles.</li><li>**Big and colourful dolls** help girls identify and relate to them.</li><li>**Colourful false fruit and vegetables** are fun to play with.</li><li>**Manipulative toys** (including shape sorters, stacking toys and bucket filling activities) not only improve dexterity and eye coordination but induce manipulation and the use of the brain.</li><li>**Action-reaction toys** (e.g. batting a ball, pounding balls, loose marbles) allow the child to understand action and reaction. It also helps improve hand-eye coordination and reflexes.</li><li>Simple **puzzles** allow for the use of mental reasoning and problem solving skills.</li><li>**Coloring** expands the imagination and increases the use of fine motor skills. Offer thick crayons and large pads of paper.</li><li>**Matching games** (e.g. card games with numbers, alphabet letters or shapes) are excellent developmental toys.</li></ul>
2 -3 Years	<ul><li>Offer **books** that ask the child to identify colors, shapes and letters.</li><li>**Puzzles** challenge the child to think critically.</li><li>**Work toys or play-doh** increase the child's motor skills.</li><li>A **toy bank** teaches math skills and the basic principles of money.</li><li>Give your child opportunities to **mimic parents** with play power tools, play kitchen sets and doctor's kits.</li><li>Offer **other activities** including dress-up clothes, outdoor climbing equipment, board games, matching patterns and so forth.</li></ul>
3 – 4 Years	<ul><li>**Play sets** (e.g. dollhouses and accessories, floor puzzles, construction toys) and **action figures** offer active play that involves imagination and encourages cooperation when playing with peers.</li><li>**Educational toys** allow the child to learn letters, numbers and simple words</li><li>Construction toys (e.g. building blocks and Lego).</li><li>**Toys with realistic parts** (e.g. medical kits) give the child something to talk about, helping initiate early attempts at social</li></ul>

	interaction. - **Books with stories and rhymes, play-doh, building sets with large pieces and stacking rings** should be given. - **Tricycles** and scooters
4 – 5 Years	- **Puppets and interactive storybooks** should be offered at this age. - **Paints, crayons and other creative designs** can be given to stimulate imagination and motor skills. - **Building sets** (including Lego, Matchbox cars, puzzles) allow the child to use and develop her brain.

5 – 6 Years	- **The best toys tend to fall in the following categories:**
	  a) Construction toys (e.g. Lego)
	  b) Character and superhero toys (e.g. Spiderman, Superman)
	  c) Toys and wheels (e.g. tricycles or bikes)
	  d) Creative toys (e.g. drawing, painting)
	  e) Toys for role play (e.g. playing dress-up, castle, kitchen sets)
	  f) Sports (e.g. playing catch, football)
	  g) Board games (e.g. Junior Monopoly or Junior Scrabble)

TIP: Smart Toys

When shopping for toys to stimulate your child, choose wooden toys more often than plastic ones. This is meant to reduce exposure to potentially harmful chemicals. In addition, keep an eye out for solid construction with non-toxic, lead-free finishes for worry-free play.

BRUSHING TEETH

PARENT CONCERN: My toddler fusses and clamps her mouth shut when I try brushing her teeth. What can I do?

GENERAL

- Caring for teeth is important to prevent dental problems and to develop healthy dental habits in the future.
- Toddlers usually do not like brushing the teeth, so of course, trying to do it for them will be a difficult task. As such, beginning to brush your child's teeth early in life may make the process easier.
- Kids are about ready to manage this task on their own when they can tie their shoes and color in the lines. Until that point, parents should brush their teeth or at least help.

HOW TO TEACH

- The best way to get started is to **let your child watch you brush** your teeth every day. Offer her a toothbrush with toddler toothpaste or allow her to brush your teeth after brushing hers.
- **Ask your child's dentist to talk to her** and explain the importance of brushing one's teeth. If she gives you trouble, then say that the dentist said "we have to brush our teeth to stay healthy".
- Allow the **child to be in control** by choosing colourful toothbrushes and allow her to select the one she wants to use. This may distract her and reduce the control issue.
- **Do not worry** about your child's technique or the condition of her toothbrush, as long as she's brushing.
- **Use a mirror.**
- **Teach your child how to brush every tooth gently**, exerting the slightest pressure against the tooth at a 45 degree angle. Brushing teeth should not be random scrubbing.
- As your child becomes more proficient in brushing teeth, you may be able to **let her take over** the morning brushing completely.
- **Supervise/check** your child's teeth after she brushes to make sure she did a good job, but don't expect good brushing until the age of 7 years. To help her feel in control, you can also let her check your teeth after you brush.
- **Praise** your child's efforts, even if they are feeble.
- **Establish a routine** (e.g. after breakfast or dinner).

- If she shows resistance to brushing her teeth, then take a **firm stance** and tell her to open the mouth to allow you to brush her teeth gently. Tell her that you have to "pop" the toothbrush in there and that it would be much easier if she helped you.
- To avoid and reduce resistance, you can make brushing teeth a fun game. For example, you can brush your teeth at the same time and see which one can brush for a longer time.

TIP: Toothpaste & Toothbrush
- Use a toddler brush that is soft-bristled and age-specific (soft or extra soft brush).
- Use toothpaste sparingly- a pea sized amount fluoride toothpaste is all you need for a preschooler.
- Share the task – ask the child to hold the toothbrush while you are brushing her teeth. Then ask her to try it on her own.

Physical Behavior

EYE BLINKING - TICS

TICS – WHAT IS IT?

- **Tics** are rapid, repeated and uncontrolled muscle twitches. They often involve the eyes and muscles of the face in the form of eye blinking (eye blinking tics can be in one or both eyes and occur in bouts), eye/mouth twitching or grimacing, squinting, repeated throat clearing or grunting.

- *They are disturbing both to children they afflict and to the people around them(sometimes regarded or misunderstood as mental illness or psychosis).*
- *The secondary emotional problem for the tic sufferer can be considerable and debilitating. It can lead to social isolation and low self esteem . The family's frustration and anxiety worsens the child's dislike of himself.*
- Tics may affect as many as 5-20% of all children at some point in their young lives and may last well into adulthood. They are more common in boys than girls with a ratio of 3:1 and rarely diagnosed before the age of two years. Tics can begin at **any time** during childhood.
- Generally, tics evolve slowly, lasting for a few weeks or up to a year and then regress again. For the most part, tics are harmless. The vast majority of tics are not the result of any underlying problem.
- There is a **fluctuation in the frequency and intensity** of tics over time. Its severity is determined by its frequency, intensity and complexity. The diagnosis depends on the duration and not the severity of the tics.
    a) If tics are present for less than one year, then the child has a **transient tic condition**.
    b) If there is a number of tics that have been present (even if not continuously) for more than one year, then it is a **chronic tic condition**. Chronic tic disorder, usually involves a combination of motor tics (start in the head and then move downward in the body) and vocal tics.

TIP: Types of Tics
- ✓ Motor tics are tics that produce movements such as eye blinking, shoulder shrugging, mouth grimacing, head jerking, bizarre facial expression and **gesturing with hands and arms.**
- ✓ Vocal tics are tics that produce sounds such as throat clearing sounds, sniffing and coughing to blurting out words and phrases and shou**ting obscenities (coprolalia).**
- ✓ Simple tics involve one muscle group or one simple sound.
- ✓ Complex tics involve coordinated movements produced by a number of muscle groups or a linguistically meaningful utterance or phrase.

CAUSES/TRIGGERS FOR TICS
While the actual mechanism of the tic is not known, it is assumed that it has to do with particular neurotransmitters and their interaction within nervous system.

- Genetic and neuro-chemical differences may play a large role in the onset of tics. Family members of affected children have much higher rates of tic disorder than relative of children who do not suffer from them .
- Children **do not "do" tic movements on purpose** nor is it the parents fault.
- Certain **medications** (e.g. methylphenidate – used to treat hyperactivity) are thought to cause tics in children already prone to the disorder. However, recent studies do not support this idea.
- Tics are exacerbated more often when the child is stressed, not when he is relaxed or sleeping. Contrary to adults, young children are typically unable to recognize situations that cause stress in their lives, nor are they equipped to deal with stress in positive and productive ways. Instead, children often exhibit stress and anxiety in physical and emotional outbursts (e.g. uncontrolled eye blinking).
- It is my opinion that eye **allergy can trigger eye blinking** similar to nasal allergy triggering throat clearing (from post-nasal drip) and nose twitching.
- **Tics & other conditions**: Tics are also seen with other conditions such as ADHD, autism spectrum disorders, Asperger's Syndrome and obsessive compulsive disorder. Similarly, there are a number of medical conditions that can produce tics or mimic Tourette's (e.g. Wilson's disease).

Tests & Diagnosis
✓ There are no tests for tics.
✓ Diagnosis is made by your child's health professional on the basis of a history questionnaire and physical examination (this is to rule out conditions such as allergy, foreign bodies in the eye, dry eyes, eyesight problems and anxiety/discomfort).

HELPING YOUR CHILD
- It is important for parents to understand that children cannot consciously suppress a tic or have little control of it.
- Consult with your chid health professional to rule out neurological movement disorder. Once the health professional concludes that there is nothing physically wrong with the child (which is found in the majority of cases), no treatment is necessary .
- The child is emotionally and intellectually exactly like other children and should not be treated as if he is disturbed, especially if he has chronic tics. He should not be disciplined into" snapping out" of the disorder.
- Support, compassion and patience will help secondary difficulties such as attention in school, decreased self esteem and social isolation- from taking over the child's life .
- Children that suffer from transient tics will benefit from stress reduction the most. Parents should try to identify and ease the child stressors or predisposing triggers.

You can help by trying the following:

o **Ignore** tics when they occur and do not draw unnecessary attention to your child's tic. If your child becomes worried about tics, it will occur more often and he will react with tension rather than acceptance.

o **Do not talk** about tics when they are not occurring; the less said, the less your child will be apprehensive about them. If your child does say something about the tics, reassure him that his face muscles have to learn to relax and that they will eventually disappear.

o **Siblings, relatives, friends, teachers or others should not tease** your child about his tics.

o **Identify the times** when your child feels pressure (e.g. homework, social interactions, and deadlines) and **remove/minimize stress** when possible.

o Help your child **learn how to relax** and maintain his self-esteem.

o **Criticize your child less** about grades, sports, table manners, keeping his room clean, and so forth.

o **Lighten** the commitments your child is engaged in by not over-scheduling activities.

o Ensure some **freedom and fun time** for your child to enjoy himself as much as possible.

o **Adequate sleep** goes a long way towards eliminating stresses.

o For longstanding tics and frequent eye blinking, **psychiatric consultation** may be necessary.

DURATION OF TICS & COMPLICATIONS

- The length of time tics persist in your child cannot be predicted in advance.
- If tics are ignored, they usually disappear in about two months to one year. If extra effort is made to help your child relax, they usually disappear earlier.
- For the most part, tics are harmless and the majority are not the result of an underlying problem.
- Tics can be very distressing to the child. Some children are made unhappy by being teased about them.
- 70 to 90% of children who suffer tic no longer have them by the end of adolescence (the reason for this is not clear-?maturation of the nervous system).

WHEN TO SEE THE DOCTOR

Consult your doctor when:

✓ You have any questions and/or concerns.
✓ Tics last more than one year (persistent and severe).
✓ Tics interfere with friendships, studies or school.
✓ Tics can involve other body parts other than the head, face, shoulders or it can be associated with other symptoms such as sounds of throat clearing and words.

TIP: Strep Infection & Tourette's?
In some cases, strep throat infections may trigger an acute onset of Tourette's syndrome or obsessive-compulsive disorder. It may sometimes trigger a dramatic worsening of symptoms in individuals who already have either disorder (recent study in 2008 refuted such associations).

Parent Concern: Is it simple tics or Tourette's?
<ul><li>When a child develops a tic, a parent immediately begins to wonder if their child will develop Tourette's syndrome. Tourette's occurs infrequently.</li><li>Generally, Tourette's syndrome involves multiple tics where at least one is vocal and symptoms must be present for one year. If the child has a history of numerous motor tics and at least one vocal tic with tics being present on and off for more than one year, then the child may have Tourette's. Also, Tourette's has more than just tics and include obsessions, compulsions and other features.</li><li>For Tourette's, medication and therapy options may help decrease symptoms.</li><li>The diagnosis of Tourette's is a clinical one, which means that it is based on history-taking and observations. There are no laboratory tests for Tourette's.</li></ul>

STUTTERING

GENERAL

- Stuttering is a communication disorder, where the flow of speech is disrupted by repetitions, prolongations and/or abnormal stoppage of syllables and sounds.
- Developmental stuttering is increasingly considered to be a speech disorder resulting from a central neuro-motor dysfunction.
- The frequency of stuttered words, the type of speech disruption, the presence and type of associated behaviours as well as time (e.g. day to day, week to week and minute to minute) and situations, varies among children.
- Stuttering occurs in about 5% of children with an onset between the ages of 18 months and 2 years and is either sudden or gradual.
- It tends to peak between the ages of 2-5 years (average age of onset is around 3 years of age), during periods of intense speech and language development. Boys tend to stutter three times more frequently than girls.
- While there is no cure for stuttering, it can be controlled with direct therapy and environmental changes.

NORMAL DYSFLUENCY VERSUS STUTTERING

Normal Dysfluency

- **Dysfluency** is an interruption in speech flow and is not always stuttering. The difference lies in the severity and pattern of speech dysfluencies.
- Most children go through a **normal stage of dysfluency** when they begin putting sounds, words and sentences together. These periods may last anywhere from weeks to months.
- The first early signs of dysfluency are between the ages of **18-24 months**. Parents must be patient with the child at this stage since it is natural for the child to experience dysfluency when trying to put words and sentences together.
- 50-70% of children who experience normal dysfluency outgrow this speech pattern after 5-6 months with it.

- How to Help:
  - ✓ **Read** the facts about normal dysfluency versus chronic stuttering to reassure yourself about whether your child is experiencing any speech difficulties.
  - ✓ **Model "easy and smooth" speech** (e.g. slower speaking, using simpler sentences, connecting sounds and words, forming sentences that are easy to follow).

✓ Parents can help **facilitate fluency** by pausing before responding to a child's conversation. This has the effect of slowing the overall tempo of the interaction and usually helps the child initiate speech, perhaps more smoothly (also see parent's help suggestions further).

✓ Consistently **follow-up** and monitor your child with a health professional.

Stuttering

- When your child's dysfluency becomes frequent, continues to worsen and is accompanied by one or more oral movements, then evaluation for stuttering by a speech language pathologist before 3 years of age is recommended.

- **Stuttering** is considered when there are 3 or more repetitions, prolongations and omissions for every 10 sentences (e.g. frequent repetition of sound syllables or short words).

- Since the child cannot easily engage with other children verbally, social development is often impaired. The stutterer's anxiety, shame and humiliation not only deprives the child of a positive sense of self (sometimes leading to depression), but seems to exacerbate the stuttering as well.

The following table outlines characteristics of normal dysfluency and stuttering:

Normal Dysfluency	Stuttering
- **Repetition** of words as parts of sentences (less than 3 units) such as "I, I, I want" or "I want…I want a candy". - **Revisions** of sentences (e.g. incomplete phrases) such as "I lost my…where is dad going?" or "I want, I want…I am going to the store". - Presence of **pauses** between words. - Dysfluencies has appeared recently (i.e. within the last 6 months). - **Repetition without effect** (i.e. no signs of struggle, frustration, facial tension or lip tension). - There are **periods of fluency** (days or weeks) when the child hesitates a little or not at all. - The behaviour does not seem to worsen. - Your child does not react and/or does not mention his difficulty with speaking. - Dysfluency is more noticeable when the child is tired, excited, talking about complex or new topics, asking or answering questions or talking to unresponsive listeners. - Follow progression if it worsens with a speech language pathologist.	- **Excessive repetitions** of syllables or sounds (e.g. "he..he…hello"). - **Lengthening/prolongation of sounds** (e.g. "mmmmom"). - **Blockage** of sounds, where he seems to get stuck on a sound. - Lasts for more than 6-12 months. - **Signs of muscular tension** or physical effort (e.g. head shaking, eye blinking, voice changes in intensity or volume, facial contortions). - Stuttering seems to be **increasing**. - Child **avoids speaking** and becomes aware of the difficulties and/or mentions the stuttering as **frustrating** and embarrassing. - Sometimes, the child displays avoidance behaviour (i.e. fear of talking). - It is typically **frequent, occurring at any time and any place** and sometimes for long durations, in most speaking situations with greater consistency and non-fluctuating. - If severe stuttering persists, then immediately seek a speech language pathologist.

CAUSES

While the causes for stuttering are unknown, there are only suggestive theories for the occurrence of stuttering. *A combination of the following factors may predispose the young child to stutter:*

Genetics: About 60-70% of stutterers present with a family history of stuttering.

Biologic & physiologic differences: Stutterers show more brain activity in the right side of the brain when they are stuttering compared to non-stutterers. Speech and language has been shown to process in different areas of the brain.

Family dynamics & anxiety: High expectations and fast-paced lifestyles can contribute to the development of stuttering, since it is a learned behaviour. Family anxiety, criticisms and pressure can contribute to the frequency and intensity of stuttering while demeaning the child's self-esteem. While it is clear that anxiety makes stuttering worse, it does not appear to be the root cause for it.

Child development: Children with developmental delays or other language and speech problems are more likely to stutter than those without any developmental issues.

Abuse: In some children, stuttering develops as a result of trauma or abuse.

PROGNOSIS
- Stuttering is usually a problem of childhood and most (40-85%) recover within 1-2 years of onset.
- Recent data show that more than 99% of children who begin to stutter during the preschool years will recover with minimal or no treatment by the time they reach their teenage years. The rest become chronic stutterers with speech impairment becoming evident in the elementary school years.
- When stuttering first begins, its frequency is equal in both boys and girls. However, more girls seem to recover or outgrow stuttering than boys. The distribution of males to females who continue to exhibit chronic stuttering is about 3-4 males to each 1 female.
- Most children who do outgrow stuttering without treatment do so between 6-36 months after onset. The difficulty is that there are no predictors of which children will persist or outgrow stuttering.

Comment: Children or adults who stutter are no more likely to develop psychological or emotional problems than those who do not.

WHEN TO SEEK HELP

You should consult your child's health professional and possibly, a speech language pathologist if:

- You are concerned.
- You see that your child is concerned, upset about speaking, avoid speaking situations or shows visible signs of struggle when speaking.
- Your child has facial or body movements along with the stuttering.
- You notice increased facial tension or tightness in speech muscles.
- Speech begins to be increasingly difficult or strained or the child stops talking altogether.

- The child is 5 year old and still stuttering (does not seem to be growing out of the normal dysfluency stage).
- Some specific patterns indicate the risk of chronic stuttering including part-word repetition (e.g. "I wa-wa-wa-wa-wa-wa-wa-want") and prolongations (e.g. "my fffffffffood").
- When your child's pattern of dysfluency changes (e.g. becomes more frequent, struggles and/or forcing), then you should seek help.

GENERAL PRINCIPLES OF SPEECH THERAPY FOR STUTTERING AND SUGGESTIONS FOR WHAT PARENTS CAN DO

General

There is no existing cure for stuttering, however treatment has proven beneficial. Treatment is designed to help children who stutter be more confident speakers and help manage their stuttering exceptionally. In particular, speech therapy with a speech language pathologist is very effective with long-term improvements. While many children will outgrow a stutter, it is better to have speech and language assessment services when the child is young (before the stuttering problem becomes well established).

Both internal and external factors affect the fluency of speech. Tiredness, anxiety, fatigue, routine disruption, and excitement can lead to increased stuttering in the already existing stutterer. However, these factors do not cause stuttering to develop.

If your child suffers from anxiety and emotional problems due to stuttering, then consult a mental health professional for individual and family therapy to ease the child's anxiety and increase the sense of self-worth.

> **TIP:** Individuals who stutter have more trouble controlling their speech on the telephone – **BE PATIENT!**

Suggestions for Stuttering Children

When your child is talking to you or others	<ul><li>Look at your child to show him that you are interested in what he is saying and that you enjoy talking to him; this will increase his confidence to speak.</li><li>Do not tell your child to slow down, stop, think, breathe, say again or relax. Instead, show him how to speak slowly and clearly.</li><li>Avoid filling in your child's words when he is "stuck"; let him finish his sentence.</li><li>By praising the fluency, you increase the child's desire to maintain a steady flow of words.</li></ul>
How to talk to your child	<ul><li>Pause for at least 1 second before responding to your child to help reduce interruptions and tension. This will also help the child finish his thoughts in a relaxed environment.</li><li>Frequent correction can promote adverse feelings in your child about speaking in the first place. Parents should not try to correct speech.</li><li>Parents can repeat using what the child said with the correct sound. This provides an effective modeling method to help develop your child's sleep.</li><li>Talk slowly and clearly using short, simple sentences. Modeling encourages him to do the same (e.g. reading a book at a slow rate with soft speech movements).</li><li>Avoid jumping conversations; simply follow your child's lead.</li></ul>
More to know	<ul><li>Be consistent in your discipline, so that your child does not think he is being punished for stuttering.</li><li>Do not call him a stutterer, especially when he is around. Increase his self-confidence by concentrating on his strong points.</li><li>Be open, calm and accepting when your child asks about his speech problem; listen and reassure him.</li><li>Discourage teasing and encourage understanding attitudes.</li><li>Do not show him that you are upset or worried about his speech.</li><li>Refrain from teaching him tricks or devices that you feel may help reduce or eliminate stuttering.</li><li>Accept that your child is not perfect, because no one ever is.</li><li>Spend time playing and talking with him alone every day.</li><li>Do not react negatively towards him when he stutters.</li><li>If you do not understand him, ask for clarification.</li><li>Avoid any distractions during family mealtime and have conversations with him during this time.</li><li>Do not tell him to think before he speaks.</li><li>Maintain eye contact.</li></ul>

PARENT CONCERNS

How can my child's teacher help and how can I help discourage other children from teasing my child?

- Let your child's teacher know that anticipation of talking is what scares the stuttering child. As such, have the teacher let the child know when he is required to talk and provide opportunities for him to orally rehearse or practice answers to questions or presentations.
- Ask the child what could be helpful for him to speak in front of the classroom.
- Ask the teacher of any other known strategies to help the stutterer excel in the classroom.
- For teasing, deal with it like you would in any other situation. Express intolerance for teasing and ask the teacher to explain stuttering to the class.

Should classmates, teachers and siblings be included in my child's therapy?

- The decision to include the above is an individual and personal choice.
- It depends on whether your child needs the extra support of those who would be included in therapy. If, for example, the child's siblings frequently interrupt him, finish his sentences or tease him, then they need to be included in the therapy process so they can learn how to verbally interact with the stutterer.
- If your child wants to include the class and teachers in the therapy process, then you could get a speech language pathologist to come speak to the class about stuttering and how to verbally interact with one.

Do stuttering counsellors help and how?

- There are many effective treatments for stuttering, most of which involve making changes in the manner of speaking.
- Most treatments are conducted by speech language pathologists.
- Sometimes, additional counselling is required, especially for older children, adults and families of small children. This is because stuttering is sometimes accompanied by strong emotional reactions on the speaker's part with no indication of psychological or emotional problems.
- Note: Emotional or psychological problems can develop as a way of coping with stuttering.
- Typically, treatments include helping the child "talk correctly".

What are some principles of stuttering treatment?

- Therapy for children analyzes the environment and the child's reaction to the environment to see which factors increase stuttering or fluency problems. This is one method in therapy which helps reduce the incidence of stuttering.
- Therapy elicits a high level of fluency by including a modeling approach (smooth speech = slower rate, correcting words), education and counselling about stuttering.
- When treating stuttering, it is important to have an idea about the possible predisposing factors or causes. In those children with actual speech problems (not due to trauma), treatment is directly aimed at speech and it is better to add emotional treatment. This is because there is always emotional anxiety associated with stuttering, no matter what the cause may be.

GRINDING TEETH

GENERAL

- Teeth grinding, known as **bruxism**, is a problem in children similar to adults.
- Bruxism is the unconscious habit of grinding one's teeth. In children, bruxism usually occurs during sleep and happens when the child clenches his upper and lower teeth, rubbing them together.
- Teeth grinding in children do not pose a major health concern. Although bruxism may directly cause damage to tooth enamel, your child will eventually outgrow all of his baby teeth and replace these with a new set of teeth. If teeth grinding continues after a new set of teeth replaces the baby teeth, then bruxism should be addressed professionally.
- In most cases, children do outgrow bruxism.

CAUSES

- It is not yet clear why some children start grinding their teeth while others do not. However, **bruxism may possibly be due to the following**:

Dental: For children 7 years and under, teeth are still in the growing stages. If the set of bottom and top teeth do not fit together (i.e. abnormal alignment of the teeth), then it can be due to the fact that children's teeth and jaws grow in phases. It may lead to unpleasant sensations in the area leading the child to grind his teeth to soothe himself.

Emotional: Stress or anxiety may lead to teeth grinding. The child may suppress anger from a frustrating day (e.g. pressure by other kids or parents, possibly schoolwork). Teeth grinding may cause sleep cycle disruptions. Tension is not always the cause of teeth grinding since babies may accidentally discover the "fun" associated with grinding. They may simply be experimenting with the sensation and sound of grinding, but will soon lose interest in the dental orchestra!

Other:
- Grinding can occur as a facial response to pain from earache or teething.
- Drugs that cause the nervous system to be stimulated are the drugs that are most likely to cause an individual to grind his teeth.
- Prescription drugs (e.g. antidepressants) as well as illegal drugs (e.g. ecstasy, cocaine) is another cause for grinding. Infrequently, grinding teeth is the result of physical injury (e.g. dislocated jaw).

Associated Conditions:
a) Sleeping disturbances (sleep talking/walking, bed-wetting).
b) Hyperactive children may have bruxism, especially later on in adulthood.

How to Help
- While the problem will likely disappear on its own, you may need to try some methods to help your child stop teeth grinding until it does disappear.
- Consult your dentist to ensure normal alignment of the teeth.
- The most common recommendation to help bruxism is the use of a mouth guard worn at night to prevent the child from grinding his teeth. Mouth guards have been found to be successful in reducing the habit, however your child may feel uncomfortable wearing one.
- In children whose grinding appears to be due to stress and anxiety, it is important to discover the cause of these feelings. Try various ways of relaxing your child before he falls asleep (e.g. warm bath, massage the jaw, read a favourite book, loving hugs and kisses).

When to Seek Help
- Consult a health professional when teeth grinding becomes too extreme or causes other physical problems such as headaches, jaw aches, sore face, and so forth.

Comment: Grinding Teeth & Parasites
- Many parents ask to check for parasites in stool tests while their child is tooth grinding (or in the cases of an itchy anus) since abnormal grinding or clenching of teeth has been observed in cases of parasite infection. These symptoms are more noticeable among children when they are asleep.
- Bruxism may be a nervous response to the internal foreign irritants (release of waste and other toxins) from parasite infection.
- Parasite infection in relation to teeth grinding is most frequently observed in countries where there is not a lot of good drinking water, though it can happen elsewhere. From my experience in practice of various countries, I have not found worms associated with bruxism.

HEAD BANGING

WHAT IS IT

- It can be terrifying to watch a child bang his head. Most toddlers who indulge in this behaviour are healthy toddlers who seem to be calmed by this skill.
- Head banging is most common from the ages of 9 months to 4 years. This behaviour can last for minutes at a time or sometimes, for hours.
- In most children, rhythmic self-comforting activities (e.g. rhythmic rocking, hair pulling, head banging), disappear by the age of 3-4 years without parental intervention.

- Boys are usually 3-4 times more likely to be head bangers than girls.
- Children who bang their heads usually do not hurt themselves and usually, it does not affect their development.

REASONS FOR HEAD BANGING

- Head banging is seen as a behavioral problem or issue, usually done to attract or seek attention from parents and/or caregivers. The more attention given to a child who head bangs, the more likely the behavior will continue.
- Head banging can be part of a temper tantrum. Typically, head banging is done out of habit or pleasure. Children who are under-stimulated (e.g. lonely, bored, deaf, blind) head bang for increased stimulation.
- Sometimes, head banging is soothing and helping one go to sleep, release pent-up energy and tension at the end of the day, and so forth. It is similar to other comforting methods such as rocking.
- Occasionally, psychological factors (e.g. frustration, desire to harm) can be a cause for head banging; other times, it may be an indication of mild illnesses (e.g. teething or ear infection) or serious disorders such as autism, Tourette's syndrome or seizures.

WHAT TO DO

- **Coercion** rarely works and often triggers an increase in head banging.
- **Refrain from overreacting**. It is probably best if you do not pick up your child and comfort him, since this may only reward the behaviour. Instead, try to stay calm and be consistent with your reactions.
- **Nothing should be said** or given to your child in the midst of a head banging session. Pretend not to notice what he is doing.
- Protect the child and his environment (e.g. move the crib away from the wall, remove the wheels of the crib, etc).
- When your child does head bang, ensure that he is doing so in a carpeted or **safe area** (if necessary). Parents may eventually leave the room.

- Understand that head banging is a **temporary act**. Most children outgrow head banging by the age of four or when the need to do so is replaced by other methods of expressing anger/frustration.
- Help the child replace head banging with an appropriate mode of reaction to moods, desires, environments and/or soothing techniques.

- Ensure the child receives plenty of love, **affection and attention**.
- Find opportunities to spend time with your child such as reading or playing together.
- Allow for ample playtime and provide acceptable kinds of rhythmic activity (e.g. dancing, swinging) or other activities (e.g. pounding on a toy) to help provide him with another way of releasing his nervous energy.
- Ensure that your child spends time playing alone or playing with peers. The child who has the opportunity to learn how to amuse himself and interact with others remains more confident and less likely to have a poor self-image.
- Ensure that your child has toys that are appropriate for his age and development.
- Offer creative outlets that occupy his time constructively, so that he does not resort to head banging.

Head Banging is...	What to Do
Part of a temper tantrum	<ul><li>Most toddlers do not hurt themselves.</li><li>If your child is in danger or hurting himself or others, move him to a safe spot and pretend to ignore his behaviour.</li></ul>
To attract attention	<ul><li>Pretend to ignore your child's behaviour.</li><li>Provide positive attention to behaviours you want to encourage (e.g. listening to music or reading a book).</li></ul>
Out of habit	<ul><li>Pretend to ignore the behaviour.</li><li>Divert your child to other activities such as clapping to music, riding in a teeter-totter or playing various games like peek-a-boo or patty-cake.</li></ul>
A soothing technique for sleep	<ul><li>Pretend to ignore the behaviour.</li><li>You can move the crib away from the wall to provide a safe surrounding (if it is close to the wall).</li><li>Avoid a bedtime that is too early for your child.</li><li>Make sure that your child is somewhat sleepy and tired when putting him to bed (this may decrease his need to head bang).</li></ul>

PARENT CONCERNS

How can I tell if head banging is part of autism?

The need for head banging in autistic children is a frantic attempt to block out the loud sounds they frequently hear in their heads, rather than an involuntary lapse of muscle control or spasm. *Suspect autism if, by 14 months of age, your child:*

- ✓ Lacks pointing (points at an object in order to get another person to look)
- ✓ Lacks gaze following (infants will often turn to look in the same direction as an adult)
- ✓ Lack of pretend play (child will begin to play using object substitution)
- ✓ Other symptoms of autism, see Autism chapter.

How do I pad the bed?

Padding of the bed or the crib is probably not required. Due to the small risk the child may not be able to breathe with all the padding or bumpers in the crib, it is usually not recommended to pad the bed or crib.

PICKING THE NOSE

GENERAL

- Generally, habits are behavioural patterns that are repeated and often done without the child's awareness (e.g. being unaware that he is picking his nose); often irritating parents.
- Nose picking is the most common cause for frequent nose bleeds.
- Children pick their nose for various reasons including curiosity, relieving stress, out of boredom and nose allergies (child constantly feels like "something" is in his nose). Itchiness or discomfort from heating or air conditioning system can dry out the nasal passage leading to, crust formation.
- It can attract parental attention or irritate parents (as a retaliation tactic).

WHAT TO DO

- Explain that picking one's nose is something that should only be done in **private** since people do not like to see someone picking his nose. For example, the bathroom is the best place to pick one's nose.
- Calmly point out that picking one's nose is **unacceptable behaviour and explain** why. For example, you can say that picking the nose can spread germs and cause infections inside the nose while fingers can spread colds around.
- **Do not scold, lecture, ridicule or criticize** your child since it will only increase his behaviour. It may also make your child feel guilty and "bad" for doing something that he is not even aware of doing.
- **Use stickers or prizes for good behaviour**. Offer rewards and make a chart for good behaviour.
- **Address allergies** or other nasal discomfort and how to relieve it by discussing with your health professional.
- **Encourage proper hygiene** by washing hands and keeping trimmed nails.
- **Direct or redirect activities** when appropriate by suggesting he picks his nose in private.
- **Ignore** the behaviour when all else fails.
- For an older child, **involve him** in stopping the behaviour by asking him how he thinks he can stop picking his nose.
- If the problem is dryness, then keep him and his nose hydrated. Try a humidifier at least at night and use saline nasal spray and petroleum jelly to combat the issue.

When caught in the Act!

- Ignore the behaviour, especially when your child wants attention.
- Act, don't talk. Simply hand over the Kleenex box or walk him to the bathroom for privacy.
- Offer choices: "Would you like to excuse yourself or do you want a tissue?"
- Offer other choices: "Will you stop picking your nose or should I leave?"
- Be firm and friendly. If he continues to pick his nose, leave without getting upset.

Comment: If your child picks his nose intensely (e.g. draws blood or the habit seems to be due to anxious behaviour), then discuss with your child's health professional.

HANDEDNESS

Parent Concern: At what age will I know whether my child is right or left handed? Is there any connection between handedness and brain function; if so, should I change my child's handedness?

GENERAL
- Left handed individual are those who write using their left hand. Some of these individuals may use either hand for some tasks (i.e. ambidextrous) or prefer different hands for various tasks.
- Hand choice is usually not reliable or stable until after the age of four.
- About 13% of children are currently left-handed with slightly more boys than girls (a ratio of 5 boys to 4 girls) being left-handed.

CAUSES
Causes of being left-handed may be genetic (handedness is not a matter of choice , but part of a child's physiological makeup) or pathological. Some children may be naturally left-handed (genetics), though it does not necessarily mean it is inherited by the parents. When both parents are left-handed, there is only a 26% chance that the child is left-handed. Various causes can lead to injury of the left hemisphere of the brain, left-handedness may result in these individuals who would otherwise be right-handed (pathological or forced).

HANDEDNESS AND THE BRAIN
- The brain consists of a left and right hemisphere. Handedness is determined by the greater dominance of one hemisphere of the brain over the other.
- Each hemisphere controls different functions .Regardless of handedness verbal language is usually located in the left hemisphere.
- With left-handed individuals, it is likely that the language centers of the brain are located on the right side or on both sides of the brain.
- It is wrong to presume that all right-handed individuals are better at analytical thinking or that left-handed individuals are more creative and musical. The thought process and problem solving skills may differ depending on which skills are dominant in the brain. However, some of the following aspects may be true:
  - ✓ Left-handed children may be highly **creative** and possess **high verbal** or **math** abilities.
  - ✓ Some report state that left-handed children are likely to have **high visual spatial abilities** and low analytical and verbal abilities.
  - ✓ There is no consistent link between IQ, reading and writing and left-handedness.
  - ✓ Generally, left-handed people are not more or less intelligent than right-handed individuals.

HANDEDNESS & AGE OF DEVELOPMENT

- Most babies begin using both hands and rarely show any preference for one before nine months of age. By about 18 months, babies may use one hand more consistently than the other. However, it is not unusual for a child to show no distinct preference at the age of 3 or 4 years. *You can follow your child's hand development by examining:*

  - ✓ Which hand is used to reach toys
  - ✓ Which hand is used to feed herself
  - ✓ Which hand is used for drawing or attempting to write letters (left-handed children typically prefer to work from the right, away from the body and to the left)
  - ✓ Which leg the child feels more comfortable standing on (e.g. the left leg)
  - ✓ Which hand is used to brush her teeth
  - ✓ Sometimes looking at which hand is used to catch and throw a ball (though not always accurate)

SWITCHING HANDEDNESS: IS IT POSSIBLE?

- Handedness is determined by the brain and not by one's hand. As such, you cannot switch which hand your child prefers to use.
- If you try to force your child to use the hand she is not comfortable using, then she will be using the less coordinated and weaker hand to complete tasks; she will feel more tired, clumsy and ineffective.
- With time and practice, the left-handed child will learn to overcome the obstacles associated with living in a right-handed world.

Tip: Left-Handedness & School Difficulties

Most left-handed children will not experience any difficulties at school. However, problems sometimes arise so you can try to ensure the following with your child's teachers:
- ✓ Left-handed scissors should be available when needed.
- ✓ your child is not positioned at a desk where she is hitting a right-handed child's elbow all the time.
- ✓ Left-handed children are more comfortable sitting in the right side of the classroom.

WHEN TO BE CONCERNED

- In the first 3-4 years of life, your child will probably use both hands for most tasks such as throwing, catching, writing, picking things up, drawing, and so forth. You may notice a preference for one side over the other that seems to grow stronger every day.
- In addition, an early preference for the left hand does not mean that your child will end up left-handed.
- If your child is not showing any hand preference by 3 to 4 years of age, it may be a sign of delayed maturation. In many cases, children will catch on later as per their own developmental pace while others need occupational therapy to help build coordination and confidence.
- If you notice that your child only uses one side or if one side moves much less or seems much weaker than the other, then you may need to consult with your health professional.
- Development of a hand preference before the age of 12 months is indicative of motor impairment in the opposite side.

ABNORMAL HEAD SHAPES

GENERAL

- An infant skull is made up of several free-floating bones connected by fibrous regions called **sutures**. These flexible connections allow the infant's head to pass through the birth canal and enable the skull to grow in response to brain growth.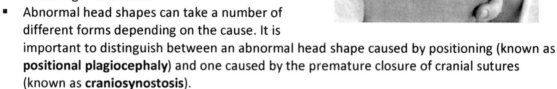
- The bones of the skull do not fuse for several months to allow the brain to grow. As such, the weight from gravity tends to flatten the head. In addition, the weight of the head itself (which is soft and malleable) can contribute to a temporary flattening of the skull.
- Abnormal head shapes can take a number of different forms depending on the cause. It is important to distinguish between an abnormal head shape caused by positioning (known as **positional plagiocephaly**) and one caused by the premature closure of cranial sutures (known as **craniosynostosis**).
- Plagiocephaly is the term used for any condition that is characterized by a persistent flat spot on the back or on the side of the head.
- Craniosynostosis refers to early (premature) fusion of any or all of the sutures of the bones of the skull. If such early fusion occurs in one of the sutures, it will restrict and distort the growth of the skull. Depending on the sutures that fuse prematurely, there will be a different abnormal head shape. For example, a long narrow head (known as Dolichocephaly) can be positional from breech presentation, familial or caused by sagittal Craniosynostosis.
- The incidence of positional plagiocephaly if striking at 6 weeks of age, increases to a maximum at 4 months of age. With the changing of sleeping positions (See Prevention & Treatment section below) improvements start to occur by 6-7 months of age.
- Early detection of abnormal head shape is important (i.e. before 4 months of age), as sleep patterns have been established and flat head is self-perpetuating.

CAUSES OF HEAD FLATTENING & ASYMMETRY

Environmental causes account for the vast majority of plagiocephaly cases. Physical deformities or genetic anomalies resulting in a misshapen skull are rare .

The most common cause of plagiocephaly is due to the baby spending long periods of time in the same physical position , which put pressure on the skull .

The following are some causes of head flattening and asymmetry:

- Sleeping on the back
- Wryneck/torticollis –is commonly associated
- Crowding of the baby in the uterus (compressive force in utero)
- Extended time in a car seat or other infant carriers
- Craniosynostosis
- Related to hypotonia for example due to prematurity
- Comment-midline occipital flattening may be normal if it is present in one or both parents.

The following are some risk factors for positional plagiocephaly:

- Male sex
- First born
- Limited passive neck rotation at birth (congenital torticollis)
- Only bottle feeding
- Supine sleeping position
- Awake tummy time (fewer than 3 times per day)
- Lower activity level

Tip: Torticollis and Flat Head

✓ Torticollis is a group of muscles that are tight on one side of the neck, causing an infant to tilt or deviate the head to one side. The muscle fibres can shorten, because of continued resting in only one position.

✓ In congenital muscular torticollis, there is a tightening of the Sternocleidomastoid muscle and the occipital flattening on the opposite side of the tight muscle.

✓ Infant with Torticollis have some limitations of active rotation of their heads away from the flattened side of the occiput

---

DIAGNOSIS

- The diagnosis for abnormal head shape begins with the health professional asking questions in **History** about birth, in utero position, neck tightness, post-natal positioning, tummy time and so forth.

- **A physical examination** will be done by your child's doctor that includes an inspection of the infant's head and palpation (carefully feeling the skull for suture ridges and soft spots – fontanel) and checking for neck tightness and other deformities. Localized hair loss is an an early indicator and if allowed to continue ,further deformity can result .

- When an infant presents with an abnormal head shape, the first step is to diagnose the cause of the deformity (i.e. due to external forces or craniosynostosis) to determine a proper course of treatment. The following table outlines the main differences between both causes for abnormal head shape:

Positional	Craniosynostosis
■ Results from preferentially lying on one side of the head ■ The ear on the flattened side is more anterior than the other ear ■ A protruding forehead on the flattened side ■ An aerial view (looking from the top) of the head shows a parallelogram-shaped head which suggests positional head deformity ■ Treatment will include repositioning/neck exercises and/or cranial orthosis. Age and severity play a big role in the course of treatment.	■ Abnormal head shape can take a number of forms. ■ The ear on the flattened side is more posterior than the other ear ■ Treatment involves surgery.

- A radiograph of the skull are only helpful when there is suspicion of craniosynostosis or when there is worsening of head shape at an age when positional plagiocephaly would be expected to improve.
- An x-ray of CT scan of your child's skull may be requested, along with a referral to a specialist if the diagnosis is unclear or suspected of craniosynostosis.

> **Comment:** Ensure that your child's babysitter and day care provider know about the importance of tummy time when your baby is awake as well as the importance of how to put your baby to sleep.

PREVENTION & TREATMENT

- **Provide Tummy time** when your infant is awake is important .Once the umbilical stump has fallen off, babies ca be placed on their tummy when awake and alert several times a day. **Limit the amount of time your baby spends on his back** everyday including time in the car seat or infant seat, swings, strollers, and so forth.

- **Change** your baby's position in the crib every night by alternating sleep orientation .Babies like something to look at and will turn their head toward the room rather than the wall. On alternate days, change your baby's position from one end to the other and check to make sure she is looking out into the room. A mobile will encourage your baby to turn the head in alternate direction.

- Minimize use of seats-babies should not spend long time in the car seats and other baby holders. Seats should not be used for sleep.

- **Rearrange toys** attached to the crib to draw the child's attention to other directions or move the crib in different areas around the room.

- **Counter-positioning:** This is usually effective in reversing skull asymmetry. It is a technique used to encourage your child to alter the resting position of his head. This includes positioning the infants so that the rounded side of the head is placed against the mattress. You can also alternate the sides of the head when the baby rests (e.g. the head is faced one way for 3-7 days and then faced the opposite way for another 3-7 days).

- **Neck exercises:** Neck dysfunction is almost universal for patients with deformational plagiocephaly. Sometimes this dysfunction is overt and infants have difficulties turning their heads midline. More often, it is subtle (the restriction of motion). One can have an idea of this restriction of neck motion by assessing the active and passive range of motion.
One hand is placed on the child 's upper chest and the other hand rotates the child's head gently, so that the chest touches the shoulders; this position is held for about 10 seconds. The head is then rotated to the opposite side and held for the same count to stretch out the muscles .The head is then tilted , so that the infant's ear touches his shoulders. Again , hold for 10 seconds and repeat for the opposite side. Do it with each diaper change. Three sets are required per exercise. If torticollis is diagnosed, physical therapist will help/show you how neck exercises can be done at home several times a day.

- **Helmet:** Helmets have used to treat severe cases. It is not clear if helmets are better than repositioning. If your child does not seem to respond to simple measures (e.g. counter-positioning), then discuss the use of a helmet with your health professional. Essentially, helmets are most effective between 5-8 months of age. Helmets are typically worn 23 hours per day for a period of 4-6 months. The helmet is adjusted as the head shape changes. The helmet eliminates the tendency for the infant to continue to lie on the flattened area of the skull and allows the rapidly growing skull to expand into areas unopposed by the helmet. It alleviates the pressure on the flattened area of the oxiput and allows the skull to grow faster in the desired direction .

- Generally, infants improve if the appropriate measures are conducted for a 2-3 month period.

TIP: If a baby still resists his head consistently in one direction, some parents use little Velcro pillows on the back of the child's pyjamas to prompt him to face a certain way.

Summary of Treatment for Positional Plagiocephaly

Younger than 4 months of age:
- ✓ Repositioning therapy is the preferred choice for patients 4 months of age and younger with mild to moderate asymmetry. Physiotherapy and positioning is preferable to watching waiting.
- ✓ Conservative treatment is most effective (i.e. aggressive repositioning and neck exercises) with a close follow-up (less than 1 month).

5 – 8 months of age:
- ✓ If head shape is mild to moderate, then the same treatment above applies. If there are no improvements on active repositioning, then you may need orthotics.
- ✓ If head shape is moderate to severe, then the use of an orthotic helmet may be required. Using the helmet at this stage is most effective since the infant's skull is still very flexible and malleable.
- ✓ Remember that counter-positioning between 4-6 months of age is less effective as the infant starts to roll and move independently.

7 – 12 months of age:
- ✓ In patients with severe asymmetry and regardless of age, moulding therapy can be considered and the maximum age to consider helmet therapy is about 8 months.
- ✓ At this age, the infant is sitting and rolling independently so the degree of flattening of the skull usually plateaus at this age.
- ✓ Counter-positioning is less effective at this age.
- ✓ The skull will continue to improve until about 12-14 months, when the sutures of the skull fuse. Around 1 year of age, the skull is more resistant to molding.

PROGNOSIS

(A) FOR POSITIONAL PLAGIOCEPHALY

- Usually, abnormal head shapes do not affect a child's neurological development.
- Abnormal head shapes are cosmetic conditions that will likely resolve.
- By the time the baby starts to sit up on his own, the head will gradually round out.
- The vast majority of positional plagiocephaly cases resolve by 2 years of age.
- The long-term consequences of positional head deformity are controversial and include an "emotional cost" of the deformity, mild to severe cosmetic deformities (these persist in 10% of infants affected by positional head deformity) and increased risk for subtle developmental difficulties in some studies (showing it could be present still at 18 months).

(B) CRANIOSYNOSTOSIS

If not treated it can result in neurologic damage and progressive craniofacial distortion. It may lead to increased intracranial pressure which may interfere with vision and intellectual development, low self-esteem and behavioral problems. Surgical correction may be needed in these conditions.

PARENT CONCERNS

What are the most important points to know about positional plagiocephaly?
- It is important to know that it can be prevented and corrected by repositioning. If it is treated early, then it can be corrected without surgery.
- Regarding any concerns about your child's head shape, speak to your health professional to rule out any other conditions such as torticollis or craniosynostosis that require different courses of treatment or surgery.

What can happen if I do not treat positional plagiocephaly?
- If untreated, head shape deformity can result in facial asymmetry. Medical issues may arise later in life (e.g. occlusion and temporo-mandibular joint problems).
- In addition, the importance of looking normal is attached to a child's emotional and social development (particularly as they grow into adolescence).

Does an orthotic helmet affect my baby 's hair growth?
- Studies show that helmets do not affect hair if you use appropriate FDA approved helmets or ones that are provided by an orthotic specialist along with proper monitoring.
- Even if hair loss occurs, it is only temporary.

Premature fusion of the sutures in the newborn skull occurs at what age?
- The skull grows in response to brain growth.
- The brain grows rapidly from birth to 2 years of age when the brain reaches about 95% of its size. After the age of 2 years, it continues to grow until about 7 years of age.
- The sutures typically involved in craniosynostosis deformities begin to close in the 3rd decade of life.
- The premature closures that lead to craniosynostosis generally occur in the first year of life.

HYPOTONIA

GENERAL
- The medical term for low muscle tone is hypotonia. This means that the muscles are weaker than they should be.
- Causes of hypotonia include neuromuscular diseases, muscle disorders and genetic disorders (e.g. Down syndrome, muscular dystrophy, cerebral palsy).

SIGNS & SYMPTOMS DUE TO HYPOTONIA
- As a young infant, your child may experience **feeding difficulties** (e.g. breastfeeding). This may be presented in problems nursing for long periods of time. He may become exhausted and fall asleep after a short nursing session since breastfeeding requires more effort than bottle feeding.
- Infants can be **floppier** than other babies without hypotonia. Babies with normal muscle tone may be lifted by placing your hands under their arms; however, the arms of babies with hypotonia will lay floppy with no resistance. Parents may feel as though the baby will slip through their fingers and fall.
- Children with hypotonia may experience **developmental delays** when it comes to head control achievement, sitting up, standing, walking, jumping, or running. Babies may be less likely to crawl and more likely to scoot along on their bottom once they get moving.
- Fine motor skills may be limited and speech may be affected as well.

MANIFESTATION OF NEUROLOGIC/MUSCULAR DISEASES
- Diseases of the neurologic or muscular systems may present in various ways as noted by parents, teachers and health professionals.
- **Developmental delay** of gross and/or fine motor skills may be an indicator of a neurologic/muscular disease.
- **Frequent falling** is sometimes an early complaint when there is a distal muscles weakness
- Teachers may report that **the child is slower** than his classmates in rising up from the floor, climbing stairs, skipping or jumping. He is **easily tired** (quick fatigue), runs out of energy quickly and unable to keep up with the other children in the class. Also, the child's **handwriting** may not be at the same level as his peers due to weakness of the hand muscles.

- Some children may **walk on their toes** (in cases such as Duschenne muscular dystrophy; see chapter on *Toe Walking*).
- **Abnormal gait** may be a presenting symptom of proximal or distal leg weakness. The pelvis is not stabilized and so the child may walk from side to side (i.e. ataxia).
- Muscle stiffness, pain, cramps, atrophy and twitching may be present in neurologic or muscular diseases.

DIAGNOSIS AND TREATMENT
- Hypotonia is typically diagnosed by your child's health professional or a neurologist who will ask related questions, examine muscle tone, motor skills, balance and coordination with reflexes and nerve function. In addition, blood tests, diagnostic imaging with a CT scan, MRI and/or EEG may result depending on possible causes.
- Treatment depends on the cause of hypotonia. The help of a physical/occupational therapist is usually part of the treatment process

TIP TOE WALKING

GENERAL

- A child's normal gait (i.e. technical term used for walking) cycle is not similar to an adult's gait until about the age of 3 years. Typically, children younger than 3 have a wide-based stance with short, quick steps.
- Some parents worry about the shape of their child's feet or legs or how their child walks.

- Many times tiptoe walking is not a cause for alarm as it is a normal part of development. It usually presents between the ages of 12 and 24 months.
- It is only when tiptoe walking is consistent or persistent (especially after the age of 3 years), that it becomes a gait abnormality and should be evaluated to rule out medical problems.

TIP: Differential Diagnosis of Tiptoe Walking

Toe walking can vary from mild conditions, which may be difficult to detect, to a serious condition with obvious features.

The main differential diagnosis in patients with tiptoe walking is mild cerebral palsy.

CAUSES

Normal Causes

- Toe walking when the child begins to stand is usually a normal part of development in many children, especially if the child is just beginning to learn how to walk (between 10-18 months of age)
- The child begins to walk flat and then goes up on the forefoot. There can be a period of time when the child walks flat for a while and then proceeds to tiptoe walking.
- There is no treatment required since it should disappear before the child is 3 years of age.

Idiopathic Causes

- The most common cause of tiptoe walking is idiopathic or habitual toe walking.
- Idiopathic causes are when there seems to be no physical or medical reason for toe walking.
- It is usually common in a child younger than 3 years of age.
- In some children, idiopathic toe walking may be simply a mimicking behavior and becomes a habit. When these children are asked to walk normally, they will place their heel on the ground first (before their toe). It is when these children are not concentrating that they seem to revert back to their habit.
- Habitual toe walking may lead to fixed contractions of the Achilles tendon (i.e. the largest tendon connecting the heel bone to the calf muscle of the leg).
- Family history of toe walking as a cause ranges from 30-71% and is considered characteristic of idiopathic walking.

Abnormal Causes

- Medical conditions that cause toe walking indicate that the nerves or muscles in the legs do not work properly. In these cases, there may be other problems that present along with toe walking including difficulty running, climbing, getting up from a sitting position, frequent falling or poor coordination.
- Neurological diseases which can cause toe walking may include Cerebral Palsy, spinal cord problems, congenital muscle diseases or localized diseases (e.g. Charcot-Marie-Tooth).
- Orthopaedic problems including congenital short tendon Achilles, hip dislocation or leg length discrepancies along with metabolic diseases may cause toe walking.
- Sometimes toe walking may act as a sign of other disorders such as Autism or Asperger's Syndrome.

Specific Medical Causes

Congenital Tight Heel Cord (short tendon Achilles)	✓ The only problem with congenital tight heel cord is that the heel cords are tight; there are no other problems with any other muscles of the body. ✓ While this can be an isolated condition, it may also be a part of Cerebral Palsy. ✓ *Treatment* may include the use of a therapeutic brace (AFO) or surgery in more severe cases. Casting may alternatively be used to correct the Achilles tendon.
Cerebral Palsy	✓ Cerebral Palsy is a group of conditions that affect the control of movement and posture. There is damage to parts of the brain that control movement and the affected child cannot move his muscles normally. ✓ Symptoms range from mild to severe; it usually does not get worse as the child gets older. ✓ With treatment, most children do improve their abilities. ✓ In Spastic Diplegia Cerebral palsy, early onset of toe walking is almost always found. ✓ Both conditions of idiopathic toe walking and mild spastic diplegia cerebral palsy are associated with premature birth, and tight Achilles tendons. However, it is a good sign when the child can walk completely normal when asked to do so. In this case, it is more than likely that the cause is idiopathic toe walking than Cerebral palsy.
Late Onset Toe Walking	✓ Late onset of toe walking begins at least 4 months after a child develops a normal gait (walking) cycle. ✓ It is virtually always due to some neuromuscular problem requiring a neurological assessment.

TIP: Running Your Own Tests
You can conduct an informal range of motion test by asking your child to lean forward and backward into your arms while keeping his feet flat on the ground. You can also place your child on your legs and gently move his heels in a circular motion.

WHEN TO SEEK HELP

Seek help when the following occurs:

- Behaviour occurs after about a month of being adept at walking and seems to be the main approach to walking
- Toes walk all the time and cannot stand on flat feet
- Toe walking is accompanied by other signs or symptoms (e.g. Autism, Cerebral palsy)
- Continues after the age of 3 years or develops at an older age in a child who used to walk normally
- Child has pain
- Unilateral tiptoe walking
- Child is unable to passively dorsiflex the ankle
- Associated concerns about developmental delays

TREATMENT

- No treatment is necessary for normal tiptoe walking since it should disappear by the time the child reaches 3 years. For other children, treatment may be necessary.
- Treatment may include **stretches** to lengthen the constricted tendons. For a child with the mild condition (i.e. contracture of Achilles tendon) , stretching exercises and physical therapy may be necessary.
- Treatment for tiptoe walking may include **physical therapy, serial casting (i.e. using a series of plaster casts on the feet and lower legs to hold them in the corrected position) and Achilles tendon lengthening surgery**.
- Overall, there is no convincing evidence that treatment is even necessary for the idiopathic tiptoe walker; though, observation is initially required.
- For persistent or more severe contractions, casting or surgery may be required; some use **Botox** (injecting the Achilles tendon to relax the muscles) to successfully treat and correct tiptoe walking.

Helpful Suggestions for Parents for Reducing Tiptoe Walking
1) **Reward** your child for walking with the heels on the ground. Reward with snacks and goodies, bubble baths, trips to the park, and so forth.
2) **Provide opportunities** where he has plenty of room to walk around barefoot on a familiar surface (e.g. living room floor) and where you can supervise him.
3) **Prompt** your child to walk on his heels by saying "Heels down" when he is standing. You could also place your hands gently on his shoulders and help him bring his heels to the floor.
4) When you see your child walking on his toes, **firmly and consistently** tell him to stop and what to do instead.
5) Have the child do **squats and massage** the tight heel cord with cream every night to relax the muscles.
6) **Praise** when he is walking with the heels to the ground. Remember to gradually decrease the amount of praise and rewards you offer for walking a normal gait cycle.
7) **Offer** a pair of shoes that have stiff soles and a high stiff heel counter to prevent him from standing on his toes.

HOW TO DEVELOP MOTOR SKILLS

It is important to develop a child's motor skills (both gross and fine motor), since this will help her perform academically and physically.

To develop fine motor skills, you can let your child:
- **Paint**: Offer both big and small brushes as well as cotton swabs (helps develop the pincer grasp required for clear writing).
- **Puzzles** help develop control over finger movement.
- **Play-Doh** is a good tool to improve fine motor skills and becomes interesting when extra props are added such as rollers and cookie cut-outs.
- **Cutting** develops hand-eye coordination. You can give your child an old newspaper to cut up with non-metallic scissors (only good to cut paper anyway).
- **Stringing:** This helps control hand movement. Offer beads or pasta to string together.
- **Blocks:** Start out offering large blocks and gradually offer the smaller blocks.

To develop gross motor skills, you can let your child:
- **Run** in a room, on the sidewalk with your supervision, in the park, and so forth.
- **Climb:** The more your child climbs, the better his grip and balance.
- **Hopping** helps develop balancing abilities.
- **Ball Playing:** Throwing, catching, kicking and rolling a ball with an appropriate ball size develop gross motor skills.
- **Batting** helps develop hand-eye coordination (e.g. baseball, tennis, racquet ball).
- **Pushing and pulling toys**
- **Jumping and swimming**

Sexuality
Issues

TOUCHING GENITALS IN INFANCY

Parent Concern: My 12 month old baby cannot keep his hands off his genitals. Is it normal that his hands are ready to jump to his genitals as soon as I remove the diaper?

GENERAL

- Touching the genitals in infancy is not the same as masturbation. It is perfectly natural for your baby to explore his genitals in learning about his physical appearance . There is no physical or psychological harm when babies touch their genitals.

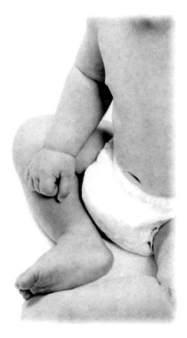

- During the first year of life, babies discover their bodies. Between 4-6 months of age, your baby will discover his hands and toes. At 7-8 months, a baby may begin exploring other parts of his body. He may discover the ears, nose, mouth, eyes and so forth. Within a few months, he will discover his genital area.
- The discovery your child makes during these exploration times significantly contributes to his later ability to feel comfortable with his body and explore his own sexuality at an older age.
- Parents should note that babies are not focused on touching their genitals as part of a sexual pleasure in the same way that an older child or adult may (i.e. masturbation).

WHAT TO DO

- By responding without anger, surprise or disapproving words, you are teaching your child that curiosity about his body is a normal part of life.
- Do not say "no" in a stern voice and move your child's hands away as you are teaching him that touching his own genitals is "bad" and that this part of his body is "bad".
- Do not make your baby feel "dirty" for engaging in such behavior due to the negative effects on sexuality and self-esteem that may result.
- If your baby seems to reach for his genitals frequently, then it is much more effective to divert his attention cheerfully than to say "no, no". These reactions will only intensify the behavior rather than reduce it.

TOUCHING GENITALS IN OLDER CHILDREN - MASTURBATION

Parent Concern: My 4 ½ year old keeps his hands on his genitals all the time. Is it dangerous? Is he masturbating? How do I stop him from touching his genitals?

GENERAL

Children's physical self-explorations and masturbations in particular, mark important milestones: they allow children a sense of mastery over their feelings and bodies. Emotional problems associated with masturbation far more frequently arise from anxious parental reaction to it than from the act itself.

- Many parents find it difficult to understand that their young child's sexuality is natural. Often times, they do not know how to react to it.
- Boys seem to touch their genitals more than girls since boys' sexuality is more obvious than the girls.
- Boys can have erections when fondling their genitals simply due to physical pleasure. Signs of sexual excitement are less obvious in girls. As such, girls may find sensation from wriggling around, rubbing against furniture or simply pressing the thighs close together.

Important to Remember

- It is important to realize that the young child is not in fact masturbating for erotic or sexual purposes.
- Preschool children touch their genitals simply because it feels comforting as well as pleasurable.
- Do not give your child the message that touching oneself is "bad" since it can create confusion about genital pleasure in the future. Your child may continue to touch his genitals secretly and defiantly if you portray a negative attitude about it. Simply ignore and adopt a cool approach.

CAUSES

- Children may touch their genitals simply because it **feels good comforting and pleasurable**. It is always going to be a part of the body that is stimulated when touched. Though the feeling may be pleasurable, it is not sexual.
- Children between the age three and five are, in many ways, the most intensely sexual they will be in their lives .Their curiosity about penises , breasts and vagina is at an all time high .

- Often times, a child may touch his genitals for **physical and emotional comfort** (e.g. when going to sleep).
- Occasionally, young children masturbate excessively due to **stress** in various areas of life. Control of bodily sensations may be used to compensate for a lack of control in other areas such as toilet training or eating patterns. Also, excessive masturbation may be due to other emotional difficulties the child experiences.
- Some children touch their genitals to **gain attention** from adults.
- It is rare that touching one's genitals is related to sexual abuse.

WHAT TO DO & WHAT NOT TO DO

- Do not tell the child that touching his genitals is a "dirty" act that is unhealthy or will cause illness.
- Do not stop your child from exploring his body.
- Do not slap your child's hand when he touches his genitals.
- Ignore or minimize the act as best you can by diverting his attention to another activity.
- Seize the moment for a little education. Tell your child that masturbation should be done in private; teach him the difference between private and public places and why certain things are allowed in public while others are not; teach him the names of body parts.
- Use a neutral tone of voice when speaking to your child and avoid punishing him for his behavior of touching his genitals.
- Do not react harshly or vehemently to public masturbation as it is counterproductive .It indices unreasonable guilt and shame, erodes the child self esteem and promote fearful attitude about sex-simply tell that public masturbation is inappropriate.

WHEN TO BE CONCERNED

- You must ensure that masturbation remains an occasional pastime and not an all-consuming passion. There are some children who always have their hands in their pants. In such cases, ask yourself why it is happening (e.g. for comfort, security, boredom, itching, infection).
- An older child who continues to masturbate openly is showing a problem.

CONSULT YOUR CHILD HEALTH PROFESSIONAL WHEN:

- Masturbation is excessive (when it takes the place of other family, educational, social or cultural activities in which the child is expected to participate).
- The child does not stop masturbating, whether in public or in private, and is using the behaviour to vent underlying anxiety (the parents task is to find out what those anxieties are or have the child engage in private or family therapy if the causative anxiety is not readily apparent).

FAMILY NUDITY

Parent Concern: Should children see their parents naked? Can nudity between parents and children be perfectly innocent?

GENERAL

- Many parents have concerns about cross gender nudity within the family, while other parents do not even give it a second thought. Feeling comfortable with nudity is, at least partly, a remnant of your own upbringing. Nudity is not the same thing as sexuality.

- Many psychiatrists believe that family nudity may be harmless in children younger than 3 years of age. The chances are good that a 2-3 year old won't form any lasting memories of nude parents or siblings. For older children, seeing parents naked may be natural though confusing since they are more curious about their bodies and sexuality.
- Nudity in the home, when handled in a respectful way, is perfectly natural. Some research shows that children who have seen their parents nude do not grow up to be emotionally scarred, but are more likely to be accepting of their own bodies and are more comfortable with their own sexuality.
- Children normally develop a sense of modesty between the ages of 4 and 8 years. As such, they become increasingly uncomfortable about being exposed, especially to adults (unless they have been desensitized to it).
- The attitude and feelings of parents about their own bodies and those of their kids is more important than the actual practice of family nudity. Essentially, the naked body should be considered beautiful rather than embarrassing or shameful.

PRACTICING NUDITY

- Help your child associate between **when it is appropriate** to be naked and when it is inappropriate. Young children have not yet acquired a sophisticated understanding of modesty and really don't care who sees them naked.
- As children begin recognizing differences between themselves and others, you should **explain** the reasons for these differences. For example, you can explain that "mommy's breasts" are for giving milk to babies such as "when you were small".
- From birth, allow your child to see you in an ordinary nude situation (e.g. dressing, bathing, showering, and using the toilet). **Being comfortable** with your own body will naturally convey the message that nudity is natural and not something to fear. Of course, there are times in life when clothes must be worn for protection, comfort and adherence to social norms – it is important to teach the purpose of clothing to children.

- **Encourage family nudity during potty training** since potty training will take off more quickly when your preschooler is allowed to go bare at home.
- **Do not force** your child to be in the nude, especially around puberty -a time of confusion.
- **Emphasize the primary functions** (e.g. birth canal, urination) of genitals to younger children.
- **Avoid exposing** the child to nude photography due to the potential of pornographic messages.
- **Don't be embarrassed** to teach good personal hygiene.
- **Take cues from your child**. Some toddlers are completely oblivious to parental nudity, but at some point, they will begin to ask questions about private parts. Make sure you answer your child's questions simply and accurately.
- Although some children do not show an interest, family nudity could become a problem by the age of 3 years when some kids unconsciously become sexually stimulated by parental nudity and are confused or embarrassed by these feelings. It is probably wise to begin using bathrobes and having separate showers by the 3rd birthday.

Additional Comments
- A benefit to understanding the naked body in the home is that when the time comes to explain human reproduction, there will be less tension from your child. They will not have the embarrassment that typically goes along with the conversation.
- Realize that not all shame is "bad" shame.
- Encourage courtesy and respect for other's standards.
- Be safe with your child and explain when and with who it is appropriate to be nude with.
- **Marital intimacy is best left behind closed doors. If there is controversy between both parents, find compromise you are both comfortable with. For example, you may agree that it is time for her to bath with the toys only when you are not present.**

ERECTION

GENERAL

- While parents may not be aware of infant erections, all baby boys sometimes experience them.
- Erections are normal reactions to the touch of a sensitive sexual organ, similar to the girl's clitoral erection which is less noticeable.
- It is reported that self-stimulation occurs as early as six months of age, sometimes even three months in boys and about ten months in girls.

CAUSES

- There are no discernable reasons why baby boys get erections.
- Your baby may be aroused from the sensation of the diaper rubbing against him or when being washed in the bathtub.
- Babies sometimes find their own ways of touching their genitals (e.g. rocking, bouncing) before falling asleep since they find the sensation soothing.
- Do not stop your baby from touching himself, particularly if it relaxes him.

WHAT TO DO
Since erections in babies are normal and something they have no control over, you do not need to do anything.

BATHING TOGETHER

- While children may be curious about each others bodies, they are not thinking about sex. As such, you can allow your children to bathe together as long as they are comfortable doing so.
- There is no definitive age for opposite- sex children to stop taking baths together.
- Let your children be your guide and see how they feel about this issue. When one of the children starts to object or begins to show natural modesty and privacy, then it is time to provide separate bath times.
- Children should be aware of the possibility of separate baths.
- Typically, modesty develops around 2 ½ years for girls and 3 ½ years for boys.
- With respect to bathing or showering with a parent, children should feel comfortable to do so. However, children will yearn for privacy at some point and may want to shower alone; this should be provided for them as a possibility.
- Be prepared to answer questions about anatomy when bathing or showering with your child since children are naturally curious about the human body.

THE NAKED TODDLER

GENERAL

- Spontaneous undressing is very common between the ages of 2-4 years of age, however, it is normal for young children to undress and resist clothing
- In various settings, nakedness may be embarrassing and frustrating for parents.
- While you do not need to worry about your child's resistance to clothing, you should set some guidelines for when it is appropriate.

WHY IT HAPPENS

- The naked toddler is generally trying to assert his independence, opinions and abilities.
- Undressing involves important advanced motor skills. When the skill of undressing is newly learned, practicing may be fun for your little one.
- Simply stated, your toddler may be more comfortable naked than with clothes on.

WHAT TO DO

- **Do not overreact** when your toddler is running around naked. This will make him feel like his body is something to be ashamed of.
- **Do not make a fuss** over a naked toddler, otherwise he may undress more often.
- **Do not laugh** when your child is running around naked, since he may come to think of nakedness as a way of attracting attention; he will then give repeat performances.
- **Allow** your child to enjoy being naked sometimes if the circumstances and temperature allows.
- Be **firm and consistent** when being naked is inappropriate. If he takes off his clothes, put them right back on. Toddlers can be persistent, which means you will need to be even more consistent.
- **Explain** that people wear clothes when there are guests in the home or when they step outside, since the human body is a private matter.
- If your child persists on undressing in public, then **dress him in clothes that are more difficult** and tiresome to take off (e.g. pants with belts, shirts with small buttons).
- **Do not ask** your child if and when he will get dressed; tell him that he can run around four more times and then get him dressed.

TIP: Potty Time & the naked toddler
Toddlers will often resist wearing a diaper when running around naked. However, allowing some naked time may encourage the use of the potty when toilet training.

EXPLAINING SEXUAL ISSUES

Parent Concern: How do I explain genital differences to a toddler who has seen his new brother's penis?

- Children are curious about everything in the environment including their bodies and the bodies of those around them, which is a normal part of development.
- Provide honest and simple explanations that boys have penises and girls have vaginas; this is usually all that is needed. If the child asks why these differences exist, then you can say that these body parts allow girls to give birth and boys to be fathers.
- Use the proper names for body parts.
- Use the same tone of voice as you would when explaining anything else.

Parent Concern: How do I explain sex and why adults engage in kissing and other affectionate behaviour?

GENERAL

- The media exposes children to many sexual images and messages. Although you may not openly discuss sexual issues, your child will know something about it.
- Excessive exposure to sexual messages causes curiosity in some children and many parents do not communicate with their children about sex simply because it is not easy.
- Accept the fact that your child is a sexual human being and will be for life. Parents must be the source of information for children otherwise friends and media forms (e.g. television) will be the sex educator.
- It is necessary for parents to have discussions about sexual issues with children.
- Be prepared to offer your child factual information about sexuality along with your values and beliefs about sex and responsibility.
- Overall, love, empathy, trust and commitment are the most important things you can emphasize when discussing sex with your child.

WHAT TO DO

- Let your child know that he can **ask any questions freely**.
- **Do not avoid** answering your child's questions; it is ok to say you are unsure and that you may have to answer at a later time.
- **Practice** talking and prepare before talking to your child so that you are more comfortable with the upcoming discussion.

- **Remain calm** during the discussion.
- Always answer questions **honestly and openly**.
- **Avoid** using nicknames or even saying "privates" since this conveys the message that the real names of body parts are naughty or embarrassing.
- Communicate the right type of information, being a **good sex educator**.

SEXUAL ISSUES: DISCUSSIONS AS PER AGE

Toddlers	✓ Sexual discussions can begin as early as the toddler stage since toddlers are learning about their bodies. ✓ Discuss body parts when the child shows interest in their own body.

Primary Grades: Elementary School	✓ Talk about "crushes" and ask if there is anyone your child likes.
	✓ You can talk about babies including information about the emotional component of making babies (i.e. sharing loving feelings and commitment to each other before having the child).
	✓ Up to the age of 8 years, you can explain the following:
	    ▪ Define a penis, testicle, uterus, eggs, and sperm, providing a base explanation. For the most part, children will accept this in a matter-of-fact way.
	    ▪ Most children will be content with knowing that a sperm cell in the man meets the egg of a woman to form a baby.
	    ▪ Do not worry if your child does not fully understand the concept of cells as long as you lay the foundation based on truth.
	✓ By the 5th grade, discussions about sex should include concrete examples (whenever possible) about emotional commitment as a prerequisite for sex.

Older Elementary Grades	✓ At the age of 10 years, the first stage of sexual awareness appears.
	✓ Talk about the love between husband and wife as parents and the joint decision to have babies as an expression of that love.
	✓ Explain that sex is an emotional act between two people who love each other.
	✓ After the age of 8 years:
	    ▪ Children may want to know how the egg meets the sperm. This is the time to talk about sexual intercourse and making babies.
	    ▪ There is one basic answer: "The man puts his penis into the woman's vagina and a sperm from a testicle comes out." You can add, "that only adults who love each other very much will do this".

	<ul><li>You can also discuss that sexual intercourse can occur for reasons other than making babies. "Adults can also have sex to show that they love each other very much". At this point, do not get into the discussion of orgasms or sexual positions and so forth.</li></ul>✓ Oral sex does not need to be addressed until later than 10 years of age, unless the child brings it up. Explain that some adults do this as an expression of love. ✓ A child who is older than the age of 11 years, explain condoms and pills.

Learning and School Issues

READINESS FOR PRESCHOOL

GENERAL

- Many 3-year-old children attend preschool, while many others enter preschool at the age of 4 years.
- There are a variety of reasons why parents want to enrol their child at the age of 4 years (instead of 3 years) in preschool. One of these reasons it that it may be overwhelming for a 3 year old to enter the preschool setting, potentially hurting any chance for the young child to like school.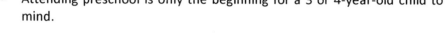
- If your child seems to be ready for preschool at the age of 3 years, then do your best to register the child in preschool or encourage creativity, thirst of knowledge and socialization.
- Attending preschool is only the beginning for a 3 or 4-year-old child to expand her mind.

CLUES FOR READINESS

To know whether your child is ready to attend preschool, ask yourself the following:

- Is your child an only child? Does she become excited if she sees other children or is she always bored?
- Does your child interact with other kids? Have an interest in learning?
- Is your child able to read the alphabet? Numbers? Recognize colors and shapes?
- Has your child been away from the parent? For how long? How often?
- Is she afraid of strangers or people she meets for the first time?
- Does she show wariness or is she afraid upon seeing the preschool?

PREPARING THE CHILD FOR PRESCHOOL

Each child is unique and while some are able to jump right into preschool, others find it difficult to let go of parents and enter the preschool system. Adjusting to preschool can be difficult for any child, even those who have been in a day care setting for a while. Help ease the transition to preschool by trying the following:

- **Plan social activities** so that your child can get used to being part of a group. You can arrange play dates with one or more peers for your child to learn how to share, take turns and play cooperatively.
- **Read to your child every day**. Most preschool classes have at least one reading period each day, making it a familiar ritual. Since preschoolers do not read

independently, they need to learn to listen and by reading along, you are helping develop listening skills. You could even question your child mid-way through the reading (e.g. "What do you think will happen next? How do you think the story will end?").

Comment for how to read: Make your voice interesting when reading to your child. Point to the story while you read it to show how you read from left to right. You can re-read familiar books so that you create a feeling of security and warmth. It is important to read to your child since it encourages speech and language development. Reading helps teach your child to listen and learn the rules of language while developing emotions and intelligence.

- **Practice listening and sitting still skills** with your child. Occasionally ask your child to sit quietly, close her eyes and talk to her about anything.
- **Ask the child** to do a series of things to teach her to follow more than one direction (e.g. take the hat and put it in the closet; go to the bathroom, wash your hands and then come help me do something).
- **Play games** that require her to listen to directions, solve problems and take turns.
- Help **develop the visual and fine motor skills** needed to write, finger point and mould clay by providing such games as connect-the-dots (for writing skills).
- **Talk** to her about what to expect (e.g. who will be in the class, what they will be doing).
- Visit the class at least once, preferably when the future teacher and kids are there.
- **Introduce the preschool gradually**, which is especially helpful for the sensitive/shy child. Even though your child may not get upset when you leave, she may later become frightened and miss you causing problems for the next day. Parents can stay with their child as long as they wish until she builds an attachment to the teacher or other children that will give her a sense of security. When parents do stay at the preschool, it is best to remain in the background.
- **Make a point of saying goodbye and not showing your own anxiety** over leaving her at the preschool. Do not sneak out when you drop her off; do not drag it out or let on that you are upset. Be firm from the start with some genuine anxiety about separating by saying goodbye once cheerfully and leaving.

TIP: Instilling a Love for Reading

A child learns to love reading gradually. *To help instill a love of reading in your toddler, you can try the following:*
- Let her pick out the books she wants to read.
- Read every day.
- Let her read to you by naming objects or making up an ending to a story.
- Visit the library often and allow her to get her very own library card.
- Sing, rhyme, talk and play with your child.

READINESS FOR GRADE ONE

GENERAL
- Starting grade one is one of the most emotional and significant transitions in a young child's life and family.
- Every child is unique and differs in maturity level and readiness for grade one. While some may be mature in certain domains of development, they may not be ready yet for grade one. As such, one must look at the overall abilities of the child.
- Since starting school can be both exciting and terrifying, parents need to know how to prepare the young child for a new school, teacher, program, recess and new peers.

READINESS
The age of 6 is the typical age for starting grade one in most countries around the world. It seems that by the age of 6, most of children's abilities are mature enough to begin grade one (e.g. sitting and concentrating for a certain period of time, cooperating with friends, accepting adult rules). However, abilities develop differently in each child accounting for different levels of maturity in children. Parents should assess the following in determining a child's readiness for grade one:

Physical (gross/fine) Motor Ability:
- Walks on a line
- Able to jump
- Climbs up stairs when one leg is on the other step
- Rides a bike (with the help of training wheels) and plays on an apparatus (e.g. ladder)
- Able to write numbers until 10, draw basic forms (e.g. circles, squares), and glues properly
- Cuts an exact line
- Holds a pencil correctly and writes her name without getting out of the lines
- *Comment:* To write comfortably and effectively, the elbow and wrist should be lying on the table to stabilize the arm. The dominant hand for writing should only have 3 fingers used to hold the pencil without excessive pressure or force. Writing should be fast and effective, yet good and readable.
- Fill forms with color and copy forms (hand-eye coordination)
- Handedness should be clearly left or right
- Closes zippers and buttons

Math Understanding
- Counts until 20
- Able to start counting from any number between 0-20
- Completes math calculations until 5
- Solves multiple problems of addition and subtraction
- Recognizes numbers to 20 with no particular order and number words up to 10
- Understands relativity in amounts (e.g. more, less, equal)

Cognitive Skills
- Check for short and long term memory (e.g. remembers what you said 10 minutes ago or what a friend said 2 days ago)
- Writes her first and last name (unless the name is long and complicated)
- Able to identify shapes and trace circles, squares, triangles and rectangles
- Imagines events in history, verbal math problems or the character of a book

Concentration Skills
- Sits when reading a book from the beginning until the end
- Able to listen up to 45 minutes a few times in the day
- Able to resist and postpone wishes (i.e. waits to get what she wants)
- Plans her actions and does not act impulsively

Social – Emotional / Peer Maturation

- Able to play with other children
- Shows empathy towards others
- Understands and takes things into consideration (e.g. understands and follows the rules of a game, accepts instructions)
- Deals with limitations, changes and pressures and behaves appropriately
- Interested in things that may be less interesting
- Presents independence and self-security

Speech & Language
- Word knowledge should be comparable to other kids of the same age (this can influence the difference between success and failure at school)
- Has a large vocabulary and a good ability to express herself in words, show curiosity and tries to decipher written words in her environment
- Recites alphabet without singing
- Names upper and lower case letters in no particular order and letter sounds
- Writes in the proper direction (from left to right) and not the inverse
- Able to separate syllables (e.g. ta/ble)
- Has general knowledge (e.g. address, holidays, body parts)

Self-Help / Adaptive Skills
▪ Able to brush her teeth
▪ Dresses alone
▪ Fixes her own school bag or room

Extra Suggestions & Tips
- Before entering grade one, parents should review the child's report and skills from kindergarten. You can help your child practice skills in art and language before beginning grade one.
- It is important to visit the school prior to starting grade one to see the teacher, classroom, gym, bathroom, and so forth to help your child feel more confident and secure in the new setting.
- You can also prepare and help your child's concentration skills on academic learning by reading, writing, number games, and so forth.
- Parents can ask the child to help pack lunches to ensure the food will be eaten at school.
- Spend some time with your child when she arrives home from school to help make the transition easier for both of you.

TIP: Vision
Good vision is required for grade one (e.g. to identify shapes, numbers and letters). It is a good idea to check your child's vision prior to beginning grade one.

Parent Concern: Should I leave my child in day care for one more year?
A child's birth date is a not a good measure for predicting maturity level for day care or school. Some children are better off staying in day care for another year while others are ready to enter the school setting. Boys also mature less quickly than girls, so you should check your child's growth and readiness in the last quarter of the year before deciding what to do.

If a child enters grade one "before her time", then she may suffer from damaged self-image and awkward or rejected social relations. In contrast, keeping a child behind by one year may allow a child to work on her difficulties arriving to grade one strong and matured. Yet, the child that stays behind may suffer from a lack of self-esteem or confidence in her abilities.

Often times, the day care teacher, health care professional and psychologist can help you assess the child's abilities and progress in comparison to other students in assessing readiness for grade one.

Parent Concern: Does my Child need to know how to read before starting grade one?
A child should be familiar with the alphabet and be able to match a picture with its first letter (e.g. cat – "c"). She should know the sounds of the letters and where to start when reading a book. While she does not necessarily need to know how to read words to be in the first grade, it is an advantage before starting grade one.

LANGUAGE DELAY

Parent Concern: If my child has language delay, should I speak one language and not two at home?

GENERAL

- Children with language delays are capable of learning two languages at least as well as monolingual language impaired peers.
- There is no evidence that suggests that children with language delays learning a second language will negatively impact child development.
- No research evidence exists that states that children with a language delay should be exposed to only one language.

- Research supports the notion that more than one language can improve a child's language and learning abilities.
- Children who are proficient in one language will likely become strongly proficient in a second language.
- Bilingual children can have the same speech and cognitive disorders as monolingual children.
- Children learn a second language best when they are exposed to the language in all daily situations and when people model the language fluently.

Parents should provide an enhanced interactive language-learning environment for their children and work with teachers to strengthen the first language.

LANGUAGE STIMULATION

GENERAL

- While language development has certain characteristics that are common to all children at similar ages, it is still a unique endeavour that varies among children.
- 95% of children use language effectively by the age of 5 years without any problems.
- It is important for parents to understand that language skills does not occur in isolation from other factors such as living conditions, family relations, health, and so forth. Developmental interference can impede language skills.

- Generally, children acquire language skills by listening and following the speech of caregivers and those around them.
- When you cannot understand your child, try to obtain clues from the context in which she speaks. You can ask her to show you what she means and if you still don't understand, then simply tell her that you don't understand.

LANGUAGE STIMULATION

Talk and speak to your child as often and gentle as possible:

- Ask her questions.
- Talk slowly, but with great interest.
- Use simple, short sentences.
- Allow her to learn by imitating your speech.

- Imitate your child and reformulate what she says to the same object (e.g. she says "uh-uh", then you say "cup").
- Take turns speaking.
- Repeat words as often as possible.

Listen and attract your child's attention.

- Listen carefully and give your child time to answer a question. If she does not answer after a considerable amount of time, then re-phrase the question and ask again.
- Maintain eye contact and attention when you are talking to your child. Place yourself at her level.
- Sometimes, you can gain attention by gently holding her chin towards you so that she is looking directly at you.

Other things you can do may include:

- **Use everyday activities** to stimulate your child's language (e.g. while bathing, clothing, playing, and walking). Talk about what you are doing, when and why.
- **Name** objects around you and repeat these words often, so she learns by imitation.
- **Categorize** objects into groups (e.g. food, vegetables, fruits, cars, bikes).

- **Encourage** the use of specific vocabulary (e.g. the child says "that one there", then you point to the same object and say "yes, that yellow ball").
- **Introduce sounds** (e.g. train goes "chou-chou") so your child can associate sounds with meaning.
- **Use gestures** to convey meanings.
- **Allow for opportunity to be with other children that are the same age.**

DO NOT...
- Criticize your child's language skills. If she says something incorrectly, then simply correct her in a gentle and "teaching" manner.
- Force her to say or repeat words correctly.
- Do not over-correct and do not give negative corrections ("no, that is not the right way to say" – correct by repeating the right way to say the correct production).
- Bombard her with questions.

HOW TO ENCOURAGE READING

Reading Stories to Your Child

- Reading stories to your child is necessary and good. In fact, the more you read, the better.
- There are several advantages to reading books to your child including:
  - ✓ Enhancing her language capabilities, thinking operations, imagination and productivity.
  - ✓ Fostering the development of a positive attitude towards reading and books, so that she will want to read interesting books on her own in the future.
  - ✓ Helps children learn to deal with emotional subjects that bother them (e.g. bullying, sibling rivalry, fears, death). Hearing stories can help children understand that they are not alone when dealing with an issue.
  - ✓ Offers opportunities to connect and bond with your child.
  - ✓ An easy and inexpensive way to spend time together.
- To make reading together a fun and effective experience, you can:
  - ✓ Start reading stories to your child at an early age.
  - ✓ Do not force her to listen to the stories.
  - ✓ Allow her to play with and hold the book as well.
  - ✓ Make reading time part of your daily routine (often before bedtime).
  - ✓ Allow her to choose the book you will read (even if she picks the same one every night).
  - ✓ Stimulate her to actively participate in reading the book with you.
  - ✓ Read the book in a dramatic and interesting way, using different tones of voice.

You can take steps to help your child appreciate books and encourage reading.

- Use **alphabet books** to teach letters.
- **Point** to words and pictures, so she can associate language with various things.
- **Point out letters** everywhere, not just in books (e.g. newspapers, magazines, bulletin boards, restaurant menus or signs, car license plates).
- Help **her hold the book** and turn the page.
- Create a **reading routine** where you read to your baby at bedtime or naptime. You do not have to read the entire story; you can just explain the pictures.

- You can **read aloud together** or have her explain the story to you.
- Take your child to a free story time at the **local library** to let her hear an animated storyteller.
- **Offer a wide variety** of available and accessible books to your child.
- Try **games** that include reading or spelling (e.g. Junior Scrabble).
- **Encourage** older siblings to read to their younger siblings.
- **Limit television** viewing in an effort to make time for other activities such as reading.
- Do not use the television or other devices as a reward for reading.

Children, who have more extensive vocabularies are better readers, so beyond actual reading, there are other things you can do to help develop your child's language skills.

- **Talk** to your child from birth. As she gets older, ask questions to encourage dialogue. Even though your child may not answer at such a young age, she will learn that she can be part of a conversation.
- **Listen and respond** when you ask or are asked a question. Wait for answer, even if all you get is a smile (a type of body language).
- **Make the effort** to pick out specific words mentioned in your baby's verbal ramblings. Babies babble and this is how they learn to make sounds on their own, so help them out by picking out the useful words. Repeat the sound of the word and let them know it is a real word to be used in everyday language.
- **Read nursery rhymes** and emphasize the words that sound the same, promoting an awareness of sounds.
- **Songs** make words easier to remember, so make up songs or find them in nursery rhymes or other resources to help your child use a difficult word.
- **Urge your child to talk back** by asking open-ended questions that do not ask for a simple yes or no answer and offer choices.
- **Give her a chance** to point to wanted objects.
- **Keep directions simple and clear.**
- Correct your child's mispronunciations **without criticism**.
- **Concentrate on concepts** such as in/out, up/down, hot/cold, wet/dry, and so forth.

How to Improve Reading Comprehension in Older Children

Help the older child improve reading comprehension by trying the following suggestions:

- Have your child **read aloud**, allowing him more time to process what is read.
- **Re-reading** builds fluency. When reading too quickly, the meaning of the text is often lost. Have your child re-read something she does not understand.
- Provide **age-appropriate books** for your child. If she stops too many times while reading, the book may be too difficult and can be discouraging as a result.
- Discuss **enlarging her vocabulary** with the teacher, especially if she is struggling to read many words. Make vocabulary lists and have her look them up in the dictionary and use them in sentences for the week.
- **Talk** about what she is reading by helping her remember and think about the book. Ask questions about the book, express anticipation for her answers and ask her to summarize the book.
- Connect with her interests in letting her **choose her own books**. Take her to the library and show her all the different types of books available for her to read.
- Set aside a **regular time to read** with her every day.
- Surround your child with **various types of reading material**.
- **Identify** any reading problems your child is encountering, so that you can help her as early as possible.
- If your child is having difficulty concentrating, then **offer a quiet place** where she can read.
- **Praise** your child's efforts.

The following are some reading strategies to help her understand the text even better:

- ✓ **Visualization:** This helps a reader make the words on the page come alive and makes the text meaningful.
- ✓ **Making predictions** involving thinking ahead and anticipating parts of the story.
- ✓ **Inferring (thinking)** is about absorbing what is known from clues in the story.

GIFTED CHILDREN

GENERAL

- A child who achieves cognitive intelligence scores in the upper 95th percentile – generally above 130 IQ - (including areas of verbal comprehension, perceptual reasoning, working memory and processing speed) is called a **gifted child**. This definition can include above average abilities in the visual arts, athletics, music or specific academic areas (e.g. science, math).
- A child does not have to be gifted in all areas to be identified as gifted.
- Each province within Canada has its own regulations and requirements for a child to be considered gifted.
- In addition, it is certainly not uncommon for a child to be gifted while having a learning disability (in reading, writing or emotional sensitivities) or developmental disorder (e.g. ADHD) at the same time. It is a fact that giftedness is often overlooked in children with disabilities and children who come from ethnic minorities, disadvantageous backgrounds (financially) and for those where English is a second language.
- Giftedness tends to run in families. Research suggests that the heritability of general cognitive ability is about 60% and the rest is made up of the environment a child grows up in.
- It is estimated that 1 in 6 children are identified as gifted while another 5 are not identified at all.

SIGNS OF GIFTEDNESS

Clues to intelligence within the first year of life may include:

- Advanced development (e.g. sitting, standing, walking, talking) - Language and use of unusual words - Good memory and observation - Creativity with toys	- Curiosity and concentration - Ability to make comments - Extensive imagination - Perceptive and humorous

Some researchers believe that the best way to identify giftedness is not by measuring intelligence, but by carefully observing your child's behaviour. The best age to conduct an intelligence test is still debatable, but most likely when the child is able to read and write. The accuracy of IQ tests is also still questionable. However, it is the single best predictor to test general intelligence. Remember, giftedness and intelligence is not synonymous. Gifted children have different abilities, talents and personalities compared to other non-gifted counterparts.

Gifted child may appear to have acquired:

▪ Extensive vocabulary ▪ Incredible memory ▪ Skills in math and reading above grade level ▪ Child complains that school is boring or easy	▪ Intense concentration (often on one area) ▪ Inquires about everything ▪ Wants to interact with older children and adults with similar interests

IDENTIFICATION OF GIFTED CHILDREN

- Typically, identification of gifted children occurs around grade 4, but can occur at any age.
- Testing for giftedness is often asked by parents and teachers through the school board or by private psycho-educational testing with a psychologist experienced in the area of giftedness.
- Developmental milestones are identified and compared to the average child in a test with one or more particularly sensitive areas such as psychomotor, intellectual, emotional or imaginative.

BENEFITS OF IDENTIFYING GIFTEDNESS

- It is not uncommon for gifted children to have social anxieties and be sensitive in social situations. Parents should make sure the child is happy in the school he is in or that he is ready to make a move to a new school because of his giftedness.
- You can work with the school to develop an Individual Educational Plan (IEP) to meet the child's needs. This may mean years of working with the school to continually meet and advocate for your child's needs.
- Pair your child with other gifted children for support.

Comment: Once a child is identified as gifted...
a) If the child is happy in a regular class, you can keep him there. You should, however, enrol him in extracurricular activities geared to areas of giftedness.
b) Arrange advanced assignments provided by his teacher.
c) Switch to a gifted program, especially when the child is gifted across a wide range of subjects.

BILINGUALISM

GENERAL

- Language is a method of communication that promotes the expression of family, culture and community.
- Young children are capable of learning to speak two languages at home, school and within the community.
- Teaching your child to be bilingual has its advantages and disadvantages. While teaching your child a second language is an invaluable skill, experts debate over when a second language should be introduced. Research studies indicate that learning a second language does not impede a child's developmental progress; thus, the decision is on you to do what feels right!
- Bilingualism does not cause language disorders. While your child may use words within both languages in the same sentence, these moments of "switching" usually disappear after the age of five years.

ADVANTAGES/DISADVANTAGES

Advantages of learning a second language:
- Knowing how to speak two languages allows the child to explore other cultures and communicate with more people within the community. In addition, a bilingual child has extended opportunities in the employment field as an adult.
- Some studies show that bilingual children may develop certain skills at an earlier age than others such as selective attention (e.g. learning to filter words when speaking one language and filtering the other).
- While it may take your child longer to fully comprehend one language when learning two, bilingual children do eventually catch up to their single language peers and differences tend to disappear by grade 5.
- Generally, bilingual children do well in speaking and understanding two languages.

Disadvantages of learning a second language:
- It may take your child a longer time to develop a large vocabulary in each language since he needs to learn more words in two languages instead of only one.
- Bilingual children tend to score lower on oral language tests.

WHEN TO INTRODUCE
- It is suggested that parents should begin teaching two languages as soon as the child is born. Rather than learning a second language, it is acquired naturally along with the first language taught. In addition, learning two languages simultaneously from birth is easier and faster than teaching an older child.

- Some experts believe that teaching children two languages simultaneously from birth places them at a disadvantage for both languages. Essentially, these experts assert that children may not be proficient in two languages when learning both at the same time.
- Some health professionals recommend teaching a second language at the age of 2 ½ - 3 years, when they already have a good grasp of the first language.

HOW TO TEACH TWO LANGUAGES

TIP: Every bilingual child is unique

- Developmental milestones of the bilingual child are the same as their one-language peers.
- From time to time, your child may mix grammar rules or use words from both languages in the same sentence; this is normal.
- When a second language is introduced, some children may not talk for a certain period of time. This "silent" period sometimes lasts several months; it is normal and will disappear.
- Children who are experiencing problems in both languages may require professional help.

- You can either use two languages as soon as your child is born or use only one language at home and allow to learn the second language when school starts.
- Provide your child with plenty of **opportunities** to hear and practice using both languages in everyday life. Remember that children learn languages best from you!
- **Read** to your child in both languages to help build early vocabulary and reading skills.
- **Be patient** with your child's mistakes or language switching moments; this is a normal part of learning two languages.
- Have one parent speak one language and the other parent speak the second language, so that your child is able to **practice both languages at home**.
- Allow your child to **listen** to his favourite music in both languages.
- Play on words when you are reciting rhymes in both languages. For example, leave out words for him to fill in with the language you are speaking.
- Talk to your child about what's happening or about whatever you may be doing. For example, while you are cooking, doing laundry, folding clothes, etc.

IDENTIFICATION OF COLORS/ LETTERS/NUMBERS

COLORS

- The ability to recognize different colors is usually seen at the age of 18 months. At this age, your child begins to notice similarities and differences in shape, size and texture, however it will still take him a while to name colors.
- By 3 years of age, most children can name at least 1 color.
- You can enhance development by asking your child to show you objects that are a certain color (e.g. red square, yellow circle, green leaf in the picture).
- As your child begins to learn the name of colors, you can point to the object yourself and ask him what color he thinks the object is. If he responds incorrectly, then tell him the correct color and encourage him to get it right later.

LETTERS

- Between 2-3 years of age, most children begin to recognize some letters.
- By 3 – 3 ½ years of age, children will know the alphabet. By 3 years of age, the child should probably know the alphabet song along with the letters, and can sing it with others.
- Between 4-6 years of age, most children know the alphabet and can identify most letters.

NUMBERS

- When your child is 2 years old, he may learn to count up until 10, though he does not understand the concept of counting objects.
- Many children will often skip in their counting (e.g. 1, 3, 4, 5, 7). Do not worry about this since he is learning how to count.
- By the age of 3 years, children should already know what number is next though not necessarily stating the correct ordering of numbers.
- Between 3-4 years of age, he is adept at counting small sets of objects.
- Between 4-5 years of age, he probably already knows all the numbers and is able to write them down.

WRITING BACKWARDS

> **Parent Concern**: Is it normal that my 5-year-old boy writes backwards? Should I be concerned about dyslexia or other learning problems?

GENERAL

- Parents are often concerned when young children reverse letters, write words from right to left or confuse letters (e.g. b, d, p) in their writing. Parents are particularly concerned when preschoolers begin reversing letters and words after having written correctly.
- This is a normal stage in learning how to write.
- The brain does not completely develop the concept of directionality (i.e. the awareness, recognition and appreciation of right/left, up/down, forward/backwards, etc) until the ages of 5-8 years. Until directionally is matured, young children can write from left to right or right to left since it feels the same to them.
- Letter reversal is normal in such young children as 5 years. Some write in mirror images, going from right to left, with all the letters reversed.
- Do not correct or make a big deal out of your child's incorrect writing. The more she writes, the easier writing will become and correct itself. Simply show her how to write the letters correctly until she begins writing it properly.

Beginning writing behaviour in young children follows these stages:

- ✓ Drawing
- ✓ Wavy scribbles
- ✓ Letter-like scribbles (resembling letters like shapes such as circles, squares)
- ✓ Development of random letters (letters can be backward, upside down)
- ✓ Letter strings (occasional single words or random grouping of letters)
- ✓ Conventional writing (readable to others)

WHEN TO BE CONCERNED

Consult your child's health professional if:

- There is family history of learning disability
- Mirror writing persists beyond the age of 6 years or older
- There is a persistence of letter and word reversals and/or inversions (upside down writing) when the child is 7-8 years of age
- Your child has difficulty memorizing sequences (e.g. home phone numbers, alphabet or postal code)
- She writes letters or numbers in unusual ways (e.g. the number 8 is written in 2 circles on top of each other rather than in a continuous line)
- She often calls objects by the wrong name

TIP: Promoting Emergent Writing
- Offer a variety of writing materials (e.g. crayons, colored paper)
- Model the writing process (e.g. model letters and numbers)
- Play games where writing is used (e.g. playing doctor with patient charts or restaurant menus)
- Encourage the child to write on her own after an outing
- Read aloud each day

Miscellaneous
Parent Concerns/Issues

PREMATURE BABIES AND DEVELOPMENTAL RISKS

GENERAL

- If your child was born premature, continue to monitor developmental progress. Various deficits may become apparent when your child reaches different milestones (e.g. walking, talking, reading); it is impossible to accurately predict who will have problems later in life (even at the age of 5 years).

- There is an increased risk of disabilities in the presence of complications such as intracranial haemorrhage, anoxia, hypoglycaemia or hyper-bilirubinemia. As such, periodic re-evaluation is important in infancy and childhood as most developmental difficulties emerge slowly over time. Certainly, the earlier interventions begin, the better the outcome.

PROBLEM AREAS

The problem areas for premature babies that are most likely to be affected are:

- Cognitive and academic abilities (intellectual ability, math/reading or learning disability)
- Language difficulties
- Motor difficulties
- Cerebral Palsy
- Behavioural and mental disabilities (e.g. ADHD, risk of Autism)
- Hearing impairment
- Vision impairment – The risk of retinopathy (*Disease of the retina,* *the light-sensitive membrane at the back of the eye.)* increases with lower gestational age. Myopia not associated with retinopathy can affect 5-20% of premature babies less than 1500 gram birth weight.
- Iron deficiency – Iron reserves are inadequate in premature babies and often require iron supplements.
- Vitamin D deficiency

FOLLOW-UP EVALUATIONS

- A premature child must be monitored very closely to ensure that appropriate treatment for any conditions that may arise begin early, especially for children at high risk.
- A comprehensive follow-up involves a close evaluation of medical, psychological and social factors along with assessment and developmental progress.
- The child with suspect neurological injury will require close evaluation of neuro-developmental functioning to investigate the possibility of long-term impact (as the nervous system matures).
- Various specialties and other professionals working with children are needed in follow-up evaluations including a physiotherapist, occupational therapist, and speech therapist.

COPING WITH A PET'S DEATH

- Children have imaginary friends and pets are real
- It is not easy for a child to understand emotions, sadness or learning to deal with the anticipated death of a dear family pet
- Allow your child to ask questions and answer those question to the best of your ability
- If the pet endures a sudden or unexpected death, then explain to you child that the animal is no longer in pain
- Do not belittle or ignore the child's relationship with the deceased pet.
- Teach your child that death is a natural part of life
- Allow your child to celebrate the life of the pet and treasure the time the child had with him. Make a happy memory of the last few days to help with sadness. Have a burial memory or ceremony
- A short period of depression, acting out or gloominess can be expected. The risk for prolonged grief (depending on the child age, relationship with the pet and emotional maturity) **in a child may be manifested when the child is:**

> - Not interested in usual activities
> - Withdrawn from friends and family
> - Eating considerably less
> - Regresses to potty training or bed-time wetting
> - Afraid to be alone or going to sleep

SHOES

GENERAL

A proper pair of shoes is important for developing all the muscles required to support the foot's range of motion. Uncomfortable and unsupportive shoes can delay the speed in which a child learns to walk. Ensuring that your child's shoes are age-appropriate is an important part of parenting.

BEFORE THE WALKING STAGE

- When your child is not yet walking, he does not need to wear shoes. Bare feet are best for your baby at this stage of development.
- You can put shoes on your baby for stylistic purposes or matching outfits on special occasions. These shoes should not be fit for walking yet and should be lightweight (made of a breathable material such as leather or cloth, not plastic). In addition, it should be flexible enough to feel your baby's toes through them and should have soft ankle support.

FIRST STEPS

- While it is recommended to wait until your baby is walking before buying shoes, you can buy shoes right when your baby begins his first wobbly steps.
- Going barefoot helps your child improve the balance and have a better feel for the floor he is walking on (as it allows your child to slightly grip the floor with his toes). Also, walking barefoot will give your child a greater sense of stability since it brings the child's feet to closer contact with the walking surface (adjusting the feet's position easily).
- Use shoes at this stage if your baby is walking around outside or on a rough surface regularly.

COMMENT: Special orthopedic shoes do not help improve or speed up walking.

HOW TO CHOOSE THE FIRST PAIR OF SHOES

- A baby's first pair of shoes should be made of **natural material** such as soft leather and canvas. This will prevent the baby's feet from sweating and rubbing against the material.
- The **sole** of your baby's first pair should be **flexible**, where you can hold the heel in one hand and the toe in the other. These shoes should **bend easily**, especially at the ball of the foot.
- Before placing a pair of shoes on for the first time, you should ask for assistance in understanding your **baby's foot scale** made especially for kids.
- **Try the shoes on** your baby by holding him in your lap, facing outwards. Slip the shoes on and encourage the baby to walk around in them.
- **Make sure the shoe fits** your baby's feet. You can feel where your baby's heel and toes are, and ensure that there is enough room in the back to slip your finger down about a quarter inch for growing room.

- **Check** your baby's feet for any rubbing or irritation.
- **Do not buy high shoes** since they are confining and interfere with ankle movement. It does not necessarily provide better support. Flat, smooth outer soles with no high ankles make it easier for your baby to begin walking and less slipping.

TIPS FOR FIT
1) The Pinch Test: Shoes should be snug at the heel, but roomy at the toe (should be the width of your thumb between the longest toe and the shoe tip while the child is standing). Determine the right fit by pinching along the sides, if the shoe is wide enough.
2) Always have your child try on both shoes since there can be a size discrepancy between feet. If there is a substantial difference between feet, then use an in sole to balance out the fit.
3) No super sizing! Shoes that are too loose are just as bad as shoes that are too tight. There is no support for the foot and may cause blisters and discomfort.

FOR THE WALKING CHILD

By the time your child is 16-18 months of age, he will be walking around unassisted. As such, you will want him to have a fitted pair of shoes. **The following are signs of good shoes:**

- **Good sole flexibility** at the ball of the foot where the foot bends is essential. Use leather or rubber soles that bend easily (e.g. sneakers are very flexible). You should be able to bend the toe of the shoe up – about 40 degree.
- Shoes that do not have enough **ankle support** can hinder a child's developing feet. At this stage, you may want to consider buying a shoe that provides ankle support.
- A **non-slip sole and leather lining** is important for a good shoe.
- **Some rigidity in the heel** with a soft edge (where it meets the ankle) is important to prevent rubbing. It is good if the top edge at the back of the shoe (above the heel) is padded or bound and the back seam is smooth .The back (or counters) of the shoes should offer firm support. Look for padding along the back edge to prevent the counters from rubbing; thereby increasing comfort.
- **Size and room to grow** - Do not buy a shoe that is too big or too long for your child since it can cause him to trip or injure himself. The heel of the foot should also remain in its proper position when walking. Similarly, shoes that are too small can pinch your child's feet or cause painful cuts or sores.
- The best fit for all is when you can place one thumb width between the longest toe and the tip of the shoe.

- **Easy on easy off**: Experts differ about whether high top or low cut shoes are preferable. High tops can be confining and more difficult for parents to put on and take off. Low cut shoes come off easily, and a toddler can pull them off at will. They also tend to slip off on their own. What is best for your new walker may depend on his / her foot shape as well as on the fit of a particular pair of shoes.
- **Light weight, non-slip, non gripe soles** – Shoes should be neither so slippery that your toddler slides when trying to walk nor so ground gripping that it is hard to lift a foot. Look for rubber soles that are grooved, like tire treads.
- The toes should not drag with each step and the heels should not slide up and down.
- **Breathable uppers** - upper of leather or canvas rather than plastic or imitation leather will allow the feet to breath and minimize moisture build up from perspiration.

TIP: Foot Notes
-Find the right fit as size 3, 4, 5 may interchange between manufacturers
-Take cues from your kids as to whether the shoes do not fit as the child may complain on soreness or try to take off the shoe if he cannot talk yet.
-You can also check for red marks that indicate that pressure has been placed on the foot.
-Extra large shoes can lead to irritation and blisters, cause unnecessary tumbles and interfere with walking.
-Use appropriate socks – stretch socks that are most likely to give a good fit.
-Consider buying a new pair when there is less than half a thumb's space at the toes or check with a salesperson.

CLIMBING

GENERAL

- Around the age of 12-15 months, the child may be able to climb up using either of his legs. He might let himself slip on his abdomen with legs first. From 18 months-2 years, the child will go up one step at a time and use his knee to open the way up and to hold his body while he is elevating his other leg.
- Above 2 years of age, the toddler can go up using handrails. Going down might be on the buttock. From 2 years of age, many succeed climbing furniture and coming back down. For certain times, he will go down furniture backwards extending the leg until he touches the floor. Going up steps is much easier than going down (and sometimes, can get stuck). After 2 yeas, your child will go down one step each time in putting the 2 feet on each step.
- Above 3 years of age, the child starts to put one leg on each step.

Safety: If your child knows to climb, it means he can reach various objects so watch for hot/sharp objects. Use security door for up and down the stairs.

WHY

Toddlers are curious creatures on an endless mission to explore the fascinating world around them. They do not understand that they can get hurt, because they have no form of impulse control. As a result, toddlers move from one thing to the next, oblivious to the dangers surrounding them.

Climbing is a common concern among parents of toddlers; however it is positive in the sense that it builds strength, coordination and self-esteem (clearly shown in the little one's face when he feels that sense of accomplishment).

WHAT TO DO

You should not try and stop him from climbing since it is another way for your child to learn about his environment and gain confidence. Rather than stopping him from climbing or allowing him to climb everywhere, try to do the following:

- Offer safe spaces for him to climb.
- Childproof your home as much as you can (e.g. bookcases are securely attached to the wall, no unstable or rickety chairs, stools hidden away).
- Supervise your toddler at all times, especially when he starts climbing.
- Allow your child to climb when it is in a safe space or simply direct him to a safe zone.

CRIB TO BED TRANSITIONING

GENERAL: WHEN TO TRANSITION FROM A CRIB TO A BED

- There is no set time to move your baby from a crib to a bed. The choice is completely up to you and your baby. It depends more on age, size, development and spirit of adventure, and whether or not there is a new sibling on the way. If the child is content in the crib and not trying to escape it, he does not have to move out until he is ready.
- Generally speaking, children are moved from a crib to a bed between the ages of 18 months and 3 years.
- If your toddler seems to be getting big for the crib, looks uncomfortable or is climbing out of the crib, then the crib is not safe and you should move him to a bed.
- A good way of helping your child transition from the crib to the bed is to take him to pick out his new bedding or pillows. If he picks what he sleeps in, then the chances of him sleeping in the bed will more likely happen.
- Moving your child from a crib to a bed may make it easier to put him to bed at night since you can lie down with him. This will help him feel safer and secure with you by his side.
- Do not wait to move your child to a big boy bed when your new baby arrives as he will not be ready and may feel displaced.

- To keep your toddler safe, you can buy the toddler side rails that keep him from rolling during the night in case he moves a lot.
- It is better to post-pone the transition:
  - ✓ If a new sibling is about to arrive
  - ✓ If day care or preschool just started
  - ✓ If in the midst of toilet training or just getting over an illness

- Look at a book that describes the journey from crib to bed and read it to your child several times.
- Involve big girl in selecting a big girl bed, sheets, or even stuffed animals (companions)
- Look at models that are built relatively close to the ground that accepts guard rails and comes with a firm mattress.
- Have your toddler say bye-bye to the crib.

TIP: Is it worth it to buy a toddler bed?
Toddler beds are impractical since toddlers grow at a rapid rate. A smaller or lower bed should be comfortable for your toddler and should last much longer than a toddler bed.

HAIR LOSS & HAIR PULLING

(1) HAIR LOSS

GENERAL

- Each baby is born with a unique pattern of hair. Some may be bald at birth while others are born with a full head of hair and some may even be bald well into their second year of life, causing great distress for parents.

- Within the first year of life, most babies will have two stages of hair growth. In some infants, the first stage of hair falls out before the second stage of hair grows (this may look as though your infant is going bald). Other infants may experience a second stage of hair growth while the first stage is ending, making any hair loss hardly noticeable.

- It is common for babies to lose their hair during the first six months of life, since hair follicles reach a resting stage at the same time (causing hair loss at once). The resting stage alternates with a growing stage where the hair follicles are replaced by thicker, often darker, hair.

CAUSES OF HAIR LOSS

- The gradual baldness of a young infant is thought to be due to **changing hormone levels**. Before birth, levels of sex hormones are high whereas these levels decline after birth, causing the hair to fall out.

- **Cradle cap** is a common infant ailment that may lead to hair loss. It is a temporary skin condition in infants under the age of six months that may cause flakes or crusty patches near the back of the head, just above the eyebrow or on top of the scalp. These patches are often red and are scaly to the touch with a yellowish tint.

- **Sleeping on the backside** may cause a circular bald spot on the back of your baby's head. Often, this bald spot is accompanied by a flat shape to the back of the head called positional plagiocephaly (see Abnormal Head Shape). It is considered to be caused by friction/rubbing the head against the mattress and is more common for babies who stay for prolonged periods of time on their backs. However, a recent study found that there is no relationship between sleeping positions and the onset of positional plagiocephaly.

> **More to Know- Causes of Hair Loss in Children**: If hair loss occurs after the age of six months, it may be due to nutritional (e.g. vitamin excess or deficiency), medical problems (e.g. thyroid issues, metabolic disease, phenylketonuria, breastfed infants exposed to drugs, fungal infections of the scalp) or other issues such as hair twirling/pulling, tight braids, and sometimes, alopecia areata (auto-immune cause).

WHAT TO DO

- In the first few months of life, hair loss is normal. Be patient and allow time for your baby's hair to grow back.
- If the cause of your child's hair loss is cradle cap, then use a mild shampoo on your baby's hair every day. This will often loosen the scales, allowing you to brush the hair out delicately. For more stubborn scales, apply a modest amount of mineral oil to your baby's scalp before shampooing and allow it to sit for about ten minutes. Use a soft brush to gently remove the scales and shampoo when done. Sometimes a cream or lotion can be added by your health professional. Note that moisturizing your baby's skin with mineral or olive oil can sometimes cause irritation.
- If your child is old and develops hair loss or you have any concerns, talk to your child's health professional.

(2) HAIR PULLING

GENERAL

- Trichotillomania is the medical term for hair pulling, which results from a psychological condition that involves strong urges to pull out one's own hair.
- It is more common in girls than boys and occurs mostly in adolescence, however it can begin in children as young as one year old.
- Children tend to pull the hair out at the root from the scalp, eyebrows, eyelashes and/or pubic area.
- Some children pull out large handfuls of hair, which can leave bald patches on the area. Some even inspect the strands of hair after pulling it out while others like to put it in their mouths.
- Hair pulling is a type of compulsive disorder, which means that children feel an overwhelming urge to pull the hair. They may also have other compulsive habits such as nail biting or skin picking.
- Complications of hair pulling may include emotional distress (embarrassment, low self-esteem), social problems (e.g. avoiding peers, avoiding social activities), skin damage and hair balls (when eating hair for too long).

CAUSES & RISK FACTORS

- The causes of hair pulling are unclear.
- There may be an imbalance in the brain's chemistry that leads to repetitive behaviours or compulsive routines. Some experts claim that there is a feeling of satisfaction or relief when hair is pulled out.
- Some of the risk factors for hair pulling:
  ⇒ Genetic factors including family history
  ⇒ Age (mostly occurs between the ages of 11-13 years)
  ⇒ Negative emotions (a way of dealing with fatigue/frustration, anxiety)
  ⇒ Other disorders such as anxiety, OCD (Obsessive compulsive disorder), eating disorders, etc.

- Cognitive behavioural therapy can help teach the child to recognize the urge to pull before it seems too strong to resist.
- Children need to learn the triggering factors to help eliminate urges to pull hair by preparing to cope with these factors. Eventually, the triggers will become weaker and disappear.
- Many individuals find it helpful to keep their hands busy with different activities (e.g. squeezing a stress ball, handling various objects) during times when the urge is strongest.
- There may be some tension or anxiety when trying to resist an urge. As such, the help of a health professional is required.

OBSESSION WITH MAKEUP

GENERAL
- An obsession with makeup is not only found in girls, but in boys as well.
- Many children are fascinated with watching their mothers put on makeup.
- Putting makeup is a type of **pretend play** and makeup is the pretend play tool.
- Sometimes, the obsession with makeup is a way to **seek attention** (even when it is negative attention). However, as is the case in many behaviours, reacting strongly only increases that obsession.
- Remember that an obsession such as this is another phase and a temporary fixation that will pass.

WHAT TO DO
- It is ok to allow your child to wear makeup. Remember that **she is playing** and that she is too young to even understand what it means to put makeup on.
- **Makeup rules and limits should be set**. You can explain that she is allowed to do it at home, but not when she is out with friends or going to school.
- Be **firm and consistent** in your rules about makeup even if she cries with tantrums.
- **Allow her only a few items** such as lipstick and blush.
- Explore your child's other interests and spend some time with her.

DROOLING

Parent Concern: My 3 ½ year old baby is drooling and chewing his hands. Does this mean he is teething or are his teeth erupting?

GENERAL

- We all know that babies drool and some drool more than others.
- Many babies begin drooling around 3 months of age, often drooling at an incredible rate (wetting bibs everywhere).
- Drooling is usually the sign that your baby will begin teething soon with teeth eruption occurring around 6-8 months of age.
- Although teeth do not erupt until about 6-8 months of age, teeth travel through the gums stimulating saliva production. As such, your baby begins drooling at a much earlier age.

- The increase in saliva production is part of a preparation process for digesting food. Stomach acid is neutralized by the saliva and the baby's intestinal lining is further developed from all that drooling.
- In addition, drool involves special enzymes that will help your baby begin to digest solid foods at 4-6 months of age.

WHY IT HAPPENS

- Your baby begins to drool when teeth are in the process of traveling through the gums, stimulating saliva production.
- The increase in saliva production is part of a preparation process for food digestion. Stomach acid is neutralized by the saliva.
- In addition, drool involves special enzymes that will help your baby begin to digest solid foods at 4-6 months of age.

COMMENTS

Drool Rashes

- Irritation around the mouth and cheeks is known as a drool rash, a common occurrence.
- You can use a barrier cream on the skin to help relieve irritation.
- Excess drool may cause irritation on your baby's bottom since saliva is a natural laxative. This may lead to more frequent loose stool and an exacerbation of diaper rashes.

Drooling & Diseases
- Excess saliva drooling can occur in various diseases due to problems keeping the saliva in the mouth, swallowing saliva or excess saliva production.
- This can be a sign of simple diseases (such as viral throat infection like stomatitis) or more serious diseases such as pesticide poisoning.

HAND FISTING

WHAT IS HAND-FISTING?

- fisting is when the hand is closed with the thumb tightly inside the palm.
- In the first month of life, your baby may hold his hands tightly fisted.
- Between 2 and 4 months of age, the baby will relax his hands more and more.

WHEN TO BE CONCERNED

A health professional should be consulted when:

- The baby demonstrates persistent hand fisting well into and beyond the 3rd month of life (especially when there are other signs of developmental delay or neurological deficits).
- If hand fisting persists beyond 3 months of age, it can signify delayed motor development, Hypertonia, or brain dysfunction (e.g. of the cortico spinal tract).
- If hand fisting persists on one side, it can signify hemiplegia (paralysis affecting only one side of the body).

BABY EYES ROLL BACK

GENERAL

It is usually normal for an infant's eyes to roll back in the first two months of life since eye muscles are still developing and not yet controlled. Generally, infants' eyes roll back when they are tired after a feeding or when falling asleep.

During the process of falling asleep, your baby enters stage one (rapid eye movement – REM – sleep) of the sleep cycle. Stage one is a light sleep, characterized by reduced bodily movements, slow eye rolling and sometimes, an opening and closing of the eyelids. In normal infants, an upward or downward gaze may also occur during the first month of life and gradually disappears.

CAUSES

There are normal and abnormal reasons why infants roll their eyes back.

Normal	Abnormal
▪ Exhaustion and tiredness after a feeding may cause your baby's eyes to roll back since she is not able to control her eye muscles. ▪ Newborns eyes roll back when they fall asleep. It should subside by the end of the second month of life since at this age, eye muscle control improves. ▪ Premature infants may roll their eyes back for a longer period of time than a full-term infant (i.e. longer than the end of the second month of life and depending on their prematurity level).	▪ Seizures may cause eyes to roll back. There may also be twitching of the eyelids or other abnormal movements (e.g. arm movement of one side or both, etc). ▪ Eyes may roll back due to gastroesophageal reflux, especially during severe reflux episodes when the back arches. ▪ A side effect of drugs (e.g. clobazam) may cause the eyes to roll back. ▪ Sun set signs may present with rolled eyes and may signify hydrocephalus*.

*Hydrocephalus is due to abnormal accumulation of cerebro spinal fluid in the ventricle or cavities of the brain. It may cause increase intracranial pressure inside the brain, and progressive enlargement of the head, convulsions, and mental problems, etc.

Consult your health professional if your baby's eyes roll back frequently or persistently and there are additional symptoms in order to rule out any possible medical concerns.

CPSIA information can be obtained at www.ICGtesting.com
Printed in the USA
LVOW121934050812

293016LV00002B/1/P